THE WAR DIARIES

Robert Raymond Davey, a son of the Manse, was born in Dunmurry, Belfast in 1915 and educated at the Royal Belfast Academical Institution, Queen's University Belfast, Assembly's College Belfast and New College in Edinburgh. He was a distinguished Ulster rugby player, and a member of the only team unbeaten by the All Blacks on their 1935 tour. He was ordained for the YMCA War Service in the Second World War, and served as a prisoner-of-war in Italy and Germany following capture in Tobruk, North Africa. He was a Chaplain at Queen's University from 1946 to 1970, and Founder and Leader of the Corrymeela Community from 1965 until his retirement in 1980. He is married to Kathleen Burrows, his wartime sweetheart, and has three children and nine grandchildren.

THE WAR DIARIES

RAY DAVEY

Foreword by Alf McCreary

THE BREHON PRESS
BELFAST

First published 2005 by The Brehon Press Ltd
1A Bryson Street, Belfast BT5 4ES,
Northern Ireland

© 2005 Ray Davey

ISBN: 0 9544867 7 3

Design: December Publications
Printed by Cox & Wyman Ltd

CONTENTS

MAPS

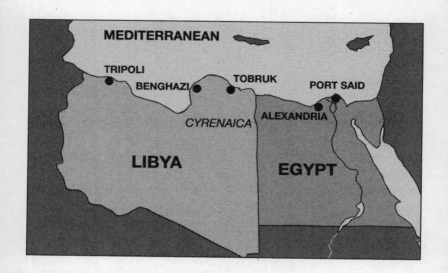

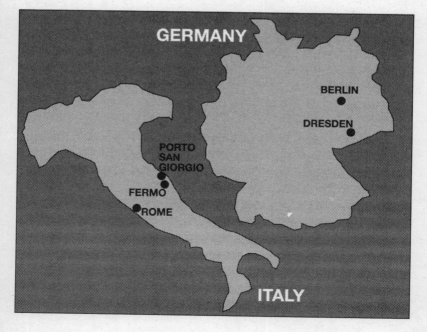

ACKNOWLEDGEMENTS

When I fled the POW camp at Hohnstein at the end of the war in May 1945, carrying in my arms eleven notebooks of diaries written in the desert, Italy and Germany, little did I think that they would become a book 60 years later. In no way could this have been possible but for the foresight, the tenacity and the devotion of a number of people.

First and foremost I wish to thank Angela Louden, who so willingly and painstakingly transcribed my erratic and sometimes miniature handwriting into readable form. Thanks also to Fionnuala O Connor for putting me in touch with Hilary Bell, whose expertise and sensitivity have seamlessly sewn together the various strands into a legible whole.

Very many others have helped and encouraged me along the way. To mention but a few: Alan Evans, Alf McCreary, Roger and Alison Curry, Susan Dalzell, Rachel Pierce, and my publishers at the Brehon Press, Brendan Anderson and Damian Keenan. To all of these people I extend my deepest gratitude.

But above all, I thank my wife Kathleen, who through all the ups-and-downs has always had faith in the outcome and supported me all the way.

A NOTE ON PHOTOGRAPHS

AUTHOR'S NOTE

Just before the war, I had formed the habit of writing up my diary for each day – the people I met, the places I went to – ordinary details like that. I continued this during the war years. These diaries begin in Belfast in 1940: I brought one out with me from home, purchased another in Egypt, and several paperback notebooks in Dresden. One of the diaries was lost when I left Sidi Birani during an Italian attack in 1941. Luckily, when I later returned it was still there, having been used as an inventory by the remaining British troops. Thankfully, when censors in Germany later confronted me over my diaries, they gave up trying to read the dense text after half a page – there is some justification for bad handwriting!

FOREWORD

When the definitive history of the 'troubles' in Northern Ireland is eventually written, and with the benefit of long hindsight, I have no doubt that the Reverend Dr Ray Davey will be confirmed as one of the most influential bridge-builders of all. His work as the Presbyterian Dean of Residence at Queen's University in Belfast, and later with the Corrymeela Community, showed a spiritual depth and vision, and a refreshing realism, which demonstrated the best of Christianity during some of the worst of times.

Under his gentle but firm leadership, Corrymeela became a light in the darkness of Northern Ireland's violence, sectarianism and misunderstanding, and in a true Biblical sense, that light was never quenched. Whatever the challenges or the setbacks – and there were many – Ray Davey and Corrymeela showed through their philosophy and their actions that, in the midst of chaos and recurrent crises, there could indeed be 'a better way'.

Many people have tried, with limited success, to quantify and analyse Ray Davey's qualities as a leader in difficult times. His abundant charm and ready sense of humour have been invaluable gifts, as have his deep humanity, his willingness to listen and to inspire succeeding generations, and his talent in finding common ground where none seemed to exist. All of these were part of Ray's considerable ability to move all sorts of situations and people forward for the common good, but these skills and gifts overlaid a firm foundation of theological rigour and a clear Christian commitment.

Significantly, Ray Davey learned the hard way. As a son of the Manse and a rugby player of great skill, he might have been tempted to follow the conventional career of a Presbyterian minister in an Ulster parish of former days when Saturday afternoon sport was almost as important to some church members as Sunday worship.

The outbreak of the Second World War changed all that. Ray served with the YMCA in North Africa and was thrown into the white heat of conflict, having to live through the huge personal and communal challenges of being made a prisoner-of-war. As he said to me recently, he was forced to make a major choice: 'I could allow this experience to grind me down completely, or I could decide to be positive and to make the best of it. I chose the latter course.'

In doing so, he changed not only his own life, but later helped to change the life of his native province. From his imprisonment in Tobruk and elsewhere, he learned about the need for human beings to develop a peaceful way of living together in community. From his painful experience of the Allied bombing of Dresden, he witnessed the awful futility of violence. He said, 'When I returned to Northern Ireland after the war, the challenge of trying to do something about conflict stayed with me, especially in my own society which was so polarised.'

This latest book by Ray Davey provides an important and invaluable insight into the mind of a bridge-builder, experiencing at first hand the need to develop the entire concept and practice of living in community. In one sense this is arguably the most significant document of Ray's writing career, for in his war diaries lie the seeds of much of what was to blossom in his life and his work later on.

Ray is one of my greatest mentors. I am delighted to be able to commend this book, which has been a labour of love for so many people. It is also a fitting testament to the vision and integrity of a remarkable man who, with the unwavering support of his devoted wife Kathleen, has taught us so much about the true nature of community and about living life so abundantly in the service of others.

Alf McCreary MBE

GLOSSARY

Acronyms

AA Anti-Aircraft

ASR Army Scripture Reader

AYMCA Australian YMCA

BEF British Expeditionary Force

CCS Casualty Clearing Station

CMP Corps of Military Police

C of E Church of England

CSM Company Sergeant-Major

DCG Deputy Chaplain General

DD Doctor(ate) of Divinity

DHQ Desert Headquarters

GMC General Motor Company (make of car)

FSD Field Service Depot

HE Highly Explosive

L/Cpl. Lance-Corporal

MC Military Cross

MDS Medical Distribution Station

MO Medical Officer

MP Military Police

NAAFI Navy, Army and Air Force Institutes (an organisation providing canteens)

NCOs Non-commissioned Officers

OC Officer Commanding

PT Physical Training

QM Quartermaster

QMG Quartermaster General

RA Royal Artillery

RAMC Royal Army Medical Corps

RASC Royal Army Service Corps

RC Roman Catholic

RE Royal Engineers

RHQ Regimental Headquarters

RS Royal Signals

RSM Regimental Sergeant Major

SA South Africa

SARE South African Royal Engineers

SAYM South African YMCA

SCF Senior Chaplain Forces

SU Soviet Union

TTS Teetotal Society

VC Victoria Cross

WD Western Desert

WO War Office

YMCA/YM Young Men's Christian Association

Terms

Ack Ack: Anti-Aircraft

Alex: Alexandria

backsheesh: Arabic term used by beggars

Boffer guns: anti-aircraft artillery

brass hats: senior officers

buckshee'd: gave away

bully: corned beef

column: moving line of troops or vehicles

dixie: cooking pot

flak guns: anti-aircraft fire

griff: news

'in the bag': captured

iron rations: basic/emergency rations

Jerry: Germans

Kilo 92/Kilo 64, etc (camps): replacements for place names

kilos: kilometres, method of location

Lights: communications

Man of Confidence: prisoner's representative to Germans

Mess: canteen

recce: reconnaissance

reveille: waking call

sapper: engineer

Toc H: society formed after the First World War to fight loneliness and
hate, and to encourage Christian comradeship

Tommy: popular name for British soldiers

tropics (ie, kit): desert kit

wadi: desert valley

whistles: slang word for shell

A page from one of the notebooks the author kept as diaries during the period from 1940 to 1945

PROLOGUE

On 28 September 1940 I did something I had done a thousand times before – I left my home in Dunmurry, on the outskirts of south Belfast, and hastened along the driveway, past the east end of the church and down to the railway-crossing. I had just said a difficult farewell to my parents. I did not know when I would see them again. As I walked the familiar path away from my home, I knew that I was heading into an uncharted and hazardous future. The war had been raging for over a year, with Hitler winning victory after victory. I was setting out for the Middle East to join HM Services as a YMCA [Young Men's Christian Association] field secretary. I think I realised even then that this day would be a watershed in my life, separating me from my youth and my dependence on others. Now I was on my own.

I had had a very happy childhood and had enjoyed many privileges. There was the spacious Manse, elevated and yet hidden among the trees, a truly wonderful playground for growing children. Here, we relived the experiences of those who had fought in the First World War, hiding in our makeshift trenches and ambushing the enemy. My schooldays were spent at the Belfast Royal Academical Institution, known to us as Inst., my undergraduate years at Queen's University, and I later attended the Presbyterian College close by. I had spent a year as assistant minister in the First Presbyterian Church of Bangor, and now I had decided to follow many of my fellow students into war. Outside the City Hall in Belfast, I said farewell to Kathleen Burrows, then just a good friend, little thinking that it would be five years before we would meet again.

From Larne, I caught the ferry to Stranraer. Security control was very strict and I was amazed, and exasperated, when a letter I was carrying from my mother to my sister was impounded. I was not even permitted to read the contents, so that I could pass on my mother's words to Emily, who was nursing in London.

The train journey to Euston was long and tiring, but no one seemed to mind – it was wartime and delays had become routine. On my arrival at the YMCA headquarters in Tottenham Court Road, I found that the premises had been bombed. A landmine had exploded a few days earlier, killing many people in a pub and pleasure garden nearby, as well as several in the YMCA itself. I was directed to Morewell Street, where temporary accommodation had been found. As I made my way there, baleful sirens began to wail and I rushed to the nearest air-raid shelter, only to discover, when my eyes became accustomed to the dark, that I was the sole occupant. I slunk back into the street, shamefaced, and quickly mingled with the crowd. The spirit of the Londoners was incredible – the Battle of Britain was being fought in the skies above, and despite some very severe air raids, the high morale of the people was almost tangible. That night, when I went to catch the tube for Slough to visit Emily, the underground platforms were crammed with people preparing to sleep. They had spread out their blankets and bedding in a great line, leaving enough room for travellers to get on and off the trains.

I learned at YMCA headquarters that we would not be leaving for some days because various arrangements had to be completed. We were to be equipped with tropical kit and, because we were civilians, we required passports and Egyptian visas. Pleasantly, this delay meant that I was able to get accommodation in Slough and see something of Emily. The weather was at its best, and each day dawned with sunshine and clear blue skies. There were frequent air-raid warnings, of course, but I soon fell in with the locals, who seemed to know when the bombers were close at hand or remote. The sky was silently marked with the vapour trails of RAF Spitfires moving across Greater London to ward off the Luftwaffe Heinkels and Messerschmitts, and the *thud thud* of the anti-aircraft batteries seemed constant.

Eventually I was instructed to travel to Glasgow for embarkation, and on 5 October 1940 we boarded the *Oronsay*, an old liner that offered very limited accommodation for its wartime passengers. We 'welfare types' had all been lumped together, and what an assortment we were. Like myself, three others were bound for YMCA duty – one was an ordained Church of England minister, another had been a London businessman, and the third had been involved in opera. In addition, there were two ministers from the Church of Scotland bound for work in the Scottish Huts in the Nile delta. A Toc H man and an officer of the Church Army completed the group. We did not dwell on what it was going to be like living together for two months, crowded in the narrow, L-shaped cabin with four double bunks and one wash-hand basin. It certainly was going to be no pleasure cruise. Nor did we voice our apprehension about the German U-boats, which had sunk a great many ships in their lethal campaign.

We must have been quite an enigma to the Army people. Just where did we slot into the system? We were not officers and carried no rank, but neither could we be described as private soldiers. The compromise was to treat us as non-commissioned officers, which happily gave us access to both officers and men. The YMCA's role in the desert was a dual one. On the one hand we provided services for the soldiers, for example, running canteens and sending messages home: the Tobruk YMCA was one of the few places that the soldiers could get everyday supplies. On the other hand we were to play a deeper role in providing a place for men of all denominations to come together in an atmosphere of community. These roles complemented each other; looking after both material and spiritual wellbeing was at the heart of our mission.

Very slowly the ship moved away from the dock, pulled by two tugs into the main channel of the River Clyde. Along the riverbanks, a few passers-by waved and shouted greetings, some offering eloquent suggestions as to what we should do with Hitler and Mussolini. As we moved into the wider estuary under our own steam, the Clyde basin seemed like a vast, beautiful arena, encircled by distant mountains and the great spread of sea reflected the blue and silver of the sky.

We all slept soundly that first night, lulled by the steady beat of the engines and rocked by the gentle movement of the ship. But by early morning the strong swell of open sea was beginning to take its toll. When the steward brought the tea round, I decided to get up and shave, but as soon as my feet touched the floor everything became unstable and I was glad to make it back to the bunk. We ignored the call to breakfast, all lying as still as possible in our cabin, in the hope that the sickness would pass.

Then we heard a terrific crash and felt a great shuddering through the ship, which seemed momentarily to lift out of the water. The alarms began to sound and there was no longer time to think of being sick as we threw on our clothes, grabbed our life-jackets and rushed to emergency positions. When we got there, there was absolutely no panic, just a stoic acceptance and even the occasional wisecrack. At least we were still alive and afloat. As we looked out on the rolling waves, we could see two destroyers circling us like guardian angels. Some wads of bread and beef, washed down by mugs of hot tea, helped to keep up our morale.

We had been attacked by a single German bomber. A bomb had grazed the hull of the ship, exploding on the waterline and blasting a hole in her side. Another had passed through a lifeboat projecting over the side, and two others had missed altogether. The side plates of the hull had been damaged and the oil feed to the pump had been put out of order. We were without power, with the danger that more enemy aircraft would come to finish us off, and there were no friendly aircraft in sight.

The German plane had shot up the deck and we were told by the crew that five soldiers had been killed and eighteen injured. These casualties were never officially confirmed at the time. It was during the crucial Battle of the Atlantic and the policy was to say as little as possible. Everywhere, propaganda posters warned that 'the enemy has ears'.

Much to our relief, in the afternoon the engines began to hum again and we slowly made our way back to the security of the Clyde waters. As darkness gathered, everybody retired to bed feeling exhausted and profoundly grateful that we had survived.

While I waited for another ship bound for the Mediterranean, I worked in the Services Club in Edinburgh. Some of my friends there urged me to become ordained. At that time I was not a qualified minister, but only licensed to preach – a sort of halfway house. Ordination would have meant going home to Ireland. The idea was appealing and I set about making arrangements. But just as I was preparing to leave for home, a telegram arrived from YMCA headquarters: 'Come to Cheltenham for uniform and stay till departure for the Middle East.' That settled it. Early next morning I caught the crowded train from Caledonian Station, and as I leaned out of the window to bid my friends farewell, the guard blew his whistle and my journey to the Desert War had at last begun.

Chapter One

VOYAGE TO THE MIDDLE EAST

15.11.40 After some delay, we embarked on HMS *Andes*. Lovely ship, Belfast-built, about 26,000 tonnes, and we have first-class accommodation. Barker and I share No. 405. All of the original party turn up, so we are set for the journey. I hope we make it this time!

18.11.40 Fine big convoy of ten or eleven, 20,000 tonnes and over. Guarded by nine destroyers and cruisers and two seaplanes. Sea is rolling a bit, but so far I have felt no ill effects, although some of the men have deserted the Mess [canteen]. Reading a lot and making contact with the soldiers. Bach and I have been appointed librarians, so that will give us something useful to do and also help us to get to know the men. Felt a bit lonely but this was only a passing phase and was soon gone away. Best to live from day to day and not look too far ahead. Times like these reveal to me my own nature and how real religion is for me. Sometimes I find it hard to understand my English companions. Ross and Campbell spent most of the day in bed. Barker and I had prayers together before we turned in.

19.11.40 Convoy zigzagging a lot. Sea still fairly smooth. Long and uneventful boat drill in morning, at which no one appeared and we just stood around. After lunch, Bach and I got busy on the library and have about 400 Penguin books, etc., to work on. Men clamoured at the windows for them. Officer Commanding Troops sent for us today and as a result we go to second-class Mess with WOs [Warrant Officers].

20.11.40 Rather a rough night, but slept quite well on the whole. None of us feels too good. Spent afternoon in bed and cut out lunch. Food in second class is just as good as first, though there is not the same variety.

I am grateful to my parents for endowing me with a very sound digestive system. Have had no pains whatever yet. I think we are sailing southwest. Clock put back an hour.

21.11.40 Things a lot better. All on the mend and weather is on the turn. Barker is irrepressible in the early hours and seems to wake up singing. Ross has a droll sense of humour and a very infectious laugh. Walks round the deck are very refreshing, as I miss vigorous exercise very much. How I would love a game of rugger. Troops have PT [Physical Training] every morning. Their life is no bed of roses on board, but will improve as the weather gets better and warmer. Our naval escort has been greatly diminished, which must be a good sign.

22.11.40 A lot warmer today. Back to food with relish. Sat out on upper deck for a long time with a very solid chap who has a high opinion of Germans and a very low one of the Turks. Had a group discussion led by Methodist *padre* on 'Reconstruction after the war'. On the whole, it was rather weak.

23.11.40 Dropped a garment as temperature rises. We are well hardened to the sea life now and beginning to like it. Took in a lot of books today and spent a lot of time on deck. The fresh air does increase one's appetite and makes one sleep much better. This is a sunny Saturday afternoon. Sea is lovely and smooth and blue. Spent part of evening writing home. I wonder when it will be possible to post. Good news on wireless about Greece's advance into Albania.

24.11.40 Sunday dawns bright and clear. Lovely weather, on deck most of the day, reading, thinking, talking. These are grand days, which I'll always remember. Parade service at 10am. Communion at 10.45am. Evening service at 8pm. Today's joke: 'Air-raid warning near a cemetery at night. Policeman notices a skeleton climbing over the wall with a thin block of stone under his arm. Asks him what it is. Skeleton replies, "It is my identity card".'

25.11.40 Seems likely we will come to a port at the end of the week – Freetown, Sierra Leone – so we are all writing letters today. These have to be censored by the officers, and we give ours to Major Dobson, chief *padre*. I wrote to mother, Beth and Emily. These letters should get home well before Xmas and will relax the strain for the folk at home. It is also hinted that we will call at Capetown and stay for four days. I hope this comes off. Heat today was pretty strong. Cold salt baths are much in vogue.

26.11.40 Pass another ship today, the first yet. Notice up about dress. Informal (i.e., shorts and shirt) at breakfast and lunch; formal at dinner – the Englishman's prerogative, of course! Had a grand half-hour under the stars. Sea has been like a lake for days now, boat scarcely rolls at all. Ship is a terrific size and down below is like a miniature city. Bakery, kitchen, confectionery, bars and bars, laundry, and dozens of people. Most of the Tommies [popular name for British soldiers] sleep in hammocks slung from beams. A cabin is a real luxury. Long discussion at night on causes of present war, which I maintained to be economic. Bach and Barker disagreed and said it was lust for power.

27.11.40 Warmer still. Concert at night in lounge. Some of the stuff was coarse, and some was very coarse!

28.11.40 This was a day of activity in the convoy. Aeroplane launched from cruiser; ships take up different positions. All sorts of rumours about. Heat is very great now and we are down to the minimum of clothing. Sleeping at night is not helped by blackout, which cuts out fresh air. Out on deck in dark for another session under the stars; a lot of flashes on the horizon, which at first we thought might be gunfire, but turned out to be a phenomenon of the Tropics called wildfire.

29.11.40 A fortnight out today. Greeks still doing very well in Albania. Sighted land this morning and convoy moved into single file to go into Freetown Bay. On the left is very flat land with a golden strand and palm trees. On the right, land is much more interesting. Sharp rising hills make a very picturesque background to the tropical trees that separate the huts. Just such a picture of an African village as one is led to expect from films and travel brochures. A lot of shipping is spread across the large bay and we threaded our way carefully through these and anchor well up the bay. This town was once a stronghold of the African slave trade. Soon we begin to sample African manhood, as our ship is surrounded by men in frail little canoes. They soon have the soldiers in fits of laughter with their antics and language, which, though witty, was obscene in the extreme. I wonder what mission they come from! They are beautifully built and developed, like bronze Greek gods. Their *pièce de résistance* is to dive in after some coins thrown into the water from the ship and they are adept at this and never seem to tire. Others of a more practical nature hawk fruit in 'tandem' canoes and have with them all the paraphernalia with which to establish commercial relations with the ship. Soon they are doing a brisk trade with their bananas and another fruit. But this was quickly forbidden by OC [Officer Commanding], by means of the loudspeaker. One thing that impressed us about these simple folk was their irrepressible good nature. We did not watch them long without seeing them smile. How we wished that we could see their homes and their country a bit closer. Theirs is a carefree life.

1.12.40 We left about 4.30pm and passed many ships of all types, some had come in since we entered the boom on Friday. So ended the weekend in Freetown.

2.12.40 Making good progress, we are on left and coastal side of convoy. Much cooler today, though we are in the vicinity of the equator. Hear we will reach Capetown in ten days.

4.12.40 Today we had the 'crossing the line' ceremony, with Neptune, bears, doctor, etc., etc. There was much hilarity at the pool and many people were unwilling victims, mostly officers, and the men did enjoy it so. I was victimised by Toc H, but was allowed to strip and be ducked with shorts on, so I did not suffer much. All wear tropics [desert kit] now and it makes things a lot more graceful. Had a fine game of chess with Campbell at night. Clock forward an hour, so less sleep.

5.12.40 Wonder what they are doing in Bangor these days? This certainly is a different world. I don't know what I would do without reading. Mixture of light and heavy stuff is best. Theology and Crime! *Romans* is almost finished and I look forward with zest to *Mark*. Paul, apparently, was a universalist. Perhaps I'll get a commentary on St John in Capetown. Have started J.R. Glover's *Jesus of History*. On Tuesday we had an alarm in the morning: 'Clear the decks, enemy aircraft in sight!' We all rushed down into cover, but it turned out to be just practice.

7.12.40 Weather quite cool. Played quoit bowls with Ross. He is an unusual type. Very clever, with a quick sense of humour, which can be very biting at times and which he does not spare on the Irishman, who often has to resort to physical means of reply. Barker is a fine solid chap, though, being English, is a little aloof and impersonal, judging by North of Ireland standards. He is a Trojan for work and has a fine way with the men.

8.12.40 News very encouraging from Greece. Greeks have driven Italians well into Albania. Wrote more letters. Yesterday a chap returned one of C.S. Dempster's books and said he would like another of a similar nature. I lent him *Commentary on Luke*. He is twenty-one, son of a Church of England vicar in Forest of Dean. Is a poultry farmer and would like to be a minister. Very shy chap. Must be a change for him to be in the Army. Think I could do a little more as far as the soldiers are concerned – will set apart one section of the day for this. Reading is very important and I'm beginning to get some better grasp of the Christian faith. What a tremendous subject it is.

10.12.40 Bach and I still run the library. We hit it off well together. He has not had a Church since the last war and has travelled the world since; very tolerant and broadminded. He handles the men well and calls them 'Sport' when they come for books and so alleviates their disappointment when, as usual, there are none.

11.12.40 News is very good now from the Western Desert. Big action seems to be imminent. Bagdolio resigns and several other crooks appear in the Italian Cabinet. Is this the writing on the wall for them? Is this the tide about to turn? Is it the bus the Axis has missed so often, really missed at last? We are to stop at Durban, Natal, on Thursday and be ashore for a few days. That will be a welcome and delightful change from the tedium of ship life.

13.12.40 Land after nearly a month at sea. Africans, hundreds of them, all sizes and all sorts of dress; skyscraper buildings and bright, fresh colour of the houses; the distinctive character of the Europeans – due, I suppose, to the large Dutch element in the population; very fresh and lights – house lights, ship lights, neon lights, traffic lights, car lights. A sight for sore eyes! Rickshaws drawn by powerful Zulus with fantastic headgear and their peculiar way of balancing themselves on the shafts and 'air wading' along. Papers, fruit, etc., very welcome, not to mention drinks and ice cream. News is very good. BEF [British Expeditionary Force] has taken 20,000 Italian prisoners in Libya, and so we retire tired and happy, and sleep with open windows and some fresh air.

14.12.40 Found a YMCA last night and were welcomed there by Rev. Perry. Off ship about 9.30am for the day and have a fine time. Buses free and people very kind. Weather is very warm. Bach, Ross, Campbell and I make a beeline for bookshop. Bach and I pick about 80 Penguins for the library. Then lunch in the lounge, and what a lunch, stood by Bach. Salad and York ham, fresh fruit salad and plenty of drinks.

Town is crowded with soldiers and on the whole they are a quiet lot, though we meet some who have had a few over the dozen, especially the Australians, who have made a rowdy name for themselves already. One convoy stopped at Capetown and the Aussies painted the town red and outstayed their welcome, so perhaps that is why we are in Durban.

15.12.40 Ten days to Xmas. What a rush there must be at home. Sent a cable yesterday. Terrific rush at post office. We were taken on a drive by Toc H members to the Valley of the Thousand Hills. Trip was marred by an early mist. Did, however, get an idea of African mountain scenery and the vastness of the land, which goes on and on. Some of the headlands are reminiscent of north Antrim, though not so rugged.

16.12.40 Alas, leave ends at 12 o'clock, so we only had a short drive. Lovely view of town and ships far out in the outer bay; looking down into 'Bowl', whose greenness would almost be worthy of Ireland. We motored along a serpentine road through the bush – saw a lot of monkeys – and down to the beach and so to the boat.

18.12.40 Sea quite rough – poor old Ross not so happy on it. News still good, though 100,000 tonnes of British shipping sunk last week. Very hot today. Bath was heavenly. Hope Egypt is cooler than this. Saw some flying fish tonight. Sunsets and evening skies are wonderful, sea absolutely still, like glass, not a ripple on it – Indian Ocean. Thoughts in my mind: How soon will the war end? How are all at home? What will things be like after the war? How will I fit in to YMCA war work? What will I do after it? Feeling that theological position is becoming a bit clearer. How to get it across to others? Discoveries: that I have little quick wit, but it improves under the tuition of Ross.

24.12.40 A lot of excitement today. Cocktail party for officers. Orangeade is very popular among the TTS [Teetotal Society]. Italy seems pretty well finished in East. Strong speech by Baldwin. Lot of liveliness tonight and lusty carolling about 2 o'clock.

25.12.40 Xmas Day. United service on deck, but unfortunately the amplifier was not working, so little was heard. Quiet afternoon and quite a decent dinner in the evening. Whist drive for the men down in the inferno.

26.12.40 Very hot indeed. Well into Red Sea now, though it is not so bad as we were led to expect, due to the fact that it is winter here. Land sighted today on both sides, so we are into the Gulf of Suez; and to the left is the Peninsula of Sinai and to the right, the desert. Saw a very lofty range of mountains and was told that highest peak was Mount Sinai. But visibility was not too good. This has been a very quiet Xmas and Boxing Day and it does seem strange not to be buying presents and sending Xmas cards. But perhaps with these trimmings laid aside, one can see more clearly the real message of Xmas and its intense reality and hope in a world and a future such as ours. We will soon be finished with the trip. It has been interesting mixing with eight unknown people and has done me a lot of good in self-knowledge, etc. But I do look forward to the freedom of shore life and doing some real work, not just passing time.

29.12.40 Arrived at Suez. Steep, barren hills on one side and harbour and town of Suez on the other. Bay is full of ships. Town looked very bright and colourful in the distance, but we are not to disembark here. We are delighted to hear that we are to go through the Suez Canal, an adequate commentary in itself on the position of Italy in the war. Had to conduct devotional part of Sunday evening service. Met one of RASC [Royal Army Service Corps] – a baker called Boyd, from Belfast. He tells me there are other Irish on board. Two letters dispatched from Suez. Left Suez in the afternoon, very interesting run through entrance to canal, past Port Ibrahim. Sight of Egyptians with the camels, the desert, palms and mudflats makes us feel that we have at last got to the real East. Canal is a wonderful piece of work and must have taken a lot of courage and faith to plan and realise. There were several ancient canals built by Egyptians and Romans, and also the freshwater canal, which runs roughly parallel to Suez. Speed in canal not above 10 knots. Steamed into Old Bitter Lake and anchored for the night. This is traditional place of biblical marsh, and that the waters are very salty is testified by the density of bath water – I could hardly immerse myself in it. But it has become intensely cold and we are all back to thicker kit and warm blankets.

30.12.40 Stayed in Bitter Lake whole day and wished that we would get a move on. Shows that we are not needed too urgently anyway! News still good: Roosevelt speech; Burma surrounded. But heavy raid on City of London; another on South Ireland.

31.12.40 End of old year and it was a day full of interest – to complete a most eventful and happy year for me. Bangor past and gone, very happy summer, in spite of war, though a lot of unsettled periods. Where will 1941 lead? We were glad to leave the Bitter Lake today and soon sped through to Lake Timsah, where we again anchored. Here we saw war memorial – Suez 1914–1918 – which, I believe, is to Australian forces. Waited for several hours in lake and became apprehensive lest another night would pass and a new year dawn while we were in the same place. However, the culprit of our delay soon emerged in the shape of the *Highland Monarch* – of Belfast. So I was not so annoyed when I saw its home port. I can't get away from home these days – since this ship is also Belfast-made. We pushed on up the canal and passed some very interesting stations. Now we have railway and freshwater canal with us on left-hand bank. Many boats pass us. Ancient sailing boats with steep prows and kite-shaped sails, with Arab and Egyptian crews, who shout greetings and give us a thumbs-up. El Kantana was a most attractive place and had the real spell of Eastern romance and beauty about it. It is the ancient caravan route between Egypt and Syria, and it is likely that Mary and Joseph passed across here. After this we had a straight run to Port Said and country was very flat – Lake Menzaleh on our left. Visibility was grand and canal stretched perfectly straight for miles and miles, with golden sand on either side. We reached Port Said and were connected to the shore by floating jetty. Soon the ship was surrounded by Egyptian hucksters, with leatherwork and tapestry.

1.1.41 New Year's Day. We disembarked at 10.30am and had to wait until 2pm for train to transport us to Cairo. Waited in a sort of concentration camp beside harbour. Arrived in Cairo at 7pm, when at last we met Jack and Mrs Massey. We put up at Minerva Hotel and went to Gresham Street YMCA for a good square meal. Got mail – one from mother dated 10 October! So that shows us what to expect.

2.1.41 English breakfast, then out for a walk. What a cauldron of life and what a mass of noise and colour! Round to YM and met a lot of [field] secretaries, etc. Hear that Bach is to go to the canal and three of us will be on mobile work in Libyan desert, with two new vans. Said goodbye to Toc H, Campbell and Ross.

4.1.41 Went out by myself in morning and headed for bazaar, which I later found to be out of bounds. On the whole, a pretty tough quarter. Native bazaar was like the *Arabian Nights*. Shopkeepers in little narrow lanes, sitting cross-legged on the counter; others drinking Turkish coffee with a glass of water. Noise, smell and colour were terrific. Then went into El Moyait mosque. Put on covering shoes. Terrific desire for money from doormen, who look on any stray Christian as legitimate plunder. Then a free run on tram down to more respectable quarters and a Coptic cathedral.

5.1.41 Sunday. Up early, at 5.45am, and as sun was not up we had a very cold hour whizzing alone through the suburbs of Cairo. Soon we left the town behind and saw the wonderful dawn spread over the East – light red glow. What an unforgettable picture it made, with the palms and minarets. Passed through many villages on the Nile, wretchedly squalid and ill set out, with every sign of poverty, not to mention the smell. Nile was a fine sight, with its slow-flowing water and graceful

boats with huge sails. Often the sails were not in use and the boats were
hauled by natives, slowly toiling along an uneven bank. We said
goodbye to Bach and left him to it. I will miss him a lot. He is a fine
chap and good company and he was sorry to leave us, but we have a job
to do. Jack Massey is a good chap, one of the most attractive YM people
I've met yet, thoroughly organised, fine sense of humour, very human
and most considerate and reasonable, with a very sane outlook. Mrs M.
is fine and very homely. She works very well with him and keeps the
books and does general clerical work in an honorary capacity. I think I
will be very happy with them at the base.

*The author (right) poses alongside a YMCA vehicle with (from left to right)
'Chips' Cummings, Harold Barker, Mrs Massey and her husband, Jack*

Chapter Two

WESTERN DESERT

7.1.41 Today we started the real adventure. We bid Mrs M. goodbye and set off fully laden – three cars in all: Massey in Ford V8; Chips next in Fargo; and myself last in Fargo. The two new Fargos, gifts from Ladies of Burma, are to be our charges for some time. Lovely cars, especially cooled and tyred for the Western Desert. Had to take road easy, as they were not run in. Passed out by the pyramids on road to Alexandria. Beautiful road through the desert; miles and miles of sandy waste on all sides. Passed through several camps and then came to some prison camps; grim-looking places, double barbed-wire fences, hundreds of Italians in their dark green uniforms and caps. Very dirty and weary-looking and unshaven, but not unhappy on the whole, insofar as prisoners can be in such a state. On through wire-fenced zone into Alex – packed streets and motley crowds. Very modern, especially on the seafront, and more Greek than Egyptian. Put up at French hotel.

8.1.41 On the road for Mersa Matruh [MM], passed many men in convoys. Job is very difficult because units shift mostly in the night and YM hut is often left high and dry, so Massey has to develop prophetic instincts. Arrived at Smuggler's Cove and put up for the night; it is about one-and-a-half miles from MM. Here we met Mr Thomas, YM secretary, and Cliff Houghton, leader of Western Desert Area. Our camp was opposite Italian prison camp and it was pathetic to see the prisoners trying to dig into the ground to get some warmth for the night, as they had to sleep in the open. But judging by their songs, they were not too downhearted. This does bring home the futility of it all, that a man like Mussolini can bring all these poor souls to this humiliation and suffering.

9.1.41 Up and on the road for Sidi Barrani, not long ago the centre of
the news! Road very, very bad in parts. Passed through MM and what
there was of it – a little Egyptian village with its square houses and
white-and-yellow walls – was hardly worth looking at. But a house is a
house in the desert! More interesting were the sights of recent battle:
road mined to pieces; battered lorries with all the valuable parts
salvaged; burnt-out tanks; white wells scarred with smoke and fire and
peppered with machine-gun bullets, and no sign of any life except an
occasional Tommy; MPs [Military Policemen] sauntering round
directing traffic. Passing this, we entered the Italian Road, which they
had unfortunately not finished and hence was in a vile state, though
what there was of it was well laid. We stuck to the desert and had some
very hard bumps. Was a wonderful sight, three cars crossing the desert
and each raising a blinding cloud of fine sandy dust in its train. Had
lunch beside a deserted Italian food dump and we discovered a bag of
onions and sweet potatoes. Arrived in at Kilo 95 [name of camp],
surrounded with Italian relics and deserted Lancia lorries. We had a look
at a Bedouin well. Water is a terrific problem here and has to be
transported by road or sea. Ration is usually half-a-gallon per man, per
day. Italians salted most of the wells on their retreat, but fortunately
missed this one. Bardia fell last Sunday, so things are going well.

I attempted to sleep outside and in the morning I was almost
chattering with cold.

10.1.41 On the road for Sollum very early. Passed through a real war
zone; terrific amounts of war material, hundreds of field guns. We
examined some and most were marked 'Genova 1918'; also eight piles
of shells, bullets and bombs, all live, guns, swords, etc. And piles of
books on the science of war. On to a bitumen road, which was very
deceptive and bumpy, covered with rifles, uniforms, *topis*, burnt-out
tanks, cars. We picked up several letters belonging to Italians, one dated
'27.XI.40'. This is the appalling human side of war. Arrived early in the
afternoon in Sollum, where we are to work from. It is situated in a bay
surrounded by a steep escarpment, which is very sharp and rocky. There
we took possession of a sort of shed, an Arab house probably, and set to,
to get things going. Cleaned the place out and were selling stuff within
two hours. This place is not a health resort, but the right place in which
to fight a war. One of the big raids on London has done more damage

than all the destruction done in this theatre of war. The boys all hope and believe this affair will be over in a few weeks.

11.1.41 Remembered that yesterday was my birthday, that is the way life affects one here! Loaded up with goods in the morning from Sollum canteen. Started out with Chips and Cliff Hodgson on the road to Bardia. Did some sales on the way. The climb up the Escarpment is reminiscent of Ballycastle Quay Hill for view and Ballintoy for the winding road – oh, to see those places again! Then into the eighteenth-century Egyptian fort at the top, where swarms of swarthy prisoners asked for water and cigs. On to Fort Capuzzo – Italian fort – pretty well bombed to pieces; rather a pathetic sight as it rises to view on the road; it had been a real work of art. Vigorous demand all along the line. We passed many camps that rise up overnight like mushrooms and are gone in a few days. Over the winding road, we swung round the hillside and saw the now famous Bardia. It fell to the Australians last Sunday. It looked very picturesque on the headland far above the sea, but it is really a very small, one-street seaside resort about the size of Groomsport. We drove up to the sentries, who let us in almost at once to cheer up the lads inside. British troops are not admitted into Bardia in case of pillaging. Main Street was Via Benito Mussolini – what a sad sight it all was! A deserted village with only a stray cat or dog about and one or two lost horses wandering aimlessly down the street. Here and there, a British Tommy sauntering about, getting used to his task of occupation. The bright, clean houses were badly pitted and scarred with shrapnel and bullets, as the town had been heavily shelled from air and sea and land. Farther down the street we saw a lovely little church with the front blown out and the altar rudely exposed. At the back of the street I saw Bardia Bay, very far down, almost like a Nordic *fjord*, and Bardia Harbour, with a boom across the entrance and at least two ships sunk in the harbour itself. After this we inspected the site for the suggested centre on the Tobruk Road. We called it 'Oasis', a Rest House by the roadside that had been used by the Italians as a post office. Now it was just a wreck – clothes, papers, furniture strewn anyhow over the floor and in the courtyard, and, to beat all, we found a baby camel, which we fed on biscuits and were loath to leave behind. We drove home to Sollum in the moonlight – a tricky job, as we could not use headlights.

12.1.41 One of the strangest Sundays I've ever spent. Visited the NAAFI [Navy, Army and Air Force Institutes] stores in the morning and bought £40 of stuff for my mobile unit. Our job today was to go round Sollum area and do as many camps as we could. For a long time I was not able to locate any camps, (a) because of good camouflage, (b) because there was none there. Lots of Italian prisoners working in one camp; one, passing the car, tapped his water bottle and pathetically asked for '*acqua*'. How useless this whole thing is! Our doss here is not very comfortable – there are two big openings like garage doors and when the wind shifts round we have a cold and sandy time of it.

14.1.41 Out along Bardia line to outer defences until I came to Sidi Omar. Here I struck a RAF wireless post. The OC was a young pilot officer, who gave me a fine reception, and when I had met the demands of the camp, I stayed for tea, and with darkness not far off, I decided to stay for the night. Was well entertained in the tent of Stockbridge, the OC's batman [personal servant]. Supper consisted of baked beans, heated over a punctured fruit tin filled with sand and saturated with petrol (all this in the tent), followed by some excellent tinned fruit. Had an interesting talk with the OC. I slept in his tent and found that he took his duties most seriously. Also, he did not stand for the usual attitude of the officer to the men. How refreshing! Pilot Officer Morle of London. I hope I will have the chance to visit this camp again.

15.1.41 It was a terrible day and sand blew in everywhere in the gale and often I could see nothing at all. Sometimes the sand almost choked me as it blew up through the boards of the car. First camp was a medical station, where I met an Irish doctor from Queen's University, Dr N. Williamson, brother of Bill Williamson who is minister of Dromore. So we were almost as glad to see each other as Stanley and Livingstone, but I'm sure they got a better day for their meeting.

17.1.41 Went to Bardia Area HQ to arrange about orderlies, rations and water. This was my first meeting with Army as such, and on the whole I was not greatly impressed, except by the location of HQ. Perfect camouflage and air-raid proof. Got rations fixed up with RAMC [Royal Army Medical Corps], who were very friendly and reasonable. In the afternoon, Cliff and I searched around looking for the NAAFI in

Bardia, but it has not arrived yet. Had another look round Bardia and climbed up the minaret of the lovely little white mosque. Cliff asked sentry if he could take some of the prayer mats and sentry said that, as he had served in Palestine, he had learned to respect the Mohammedans, so Cliff took no mats!

18.1.41 Cliff and I set off on Tobruk Road to do mobile work and to try to locate NAAFI. Tobruk has not fallen yet, so of course we cannot go the whole way. Road to Tobruk was once Mussolini's vaunted Libyan pride, but I doubt if he would recognise some parts of it now with shell holes, etc. Sandstorm was so bad we could only crawl along. On until about 16 miles from Tobruk, where I served for two hours without a single break. Had to ration the chocolate. When we were about three-quarters of the way home, darkness and sand combined to make visibility nil. Ran completely off the road once into shell holes, but came out none the worse and just missed a big lorry a few minutes later. But it was worth it for a good bed and warm stew. Got a cable from home yesterday, with birthday wishes and saying that all is well. I do hope letters will begin to come soon.

20.1.41 Off to Sollum to scrounge stuff from the NAAFI with Scotty, a fine big Scottish chap attached to YM; very solid and useful. NAAFI did not receive me gladly and a lieutenant said that he had orders not to serve YM when stocks were low. Back to Bardia and had some cheese and biscuits (called 'dog biscuits' by the men) – a regular part of our ration, which, apart from the tea made with salt water, is quite good when one gets 'run in', to use a motoring expression. But I'm thinking that after all this, I'll not want to see anything out of a tin for a long, long time.

Now we are getting fairly well into this new life and not feeling the change so much. It is a very strenuous life and very exacting, but now that meals are more regular and sleeping accommodation better, things are not so bad. It is a hard life for the soldier, most unnatural, no recreation of any sort, all work and sleep. Surroundings unnatural, nothing green, just desert and dust, and what houses there have been are mostly bombed and putrid inside. Still, the amount of good cheer and humour is always apparent where least expected. I do wish we had time and opportunity to do some social and religious work. Sunday is the same as every day and many of the chaps say how they miss services.

21.1.41 Supplies very low and demand increasing all the time. One fellow said very pathetically, 'You know, it's three or four days since we have had any chocolate, chum.' We arrived at Kilo 64 to find no stuff there but a convoy was expected in the afternoon, so we decided to wait. A Pioneer Corps of Cypriots and Palestinians, composed of Jews and Arabs, kept jabbering away and seemed to be arguing all the time. Also a lot of Aussies around, not bad fellows when one takes them the right way. Tobruk will hardly last much longer. We could distinctly hear the dull, quivering thuds of the guns, though 40 miles away. What will the next step be after this? Benghazi? Tripoli?

23.1.41 Life at 'Oasis' is comparatively luxurious. Job for me is to go back and draw supplies from Mersa Matruh and come up as soon as possible. Cliff started off with me from Sollum, driving the Ford, and Nobby led the way in a pinched Italian lorry, which the boys have dubbed *Betty*. However, *Betty* had pretty well fought the good fight and petered out several times. She was eventually deserted and left as a memorial on the roadside. I took to the desert and hit quite a good track and soon got to Sidi Barrani. It is quite the most pathetic of all I've seen, a nice little village, with every feature of the houses mutilated. No roofs at all; windows only rude holes and spaces; walls half down and those that stand are pitted and seared by shrapnel and machine-gun fire. This village was the limit of the Italian advance, marked by a sort of obelisk on the roadside. History will always ask why they stopped there, as I hear from all sources that we were badly prepared for any advance and Alex could have been taken. The road improved, though it was badly shelled in parts, and I got to Kilo 44. Passed a lot of Indian Corps on road-mending work. Very picturesque in their turbans and fine black beards.

MM looked very lovely as I approached it from a winding descending road. Blue lagoon, white mosque and flat-roofed buildings and the wonderful red glow of the departing day. It had been quite a big town. There was a lovely little mission compound, RC [Roman Catholic], I should think, and much of the town was undisturbed, but eerie in its stillness. I immediately thought of Goldsmith's 'Deserted Village'. There were some palm trees about, which were a sight for sore eyes. Beyond, I saw barbed-wire entanglements and tank traps, looking like a cemetery stretching away across the country. On into the camp and Mr Thomas. Had a quiet evening and a good rest with him.

24.1.41 On the road as soon as I could get away. But first we gave out chocolate and cigs on the hospital train. Boys were wonderfully cheery, though many of them had been on the road four days from Tobruk. What an ordeal it must be for the wounded.

25.1.41 On the road from Sollum we passed dozens of lorries crammed with Italian prisoners from Tobruk, which fell yesterday.

26.1.41 Up late and off to NAAFI, where we got naught, and so into Bardia, where we had a council. Cliff is to go on leave tomorrow. Chips to take over in the interim. Problems are (1) supplies, (2) transport, (3) personnel. Had an urgent call today to go out into the desert and bring in a Tommy who had accidentally shot his ankle with an Italian gun. Said he had walked over it by chance. Soon had the lad back in the hospital. Long discussion between Cliff, Jim and self about YM Christian aim. How can we meet spiritual needs of the men in these exacting conditions?

27.1.41 This ink is Italian and all that I can find. Took Cliff down to Sollum on the first leg of his journey to Alex, on leave. We passed an aerodrome and I suggested that he should ask if any planes were going his way. We were told to 'run like hell' to a big, double-engined plane about to take off for Cairo and ask pilot if he had room. Pilot consented, and in a few seconds Cliff left me lonely and envious as he flew off to Cairo.

Back to Bardia. Italian prisoner lorry had capsized on the Escarpment and caused a long delay. There seemed to be a good few casualties. All sorts of rumours today. Germans have apparently entered Italy. Bardia taken. What a cauldron it all is just now! Let's hope the business is soon cleared. This is no country for large groups of men to live in. It should be left to the Arabs and the camels!

28.1.41 On the road to Tobruk we spotted the Australian YM unit that had been machine-gunned. It was a complete wreck and everything movable had been taken from it. It is believed that the secretary was killed, but this has not been confirmed. We had many enquiries for him in Tobruk from Aussies. We passed a big aerodrome, which was crammed with prisoners, thousands upon thousands, behind the barbed wire. The defences of Tobruk, some built since 1936, were very strong and deep. It is difficult to see how an enthusiastic army could be ousted and routed from them. Though Tommies were guarding it, they let us through with no ceremony and we toured round and eventually went down to the docks, which were quite busy. Six or seven Italian boats had been sunk. We met NAAFI authorities, who told us of great plans there – canteens, wholesale and otherwise – but we'll wait and see. My faith in that body needs a distinct revival. I met Pilot Officer Morle, whose men have been transferred to Tobruk, so I hope to see more of them, if our unit ever gets there.

The town is the biggest we have seen yet, but what a state it is in! Shops, a laundry, a bar, a blacksmith's shop – all were utterly ransacked. I went through a villa and what I saw was more like fiction than fact. Everything was strewn on the floor, all glass and light woodwork broken. Nothing of any value remained, as the stuff had been ransacked again and again. I feel bad that soldiers under our flag could do such things and get off with it. A small RC chapel was untouched, except for a little side shrine that had been ransacked, but we were told that a guard had been put on the church some time ago.

29.1.41 Chips met NAAFI staff and we shared our rations with them in their Tobruk HQ – a lovely Italian villa, with a veranda overlooking the bay. They have promised us support. Camp commandant gave us permission to begin operations and set up a centre as soon as possible, so things look bright all round and more than canteen work seems to be on the horizon.

Derna has fallen and Marshal Grazani has packed up. This is all a queer business, and it becomes more evident that the Italians have little heart for the fight. For me, now that I'm fairly well acclimatised, it is all a big adventure. The next move will be up to Tobruk and get into the job there as fast as possible.

30.1.41 Tobruk today! Two Fargos set off with equipment to set up a centre. First job was to get HQ for our work and got fixed up with a three-storey building; four flats in all, so we have plenty of rooms, though none of them big; also, a roof garden that has a good panoramic view of the town. The place was in a filthy mess, books, clothes, sand, rubbish and wreckage strewn all over the passages and rooms. The little furniture that was there was mostly broken and useless. However, we are next to 2nd Field Butchery and their captain has been very decent and has promised to help us to get equipment tomorrow. We did what we could before dusk and got our stuff into one of the rooms. We had little food with us and finished the day with the terrible blackish liquid called tea, made as strong as only Scotty can make it, cheese and crusts and burnt baked beans. It satisfied our hunger and after prayers we went to bed.

31.1.41 A month today in the Middle East and on the whole I like it well and would not be at anything else, so I hope the scope of our work extends. I do not want to be a car driver and canteen server all the time, though I am ready to do that. But I do agree with Cliff that this is practical Christianity and it is appreciated so much by everybody. The place almost looks like a YM now. We got the services of ten Cypriots for the morning. But it was a job to look after them, as they gabbled and mitched off at every opportunity. Scotty and I went round countless shops and collected about 40 wicker chairs, 15 tables, 15 wooden chairs, 3 wardrobes, etc. What a depressing job it was going round places that had until recently been homes, and we became very tired of the amount of pilfering that went on. One poor lad had a very costly and, I fear, tragic lesson. He was in one shop and walked into a booby trap, which went off with a thunderous explosion. His face was very badly cut and he could not see. Some Tommies rushed him onto a lorry and off to the RAMC. I think we will all give the shops and houses a wide berth in future.

In the afternoon, having dispensed with the services of the Cypriots at the cost of ten Woodbines and a bar of chocolate, we set about putting our own quarters in order. When we were at tea, three big planes passed over very low and suddenly the AA [Anti-Aircraft] guns started and tracer bullets floated across the desk like shooting stars, but it was too late, the Italians had been over. Was this the prelude to the evening's performance, we wondered.

The house is well equipped now and we have two rest rooms on the ground floor, as well as a canteen. On the second floor we have equipped a room as a chapel, as we hope to hold Sunday evening services. Problems are (1) crowds of men, (2) *padres*. The going is a bit rough at the moment, but pioneer work like this always is.

2.2.41 Loaded up both Fargos with what little we had and set off for Derna. Road quite good, except for two bridges that have been blown up. We counted ten plane wrecks scattered round, and frequently along the road we found other wrecks. Kept our store up as long as possible, but decided about 75 kilos [kilometres] out to return home and dispose of the rest on the way. Home about 4.45pm. Had a little service in chapel: Harold B. conducted it, Hugh Bell read the lesson, and I gave a short address on Paul's words, 'For me to live is Christ'. Lot of boys stayed for tea after and we had a yarn. Nice little fellow called Davis, keen on Toc H and Methodist Church. It was the first day that I felt we had tried something of the wider YM objective.

3.2.41 NAAFI flat. Australians kicked up a row the other night when the beer had been circulated too lavishly and the place had to be rescued by CMP [Corps of Military Police]. The canteen eked out an existence through the morning by means of very rigid rationing, but mobile units were idle. In the evening ASR [Army Scripture Reader] took prayers, which he turned into a real hot Bible-punching show, much to the embarrassment of Barker.

4.2.41 We got it really hot about 4.30 this morning and it lasted for over an hour. I stayed on in bed and put steel hat on. It was very close several times and I did have the wind up properly. I stayed on right through, believing the others were in their rooms, and at last went down and found them all in the shelter. Sometimes the noise was thunderous, with the terrific *thud* of the bombs, the drone of the planes, the *crash* of the big guns and the *ack-ack-ack* of the smaller, faster guns. Someone started with a Lewis gun nearby, joining the concert! At 5.30am peace came, but just then *reveille* blew for the troops. Needless to say, it did not need to be very loud.

5.2.41 Each day now has its own little thrill and today was not to be an exception. We got off fine for about 20 kilos until we began to pass a long convoy of Italian lorries, which are very broad. The drivers would make good unionists, as they would give 'not an inch'. We passed a couple all right and approached the third. As we were negotiating the pass, our car skidded and shot right across the bows of the lorry, hitting its wheel. We rocked back and forward across the road and plunged into the desert, passing over shell holes and ditches, and finally came to a standstill, laughing in amazement. Harold was much amused when I ate a bar of chocolate, saying that I needed some nerve food.

Got some stock today, which we augmented by a visit to the Australian NAAFI; and so the canteen is hard at it while the going and getting is good. Then Scotty discovered that his Fargo had been pinched. We got into mine and set off to hunt for the lost car, but could find no trace of it. Five cars in all had been taken. Scotty was naturally a bit upset, as he had left his ignition key in the car and so was partly to blame.

6.2.41 'Canteen closed until Mobile Tea Car has been returned' was notice put up on board the next morning. We set out on the trail again and were told the car was in an ordnance place on Derna Road. Most uncomfortable day imaginable, wind and sand made driving almost impossible. Went to the place and, sure enough, there was the car, but in a mess, and the report was that it had been overturned and two Australians had been seen running away from it. Right-hand windscreen was smashed and looked just like a spider's web. It had been smashed from the inside and most likely by a bottle; left lock was broken, mudguards were badly bent in, oil was all spilt out. We brought the car home, relieved that it was not worse. Much indignation among the men about the car.

7.2.41 Derna is a lovely town situated on the Mediterranean seaboard, at the base of a very steep escarpment. Ascent is very steep and windy. The town presented a fine picture from the top, white houses, palms, blue sea and sandy coves, fine streets. The place, when we got there, was usual bad picture, deserted streets, stray dogs, battered houses, mostly empty and bare. We moved slowly through the town for some place to dock for the night. We found a villa with water supply intact and Scotty cooked a supper of tinned soup, fried bully [corned beef] and tea. Both of us slept in the cars to make sure no one ran off with them without us.

8.2.41 Up and in action about 9 o'clock. Met a chap from Sandy Row, who treated me like a long-lost friend. I was given a present of Italian cigars. Run home was pretty stiff going, as it was dark when we had done about 50 kilos. But we used headlights a bit and moved quite well, until we got entangled in a seemingly endless convoy of huge lorries that were very difficult to pass. Finally we did worm our way through them and got a clear road.

9.2.41 Canteen at full blast all day. Benghazi taken. Now for Tripoli. Service at night. About sixteen turned up and it went off quite well. After the service, the lads came into the common room and we had a singsong led by an Australian opera singer. He sang from the *Barber of Seville*, 'Ole Man River' and some other songs, and for unaccompanied singing, I've not heard the like.

10.2.41 Went to north of Tobruk to naval tower. Here the place looked as if it had had recent seismic shocks, terrific cavity in the ground, littered with huge chunks of rocks and masonry scattered round a quarter-mile radius. Nearby was a very neat Italian graveyard with uniform crosses on each grave and one big cross on the wall. It was good to see that it was entirely unmolested. Today and yesterday have been very wet and cold, almost like winter at home, and when it rains here, it is no Irish mizzle.

11.2.41 This has been a day of changing plans. Last night we had decided that if we got insufficient stuff from the NAAFI, we would visit Bardia. But Scotty got quite a haul and so we decided to stay put and open canteen, and as it turned 4 o'clock, in walked Massey and Thomas. Grand to see them. Four letters are a real tonic.

A Palestinian Jew came along tonight and had a talk. He wants to become a Christian. Comes from Austria, which he left five years ago. His family are Christian and he and his brother were Zionists and believed in the future of the Jewish race in Palestine. But now he despairs of Judaism and wants to be a Christian. But to declare this openly in the Army will mean very severe persecution and suffering. He is prepared for this and willing to take the step, but his brother is not. He seems to be a very sincere and plucky fellow. I gave him two New Testaments and he is to come back with his brother.

12.2.41 Chips and I went across the big aerodrome near Derna and examined some wrecked planes. Most had been machine-gunned on the ground, as shown by the state of the propellers. One Savoia Machetti bomber had been stripped of everything of value, as indeed had all the others. I tried to cut out the Fascist badge with a tin-opener, but it was too tough for that. The wings were made of plywood and the planes did not impress, though the Fiat fighter was a better job and looked capable of giving a lot of trouble. One might call this the grave of Mussolini's Special Empire!

On to Derna, which really looked lovely today with the sun full up and a lot of the Libyans back in the town again. We got fixed for the night by a RAMC unit, which was preparing a school for a Libyan hospital, where seven Italian prisoners unloaded the car. And then dinner, and what a treat! Sardines on toast, eggs and sausages! Then a bath, a real bath, with hot and cold water and – words almost fail me here – electric light all over! We have been told that prison cages in Tobruk and Bardia were prepared for the British troops. What a vivid imagination they have!

13.2.41 Grand day on the road for Benghazi. Very interesting journey and countryside much more colourful. On our way we passed literally hundreds of white villas owned by [Italian] colonists, and met many Libyans making their way back home, as confidence was gradually restored. Not a few Italian cars passed with Italians [i.e., civilians] going back to the towns. Chief points of interest were an old Italian fort, which made one wish to know something of the history, as did considerable Roman remains farther on, a very well-preserved aqueduct and sarcophagus and many other buildings. Passed through several small but interesting towns and, on the whole, normality was rapidly being restored. Indeed, it was very difficult to realise that we were approaching the front line, as things seemed to get more and more normal as we advanced. It was often difficult to imagine that war was so near, as there were so few soldiers about.

This journey was rather distressing for us because of the incessant demand from the men for the stuff that we had to take on to Benghazi. At last we shook off the hills and raced down onto the broad seaboard plain. Scenery soon became very Eastern – sandy coves almost on a level with the sea, while the road was verged with palm trees. Soon we approached Benghazi. We could see the two mighty domes of a RC cathedral for a long distance. City was completely flat and almost all at sea level, divided roughly into native and Italian quarters. We located the town mayor and later went out to serve CMP, who were camped about 10 kilos from city, passing an aerodrome, where I counted roughly twenty wrecked planes.

Back in dark and all but rammed another car head-on. Had a grand meal in an Italian hotel and got very nice quarters nearby. On the previous night there had been a very heavy raid and landmines were dropped – one had done a lot of damage and many windows were broken. One mine had dropped in the harbour and the waves had gone down the street. Soon got to sleep and only had a short raid during the night, which did not worry us much.

14.2.41 Continental breakfast, which I find rather frugal, and spent most of the day selling stuff. Big demand for cigarettes. Had a most welcome haircut in an Italian barber shop. Chips speaks Italian and we had an interesting talk with the hotel chambermaid, whose gesticulations and imitations of HEs [high explosives] were a treat to watch. She had little use for Australians, Mussolini, or Fascists, and seemed to be sincere enough.

15.2.41 4.30am when a bombardment began, some 'whistles' [slang word for 'shells'] fell rather close, but we stayed put in bed and though building was shaken nicely several times, we were none the worse. This was the worst for me so far! Guns of all sorts were going off, though AA defences do not seem to be adequate. Sounded like Germans were dive-bombing, according to Chips. Got clear of Benghazi about 9.30am. Back to Derna and RAMC, which was a bit noisy, as Aussies nearby were amusing themselves with hand grenades.

16.2.41 Another Sunday. Prepared for the service and had a most encouraging turnout of about forty men. Singing was an inspiration and the Aussie tenor sang a solo. How we would love a piano. I spoke on *Hebrews* 12:1. Sermon on life as a race and it seemed to hold them all right. Fine singsong after. *Padre* Doyle, Church of England (Australian), comes in on Monday, Wednesday and Friday to talk to any of the lads. He is to baptise the Palestinian on Friday.

18.2.41 Got a fine load from the NAAFI and so I persuaded Barker to go forward with Scotty to Derna and I took over control here in Tobruk. It was a hectic day. We have now acquired two Italian prisoners to help in the work. They are both '*marinos*' (or sailors) and handymen. One is a magnificent specimen of manhood and both are very friendly. It must be a galling experience for them. I have conversations with them and by gestures I can convey quite a lot, and the closeness of Italian to Latin helps me to remember many words. *Canis*, dog; *panis*, bread, and so on – makes conversation a real discovery!

I was in canteen most of the day. One does appreciate the British Tommy in this job, as he compares favourably with the others, though the Aussies are not bad. The Palestinians are a bit hard to handle. They come in waves and have little manners, shout and argue, though some are very nice fellows and many are Jews from Austria and Vienna, so one has to be patient. The most trying of all are the Libyans, who know no English, are very persistent and suspicious that one is trying to do them.

23.2.41 Sunday. Two Aussie YMCA secretaries arrive – MacLaughlin and Mallyon. They bring us some stuff from Alexandria and decide to stay with us and we have a good *craic*. They are Presbyterian and so we have a lot in common, and Barker is in an Anglican minority for once! Both are Home Missionaries and doing a course to become fully ordained ministers. Both are married and Mac was in the last war. They had a gramophone and some fine records, which they played at the service and after. Position of Australian YM is very different from ours. They are officers without rank and therefore part of the Army and attached to definite units – six YM to a division of 15,000–20,000 men. They do not do canteen work, but confine themselves to social and religious work. I sometimes wonder who is right and if we are wasting our time on so much canteen work, but the work in Tobruk demonstrates that all these jobs can be combined and one fits into and helps the other. I believe the Aussies feel this also, but they are forbidden by the AYMCA [Australian YMCA] to sell anything because of the criticism of canteen work in the last war.

24.2.41 Had an interesting chat with an Italian sailor, in broken French and Italian words, in which he said that he had no wish to fight against the British, but had been forced to by Mussolini. Had a walk through

Italian tanks and lorries in Bardia. What a scene of desolation and waste!

25.2.41 Went to Sollum and got £144 worth of stuff, though no chocolate, or sweets, or fruit. Magnetic mines dropped in Sollum Bay, and barge with 250 men blown up some days ago. Back to Tobruk. Arrived in to hear of severe enemy action last night. Destroyer *Dainty* sunk in the bay by a direct hit. Field Bakery hit: several killed and many wounded with jagged shrapnel. Very heavy bomb fell at foot of our street and some of our windows and doors blown in. Dolly in hospital with wound in the arm. Not serious, though it has given him a bit of a shake-up. *Terror* has also been hit. Things are in a queer position now. Little news in circulation, but multitudes of rumours of all sorts. Apparently the scrap here is about finished. 7th Armoured Division is on the trek for Alexandria and today I passed hundreds of lorries and cars of suntanned men with black berets, all looking tired and covered with sand.

26.2.41 Alarms last night and this morning. Got us up in nice time. Went up to hospital and saw Dolly, who hopes to go to Alexandria in hospital ship in a few days. Distributed about 15,000 Woodbines among the patients. Some bad cases from the *Terror* and the *Dainty*. Brings one up against reality. Met a RAF chap, Dodds, from Lisburn Road, who tells me Jack Tannahill is in Greece. Lieut. Gray of Bangor turned up in the evening and it turned out that I had met him, so we had a grand yarn about home.

27.2.41 This was a lively day. It began with a warning at 6.30am, which did not develop, but got us mobilised for the day. Then when I had just filled up with petrol, the traffic suddenly stopped and drivers rushed into the side trench, which was practically useless, but the raider plane was well up and plastered with AA. We saw the plane with puffs of smoke bursting all round and so the danger was past.

Today we acquired a piano from the Palestinian canteen, which has ceased to function. Last night Army Scripture Reader stayed for the night and today we started off with a prayer meeting in the chapel, to which ASR brought his dog and his cup of tea, much to the annoyance of Barker. He is going back to base for more tracts, etc., and another wireless. Aussies pinched the last one. An interesting visitor and one who made his presence felt!

28.2.41 Another day issued in with an air raid. 'Eggs' [bombs] fell on the other corner of the square and considerable damage was done. No alarm was given and suddenly I heard a whistle and a terrific grating crash and flash, then another. It was unnerving and we all rushed downstairs with little or no clothing on. However, it was all over in a few moments and once again we were in good time for breakfast. The Field Bakery lost another man today, making a total of four in Monday's raid. Wally and I went off to hospital and did mobile work. A really useful bit of work and much appreciated. One poor lad from London, from HMS *Dainty*, asked to see me and we had a talk. He was an Anglo-Catholic and wished to have Communion again. What a brave, plucky fellow, and what a tragedy!

1.3.41 Five months from home today and two months on the desert. Another nasty storm with gusts of wind and sand, like yesterday. Last night we slept in air-raid shelter, which has been made for four berths. Got a slight sore throat, but hope to banish it with Aspros. A little stock today, so work is still ticking over. A navy officer, named Brown, who lives on Malone Road and was at Inchmarlo, knows the Higginsons and tells me there are many Irishmen down in Alexandria. A few warnings today, but little happened. Last night there was a lot of AA fire. Most of the troops have been evacuated to suburban camps around the area.

We had to take back our two Italian prisoners, Bruno and Raphello, so that they can sleep in prison camp. But they will come and work each day. They are attractive fellows, with very nice manners. Raphello is a splendid big fellow, as gentle as a lamb, and when he says 'Bruno', it's like a distant rumble of thunder. We had a grand English–Italian lesson last night, which we all enjoyed. Poor lads were upset when we took them to the prison camp, which was filled with soldiers and pretty shaggy specimens of humanity and I could understand their reluctance. It was amusing packing four of them into back of Fargo, with Wally and corporal from next door with guns to prevent them from escaping. All enjoyed it thoroughly, and it seemed like a Students' Rag Day rather than a war. Tommies are very decent to prisoners and they get plenty of freedom. Reason for this restriction is because signalling has been going on and wires have been cut.

This part of the drama is finished and all indications are in the line of the Balkans, via Turkey. We do not expect to be here long now. Chips has gone down to Mersa Matruh, so we expect developments. One recalls what Donald Hankey said in the last war: 'Out here the issues of life and death are close, but we take the first step in faith and God does the rest.' Although these conditions are nothing like his and the people of London are passing through a worse time. Yet one often does think of the possibilities and the Faith does make a very great difference in the sense of Someone behind who cares. I have been reading *Luke* lately and go back to it with the greatest relish. It lifts my mind onto another level and makes me look forward to post-war days. Services give me food for thought here. What is one to tell the men that will really help them? The one thing that they want to know is if Christ's power is a real, dynamic power in the lives of ordinary men. All this makes me feel that I am a poor Christian and how much I need some power beyond myself. From Barker I've learnt a lot of things: his unselfishness – Tommy is always first with him – and his even-temperedness. I look forward to running a centre of my own and look on all this as a sort of probationary period. Another remarkable thing is that I'm not worrying about the future – perhaps this is indifference, but I believe the advice Father once gave me: 'A day's work in a day.' I will be glad to get some letters from home.

3.3.41 Spent the day in bed. Got a letter from home dated 5.12.40. Notes from Mother and Father, both in Portrush. Great comfort, especially coming at a time like this. Both seem very well and in the best of good spirits. Judging by the letter there is at least one mail that has not come through.

4.3.41 In bed all day today, but in the afternoon throat got a bit easier. Capt. Richards, RAMC, brought down a straw mattress, which eased things a lot, as lying on springs with a couple of blankets between is poor comfort. Tablets from hospital are a great help, as is lime juice cordial.

5.3.41 Got up today though I felt just rotten, but hope to shake the feeling off as the day goes on. Took some sun out on the roof garden. Bit of excitement last night when CMP thought they saw someone in the house signalling to the enemy. They rushed up the stairs and are still looking for the man.

7.3.41 A good bit better today. Went out to Tank Corps on desert and sold stuff for most of the afternoon. These lads live a very hard life, in the desert all the time, iron rations [i.e., basic rations] all the time, sand, noise. Most of them look wonderfully fit. Lieut. Dunstan, who entertained me, was a very bright young Londoner who attributed his fitness to alcohol in various forms and quantities. This seems to be their one form of relaxation.

9.3.41 Not in best of form as yet, with a rash and sore eyes. Using as much Optrex as I can get. Long and pointless talk with Massey, who is not clear on situation at all, but advocates tea and social side and fears that I am doing *padre*'s work. But what is the difference between YM and *padre*, especially when there is no *padre*?

10.3.41 Mobile work – had a long yarn with captain in 'Lights' [Communications] who knew a lot of Belfast people. Told me he found that most unhappy men in East were those engaged or married. The Aussie YM passed through *en route* for Alex yesterday – Mac and John Mallyon. Jokingly, they asked me to join Aussie YM and in some respects I'd be glad to. These lads do cheer me up a lot, they are so human.

Had a talk with Capt. Jackson of the NAAFI. Very interesting chap and frank. Talked mostly of religion and we covered a lot of ground. He's the old type, decent, wouldn't see anyone stuck, doesn't see any need for a personal religion, yet sees it in a wider sense. Does not believe in immortality at all. Very keen on ascetic approach to life.

12.3.41 Wireless in action and tea on sale, so we are doing something worthwhile. Library restocked for Massey's visit. Mostly Aussies who use the library.

16.3.41 In bed all day with a gyppy tummy. Managed to scrape through the sermon in the service on 'I have made and I will bear'.

19.3.41 No. 15 CCS [Casualty Clearing Station], Derna. Doctor. Admitted into dysentery ward immediately, though it is only a slight touch.

20–23.3.41 Had no difficulty in settling down here: (1) comfortable bed, (2) no biting mosquitoes, (3) feeling that I was in proper hands. CCS is in fine surroundings, and trees and birds remind me of home and the springtime.

After Tobruk, Derna is like the Promised Land. I have little pain and feel in fine form and try to do some thinking and meditation each day. I'm in a two-bed ward and have as companion a New Zealander called Lee – a decent sort of fellow and we soon struck up friendship. Chips and Scotty in to visit me. Chips is at his best at a time like this and Scotty is a gem. Felt a bit depressed at times over the whole show and our work. Keep thinking of home and of the sort of food one gets there when ill, and attention, but it wears off as I come back to form.

Hospital routine is amusing. Of course, we have no female influence here and the place is run by medical orderlies who are the most careless crowd of individuals I've encountered for a long time. They are assisted by several Libyan civilians and some Italian prisoners. Three sets of men with little or no means of communication. I was on a fluid diet the first couple of days, but at mealtime the Libyan brought round the full diet as regularly as clockwork. Lee gets his meal back to front – tea, sweet, meat, etc. And one simply can't explain what's wrong. Then the doctor put me on to light diet and I got what Lee got. But it all adds to the variety, though I'm glad I'm not really ill, as this food would not encourage one to get better. The doctors are very decent and painstaking.

Nearly three months in action now. Time to think has helped me to see the position more clearly and, on the whole, I feel a bit disappointed. This is due to the fact that I'm not sure what the YM wishes to do here and Massey is very woolly on policy and no one knows what he wants. As far as the Army is concerned, our main function is canteen work, and if we did have sufficient stuff, we'd have no time for anything else. No stuff up now, so at Tobruk we try to keep other end going. I suppose we have to expect these problems, but I would like a clear declaration of policy. I feel that the most effective YMCA work is done in base camps, though Tobruk and Tobruk alone has done a little more up here. What is one to say to the chap who is decent, moral, glad to do a good turn, etc., but feels no need for religion or Christ? And what hope has Christianity to offer, more than personal salvation? Army life has not made me take a higher view of human nature. No doubt decency and unselfishness is there, but it takes the worst circumstances to bring the best out. In day-to-day life, Tommy is pretty much self-centred and out for his own ends. One does, of course, meet frequent and delightful exceptions, and one is amazed and thrilled at the way most of them treat Italian prisoners when they get to know them.

24–25.3.41 Still in CCS, though I feel like the Young Pretender and wonder if I'm keeping any more deserving cases out. Wandered round the grounds and sat about reading. Very hot in the open. Went out in evening and cadged a lift to YMCA, where Scotty gave me a hearty welcome. Stanley and Nobby arrived back from Alex with a lot of news but, above all, with a splendid mail for me – eight letters and two books – so I had a great feast of news. This was the best tonic of all and I could hardly settle down in the CCS for the night, but wrote a couple more letters and so soothed my excitement. I am to be discharged tomorrow.

26.3.41 Went before the Lieut. Colonel and was discharged. News of Axis Non-Aggression Pact with Yugoslavia came through.

28.3.41 YM busy, with chaps in to hear the news on radio. Yugoslavia revolution and new government in. Two big victories in African war. Bruno and Raphello said farewell a few days ago, as they were being sent off to Alex by sea. They only got as far as Tobruk Bay and the ship hit a mine. Sixty-two lost. Bruno and Raphello swam for it and Raphello rescued Bruno as he was sinking. Poor Bruno looks badly shaken up and both have lost all the little they had. However, they do seem happy to be with us again. I'm to go back to Cairo with five orderlies; Cummings and Scotty will follow and Barker will stay on at Tobruk until situation clears. My immediate reaction was joy, with a slight tinge of regret at leaving the desert. But I hope everybody will soon be out of it to more healthy climates.

30.3.41 And so we leave Tobruk; a place of mixed memories for me. It looked at its best as we left, as if making its last appeal. Made Bardia and Sollum with no trouble, but tomorrow is the real test. NAAFI put us up in their quarters. The staff here is languishing in boredom with nothing to do, but the base is necessary to receive goods from the occasional ships that get through. They gave me a very comfortable-looking bed, but after a short time I discovered fleas and spent a most uncomfortable night and was glad to be up at 7 o'clock.

31.3.41 Sollum was a delightful sight, a wonderful calm everywhere, nobody about and the only sound was the waves lapping the beach across the road. Even the Escarpment seemed almost friendly, now that it has been once again left to its ageless solitude. The sea is a wonderful reassurance of the things that are never-changing and it always has a soothing effect on me. However, the peace of the early morning was soon shaken from our bones on the boulder road to Sidi Barrani and we wondered if the old car would stick it. At last we made Sidi Barrani, or what was left of it. What a desolation it is!

On to Mersa Matruh. Road bad until Kilo 44. But when we did get onto the good road the car began to chug and we knew it was running on two cylinders. Nobby eventually got it into good form again and we reached NAAFI, 12 kilos from Mersa, where we had very welcome eggs and chips. After a lot of wandering in Mersa an Aussie captain (trust the Aussies when you're stuck) fixed us up with six new plugs and told us if we'd any more trouble to 'burn the car and keep the plugs'. Now onto the main road for Alex – 280 kilos.

The Med was a constant treat and its colours were heightened by an almost continuous reef of white limestone, which formed a lagoon along the beach. Very rocky country and the switchback road did not add to our comfort, but frequent stoppages to refuel with oil and petrol gave us respite. The vegetation increased as we neared Alex. Clusters of palms relieved the monotony of the desert and in one place there was quite a carpet of pretty, brightly coloured poppies. We passed many Bedouin tents, which have hardly changed since the time of Abraham. Arabs are a wonderful people, living on the desert with their herds of goats and sheep and camels.

We approached Alex through a network of camps, quarries, roads, railways, factories, and went straight to Kosta's, where we got a grand meal of steak, chips and eggs from a very decent fellow who really made us feel welcome. Then the lads parked me in the Gordon Hotel, and after a bath I went up to Scottish School for supper. After supper, I went to the pictures – *I Married a Nazi*, not my choice!

1.4.41 All Fools' Day, and I felt one after waiting two hours for the lads to come from the garage. They turned up at 11 o'clock. Terrific naval action in Ionian Sea, in which several Italian ships have been sunk. Car went very well and at dusk we saw the outline of the Giza pyramids and so Cairo once again.

2.4.41 Breakfast in bed. When I clap my hands, Mohammed or Abdul glides, ghost-like, through the curtain with turban and flowing robe and breakfast appears in a few moments.

Massey decides I am to go to Greece. I spend most of the day trying to arrange for overhaul on GMC [General Motor Company car]. Got it arranged at 8pm when I finally met an Irishman who had a brother in Derriaghy and knew the Lowrys in Bangor. When Greek meets Greek, things are done!

4.4.41 Massey has gone up the desert to have a look at the situation. Today the news comes through that Benghazi has been retaken by a united German and Italian force. I am making preparations for Greece, have to take Brenton car, a reconditioned Ford V8 and supplies, as much as possible. In the afternoon I decided to see the Citadel and Mohammed Ali Mosque. Passed some very fine mosques, stately and majestic. Went up to Citadel and was relieved of my new Falcon camera, much to my disgust. Mohammed Ali Mosque is breathtaking. Usual courtyard, with ablution fountain. Inside, a wonderful sight. What impresses is the great height of the roof and the effect is maximised by the low circles of lamps, all round globes. Passed under the lectern and had my wish. Guide was rather attractive and seemingly a devout Muslim. Mohammed Ali's Palace is a bit mouldy now, occupied by troops for a long time. Wonderful view and terrific buzz of human voices rising from the teeming streets and houses far below, and the Nile waters gleaming in the evening sun.

5.4.41 Waited all day for Youssef to come from Alex with Brenton car, but he did not arrive. Went to Gresham Court to sleep and met an interesting Tommy. We had a very pointed talk, as he started off by saying he was afraid of his past and scared to die. It is such a pity that one sees these fellows and then passes on, but all that can be done is to make fullest use of opportunities that come along. Wrote to Mother and

John, with cryptic references to my new destination culled from *Acts* and *Paul* on Mars Hill. Big sea battle off Greece.

6.4.41 Sunday. I hoped to get to church today, but no luck. Youssef turned up and said, as excuse for yesterday, that he 'was not good inside'. Nearer the truth than he knew. Germany declares war on Greece and Yugoslavia, and it seems I'll have a front seat in this new act.

The author, pen in hand, in YMCA uniform

Chapter Three

SERVING AT THE FRONT

8.4.41 Orders to embark at 4 o'clock, so spend a busy day getting things ready and down to dock, with the help of Scotty, Nobby and Stanley. Got supplies from Kosta, who is a fine fellow and eager to help. Down at dock, things were in a mess and car was loaded, unloaded and then loaded again. I got accommodation in a two-berth cabin with two officers – lucky, when one sees the ordinary soldiers sleeping under the stars. Boat is an awful old tub, the *Custodian*. Discovered I could go on shore for the night, so eagerly went back to Mohammed Ali Square and sought out the YM and was lucky enough to find John Mallyon & Co., my Australian friends. We had a posh dinner in a French restaurant.

9.4.41 Back to the boat at 7am, where we did nothing all day but wait, so I went ashore in the evening again to pass the night.

11.4.41 Very tired with waiting. No news of sailing and on six hours' notice. Had an air raid about midday and a lot of shrapnel was dropped. Is this the shadow of things to come? Today is Good Friday. What a thought it is amidst all this. The war atmosphere, especially as we have nothing to do and the news is not so good, gets us down a bit. I do not know what I would do if I had not the Easter message to hang on to.

Have had a real problem to deal with – pilfering by Egyptian dockhands and caught several red-handed. Car has no lock and when they were down in the hold storing stuff, they used their opportunity and several cases were broken into and some chocolate and biscuits taken. I very nearly punched one of them on the jaw, but what's the use! My respect for Egyptian morals has sunk below zero.

12.4.41 Still here and feeling pretty blue. Wrote to Father, John and cousin Katie. Flies today have been almost unbearable and I smoked like a furnace all morning, but still they came on. Fortunately, definite news came through that we would not sail until tomorrow and so we all took the night ashore. It was a good relaxation and I made the best of it. Posted letters and found my old Aussie YM friends still in Alex, washing their dirty linen with the Commissioner, who had flown from Australia. But they decided to leg it and we dined in the Cecil and took four New Zealand nurses to the cinema and then had tea. The evening did serve to lift my mind, but rather a poor preparation for Easter Sunday.

13.4.41 Easter Sunday. The service was a memorable one, held on the forward hatch and surrounded by big Chevrolet trucks, with the crane poles just at head level and the wind blowing across the harbour. I used the King's quotation – 'I said to the man who stood at the Gate of the year – "Give me a light that I may tread softly into the Unknown." He replied – "Put your hand into the hand of God and that shall be for you better than a light and safer than a known way"' [quoted by George VI in his first Christmas speech] – as it seems especially suitable now that all of us go into the unknown.

News that we will not sail till tomorrow gives me another glad release from the ship and I hasten downtown to worship at St Andrew's, Church of Scotland – a fine little church full of Servicemen. Rev. McKean conducted a helpful service and I stayed on for Communion and was indeed grateful for such an opportunity.

14.4.41 More activity on board and presence of tugs raising high hopes. But our captain would not go out as there was a high sea running all day and some risk of taking the boat through the channel in such weather, so we still wait. Spent most of the day reading and looking at Greek grammar. Little did I ever dream that classical Greek would be of such practical use, though there are vast changes from the language of Plato's time. My mind is in a strange state these days, keen to be on the job and I'm feeling exhilarated about the future adventure, wondering what it will be like and how I will react to it. Food today was salmon in three acts: fish cakes, potato and salmon, and salmon and potato.

The Aussie officers are an attractive lot of men. I find it easier to make contact with them than the English officers. Especially as most of them claim some Irish blood. But Lieut. Barnicot, the only English officer aboard, is a fine chap and most friendly and looks after his men well. They are on the Ack Ack [Anti-Aircraft] and are on duty all the time. German units have penetrated to Sollum, though Tobruk is still in our hands. Crack Nazi Armoured Division thrown back in Greece. Massey was to fly to Greece today – I wonder if it came off?

15.4.41 Woke up today to the music of the turbines. We moved off at 7am, and when I went on deck, the harbour of Alex was well astern. And so, after a week's delay, we get on with the job. Moving about 5 knots and eventually pick up another convoy and now we are part of an imposing fleet. Like old times. News from Tobruk is good; strange to think of the struggle that goes on and of enemy focus on Derna.

16.4.41 Rather a nice day and sea on its best behaviour. Some machine-gun practice in the afternoon shattered our siesta. Then the signal went round: 'Expect air raid soon.' Apparently a plane had been over on *reconnaissance*. No raid for a time and message goes round, 'If no raid before dusk, may come in moonlight', so we live on in hope! Captain says tomorrow will be tough going, but everyone is cheerful about it all and takes it as a joke. Getting used to wearing tin hat and carrying lifebelt around.

17.4.41 An uneventful night. But we waken up to be told at breakfast that we and three other ships are to turn back to Alex. Message came from the destroyer and naturally caused a lot of disappointment and speculation. Turned back at 11 o'clock and bade farewell to the other ships. Weather was very bad, rain and wind, which of course was most welcome to us in such a position. Ack Ack cruiser came up yesterday and we will be conducted back by one of the destroyers. And so we are not to see Greece, not yet anyway. I felt a bit annoyed about it, especially as it means more hanging around and waste of time. However, someone probably knows more than we do. So we are cruising back across the Med, bound for Alexandria. Interesting to think of those who sailed these seas in the past. I would like to have seen a few ports.

News came through of a very heavy raid on Ulster, and especially Belfast. This is the second and I suppose it had to be. It is hard when one can have no details and can do nothing about it. London also had its heaviest visitation last night. Poor Emily must be having a gruelling time in the midst of it all.

Owing to the heavy weather, we passed on our way unmolested. Got hold of H.G. Wells's *Fate of Homo Sapiens* and read it most of the day. Not a very cheerful book to read under the circumstances. Almost like reading a book on surgery while appendix is being removed. His diagnosis of human situation agrees with prophetic theology, but his methods of readjustment on his own is the old humanism writ large. Valuable points in his book are passage on Nazi Germany maintaining that they 'have not brutal strain' in their make-up, but that it is the creation of circumstance. His onslaught on the British oligarchy has much truth in it, though he says little of its good points.

18.4.41 Weather dawned bright and clear. Had two 'stand by' alarms for enemy aircraft and destroyer opened fire on one, which passed hastily on its way. Mine sighted and destroyer accounted for this with gunfire. Then at 4 o'clock we saw a fine sight, the Mediterranean fleet in full sail, going where? Fourteen ships in all. One aircraft carrier and the rest made up of battleships, cruisers and destroyers. Someone is for it and I was glad to be on a British ship. Wonderful to see the carrier surrounded by its escort, like a Queen and her courtiers. About an hour later a destroyer came up, apparently to catch up the fleet. It was in full cry and ploughed up the sea, spray breaking over its bows as it bore through the water. Capable of 32 knots. Lieut. Barnicot seems almost disappointed that we've not had anything to shoot at. Everyone is in the dark as to this move of ours. The lads in Greece will be wondering what is holding me up.

19.4.41 Sighted Alex and took up Egyptian pilot. Sailed slowly through the channel and got in about midday. Car and goods will not be moved until tomorrow.

20.4.41 Lot more stuff pilfered. Slapped one Egyptian face, as I caught him in the act. Just managed to make church and the sacrament after. In the social hour after the service I met a lot of Ulstermen: Jack Thompson of Fortfield, Dunmurry; Moore of Derry, who played tennis at Castlerock in the old days; and some Ballymena chaps.

21.4.41 Still waiting instructions for movements. Went out to Stanley

Bay with Selsa Blue and Dilys Williams. Very pleasant day, had lunch there and a bathe. Spent morning getting Youssef to fix the car. Dinner at Scottish School and evening there. Had to take lads to Transit Camp again. Greece position is pretty unstable, as we are losing a lot of ground there.

22.4.41 This was a day of wires, two from Massey, (1) not to go to Greece unless I was strongly convinced I should go, (2) not to go at all, so back to Cairo.

25.4.41 Out to Mustapha Barracks and bought some clothes, including a battle dress. Thrilling news came through that Father has been awarded DD [Doctorate of Divinity].

28.4.41 Floodtide of letters from home. Bought Voitlander Bessa, which should do a useful job: 6.5 lens, delayed action. I have to go to Western Desert and organise work there as best as possible with three cars and Major, Clarke and Scotty.

29.4.41 Collected car and took it to Abyssia to have it camouflaged and recanvassed. Chips is back. Seems to be in good form after his leave in Palestine. He is to come to Alex with me and look after Sidi Bishr. News these days is discouraging. Evacuation of Greece. Tobruk holds out against Nazis. Barker and Tank still on the job there.

30.4.41 Spent three hours walking round Abyssia looking for depots and sub-depots, all in the heat of the day. Finally found the car in the hands of four Egyptians, who were enjoying themselves splashing paint on it.

Got off about 5.30pm. Interesting chat with Massey. My respect for him increases as I get to know him, a very likable, human man. About 60 kilos out engine began to weaken and petered out about 40 kilos from the Half Way House. Getting dark, so Chips set out by foot and I tried to fix the car, but had to give it up and wait for something to turn up. At last a lorry did turn up and it was a breakdown, so I was soon at H.W. House. Had a good meal and two Tommies fixed car, where I slept, as it could not be locked. Very cold and tried to keep warm by piling up magazines all around.

1.5.41 Arrived in Alex about 12 o'clock. At 9.20pm Ack alarm and then from the roof we saw a real firework display. Alex boasts the best defence in the Middle East. Searchlights all round the town and guns sending up a fierce barrage. One plane was caught in lights and commonly reported to be shot down. Dilys Williams calmly watched this performance from the flat roof, commenting on the beauty of it all.

2.5.41 News is not so good these days. Iraq at war with us and evacuation of Greece almost completed.

5.5.41 Some mobile work done today towards Bagush. I set off to visit *Padre* Cecil Henderson, who is in Mersa M with Church of Scotland canteen. All goes well until I have a flat near Mersa. No spare wheel, so come back for one. Back to car to find dynamo, petrol tin and sand mat all stolen. Nobby tows me in to Mersa and we search in vain, and I return in utter disgust.

6.5.41 A memorable day. Had hoped to go to Sidi Barrani to arrange forward work, but lo and behold, a horrible sandstorm darkened the sky. Nobby and I set out to see what the going is like. It is very nasty – sand sweeping across the road, obliterating everything, and motoring very unpleasant and dangerous, especially with minefields about. So when we got to Mersa, we called it off and I went to Lido Hotel, where boys say Duke of Windsor once stayed.

Back to camp and stay in during the afternoon until the tent is blown over. What a wreckage and mess. Paper blows all over the desert and bushes blossom with leaves – of YM notepaper. We salvage what we can, but storm forces us to retire into the car. Scotty and Stan come back and situation is almost too much for Scotty who lets loose on us and everything in general. Soon the storm lessens and Stan goes off for help and returns with car filled with Arabs, much to my amusement, and so the old carcass is raised from the ground and life restored to its normal course again, though Scotty takes time to forget. Sandstorm is over and all is peace once again.

Another very heavy raid on Belfast and here we are living in comparative safety! What a war! Wonder how Emily is in London these days.

7.5.41 Started off with Nobby before 9 o'clock. Weather seemed to be an atonement for yesterday. The freshness of the morning and the stillness of the evening are two lovely features of desert life. It is then that one forgets about the war and all its gruesomeness. Road to Mersa heavily fortified with tank traps, barbed wire, and minefields all over the countryside. It has the look of a real battlefield. Sentries check identification cards at each defence. View of Mersa by direct road is wonderful, deep blue of the open sea and light yellow-blue in the lagoon. The mosques lend distinction to the outline of the town, which by now is pretty well battered about. It is an Australian garrison. Soon out on the road to Sidi Barrani, which is 137 kilos away. Few troops about, except occasional patrols and camps. On look out for enemy aircraft. Sidi B. a desolate ruin and on to the road for Bug Bug. A rather ghostly experience, as there were no troops at all in this area and no sign of life. Nothing but endless sand hills and deserted lorries and cars, now completely pilfered and destroyed. Eerie feeling all the time – Nobby loaded his rifle and we almost expected to meet a German patrol over every hilltop. Two men met us at the appointed spot and we were welcomed by the major and sold for two hours. Down to another unit and off for home at 5 o'clock. Arrived in at 9.40pm, having covered 400 kilos. Glad of tinned sausage and tomatoes, which Scotty cooked for us, and felt the day had been worthwhile.

8.5.41 Back to see the Ulster Ack Ack brigade at Lido Hotel. The lovely beach presented a gay spectacle today, crowded with suntanned Aussies swimming and sunbathing.

9.5.41 Hoped to go to Bug Bug with two cars and started off from Quasaba, but another really atrocious day, with sandstorm and heat. Abandoned the idea at MM. Spent most of the day in the tent. One driver arrived in exhausted; it was his second day on the desert and what a day. The sand lashes across the desert and scorches us like the blast of a furnace; temperature yesterday was said to be 125. In the evening the wind died down and all was still again. We are getting settled down into our stride. I'm glad to be on my own and to run things in my own way, though the lads, having so much knowledge of the job and having been on their own so long, need tactful handling.

America seems to be putting on full steam and may be in the war very soon.

10.5.41 Went to Indian camp in Mersa to get a haircut and got a grand reception. Great interest and pleasure taken in my haircutting, which gathered a large crowd round the 'mango' tree. Cigarettes offered and accepted; unfortunately, no medium of communication except smile and gesture. But it goes a long way with these fellows. They are an attractive crowd, with their beautiful teeth and flashing smiles and dark bodies. I wonder what real interest they can have in this war. All went well and my shearing was almost complete when guns started and plane came over. What a rush and scramble – Scotty and I found ourselves in a tent trench. Soon the raid was over, and with great merriment the clan collected again and my hair was finished and I felt a better man. I offered to pay, but they would have none of it and with more smiles of goodwill we took our departure. My last three haircuts have been performed by Italian, Greek and Indian. Who will come next, I wonder.

11.5.41 Massey and I go out on mobile to Mersa and beyond. Terrific demand, and in spite of ration, our fruit goes like snow in the desert. Up to Kilo 44 on a further quest. Had lunch of mangoes and sausage and water. Today much cooler and pleasant. Talked over plans for future with Massey. Probably will send up another secretary. Lots of stuff going up, so something's in the air.

12.5.41 Little mobile work in Mersa. Saw Ulster Ack Ack and met Bob Thompson of Belfast, who was at Inst. and very glad to see me. This crowd are to move down to Quasaba.

14.5.41 Breakfast at the cookhouse, though tea was barely drinkable, so strong and sweet. Started for Bug Bug, but got about a mile along when I was stopped and men ran from all directions to mobile. Eventually, when there was a lull, I beat a hasty retreat into the desert. News: Hess captured in Scotland; action in Sollum.

16.5.41 Got as much stuff as possible on the two cars and set off on road to Sidi Barrani, resisting all entreaties to stop on plea of greater need at the Front. Most of the soldiers and officers accepted this and let us go on without protest. At Sidi B. we examined an Italian cemetery. Many graves left unoccupied. Several unknown British buried also. One felt that death, at least, unites all men. What a pathetic site Sidi B. is with its roofless ruins and wrecks of cars, guns, and odds and ends strewn over the desert. Only place with a roof is old NAAFI hut. Passed several German prisoners in trucks, with their distinctive tin hats. Set out for Bug Bug and got there after a blow-out and another puncture. We fixed up for the night with anti-tank unit. Got a good meal and just as I was talking to a staff sgt. from Cork a plane loomed up and I said, 'Do you know, I haven't seen a Jerry [German] plane yet?' No sooner said and a whistling sound was heard and boys rushed for any available cover. Ginger and I took shelter under the car. Three bombs dropped in a line, one about 150 yards away. Boffer guns [anti-aircraft artillery] opened on him and he cleared off. And so I have seen a Jerry plane! One man from RASC was killed.

17.5.41 On to mobile car about 7.30am. This area is crammed with camps on both sides of road, and at every turn we were besieged. From time to time, officers and staff cars stopped and asked us to go to certain camps and we obeyed as far as it was possible. Some of the scenes were almost pathetic. We drove into one place situated between three hillocks and immediately, from all sides, men rushed down and queued up. The poor lads looked pretty well done in. No one we met the whole day was shaved except an occasional officer. One felt that here was the real job and how much we would have given to have a 10-tonne truck to get to grips with the job. This is the closest I've been to front-line conditions. Stanley said that the YM had never got up as far before and never had the demand been so great. Got back to poor old Scotty, who had kept a hungry and lonely vigil while we were away.

18.5.41 We load up with 60,000 fags, etc., and set out. Scotty is a bit upset as we pass some troops on road, but one has almost to be hard-hearted to be kind in this job. Get to Sidi B., where van is besieged by Scots Guards, Tanks, etc.

Several big bombers over at night; after heavy raid on Jerry, one made a forced landing nearby. We are rather doubtful when these things pass over our heads and are most reassured to know they are British. Today was Sunday.

20.5.41 Up at 6.35am and feeling excited at going 'right up'. Followed pick-up truck over hill and dale to Bug Bug salt flats, and passed some British tanks which had been trapped in the soft ground in an early battle. We are told to follow to Hell Fire Pass, which is much in the news these days and is right on Jerry's lines. This experience is one I'll never forget – up, up, the rough road wound from the Escarpment, heat was terrific, below lay Sollum, now a deserted no-man's-land of charred petrol dumps, wrecked vehicles, sanded trenches and rocky dugouts. Beyond, the lovely beach and the sea looking bluer than ever. Up we went, passing little groups of sun-scorched men, with promises to stop on the way back. Near the top we served several big tanks, who were most glad to see us. 'Good show for YM to be up with us!' 'Grand job you fellows are doing!' 'When will you be back?' Sold all we could to many units, which appeared from nowhere, almost like an ant hill of a gathering of the clans. Issue of socks was greatly appreciated. I was impressed by the Tank officers, who muck in with the men and were most appreciative and friendly to us and asked us to begin there the next time, which we will do. When proceedings were in full swing, someone shouted, 'Planes!', and everyone dived for cover. We saw three Heinkels far up in the blue, off on the hunt. No stuff was dropped. We had some very welcome tea, and with a much lighter cargo, set out downhill. Several stops on way down and sold out most of kit. On the road for Quasaba we saw a staff car that had hit a road mine.

My opinion of Army life goes up by leaps and bounds these days. But I am not impressed by a certain type of English officer; indeed, many of them represent a type of English life that must go forever if England is to fulfil a worthy destiny. I see it in how little they think of their men, how they treat them and what they expect of them. I wonder what they are fighting for. Is it to get back to the old life of high society, hunting, etc.? What do they believe in? Themselves – alone! Do they want to see a better world, better social conditions at home? Certainly their attitude in the Army reveals no hope for the future, if such are in the majority. Reaction among the NCOs [Non-Commissioned Officers] and lower ranks after the war will take a lot of handling.

23.5.41 It was a very nasty day, with sand and wind. The heat was terrible and we managed to get to Kilo 50 on Sidi B. road, when we had our first puncture. This mended, we had a blow-out a few kilos later. So we decided to come back and got the GMC tyres changed and ready for tomorrow.

Fierce battle in Crete. France gives more concessions in Syria.

24.5.41 Got off today, though sandstorm was still raging and engine heated up a lot and we had to stop several times to let it cool. In MM saw a lot of South Africans, who are relieving Australian 7th Division, who are off to Syria and aren't they glad about it! Got through to Sidi B. with our load practically intact, as we want to take it right to the Front and work back. Camped for the night near Bug Bug with a bunch of RS [Royal Signals], who maintain the lines. A happy crowd, who did us very well – steak and potatoes. The funny man of the bunch, a flaxen-haired regular, tattooed all over the body, made the evening go in quickly. Slept in one of the big-wheeled Italian desert cars. Life in the desert certainly has its moments.

25.5.41 This is a much better day and we soon get on the move for the Front. We are not to go up Hell Fire Pass, as it is being shelled and units up there will send down. By the time we had served three units, it was well on towards evening. Lot of shelling going on, especially by our batteries, and it took some time to get used to the crash behind us. Officers would not allow crowd round van in case of shelling. Enemy are reported down in Sollum and so we were within 2 miles of them and perhaps nearer their punch on the Escarpment. However, he kept on his best behaviour while we were there.

The lads are quite cheerful, but terribly fed-up with life in and around Sollum and on the desert in general. I heard a lot of gruesome stories and got the impression that these fellows were confident of success. Most are eager to hear any news and with the wireless on the Crailsham I was up-to-date and often had to broadcast it to quite a crowd. Seemed too ludicrous to be in one of the main theatres of war and to tell the soldiers in action what was going on there. Drove back at night over the salt flats. I don't know how Stan kept the car going! However, we came to an abrupt halt when we found ourselves right up against a white barrier. It turned out to be one of the silver sand hills on the Salt Lake coast. Here we found ourselves in a camp and beside a cookhouse, so there we dug our well and pitched our tent, and all night we heard a persistent rumble, and often it was more than a rumbling.

Someone was getting it hot.

26.5.41 Shared a breakfast of bacon and beans and set off, doing some units as we moved back. NAAFI has got some large mobiles through, so this area is comparatively well off. Served quite a lot along the road, who were greatly surprised when we told them we had been right up to the Front. Got in about 4 o'clock and found Scotty in good form.

Ginger very anxious about his girl in London. He has had no news of her for two months, though he has sent several pre-paid wires. Poor lad thinks that something has happened. Unfortunately, he tried to drown his sorrows and came home under the care of two CMPs. After they went, he spent a couple of hours talking about her and wanted to go up to Sollum and take it out of the Jerries.

28.5.41 Ginger and Scotty go off on mobile, while I hold the fort here. Heat and flies pretty bad. News of terrific battle in Crete, sinking of *Hood* and swift retribution in the destruction of the *Bismarck*. Roosevelt's speech assuring freedom of the seas and that British will get the goods.

29.5.41 Ginger and I go off on a mobile run on Sidi B. Road. Glad to do this district, as in the race for the Front a lot of these camps are forgotten. Broadcast news to water-carrying unit, who had had none for days. Many casualties had passed through from Coldstreams. On our last visit to Sollum we just got out in time, as Jerry made a sudden push with tanks, artillery, troops, etc., and our boys had to bolt for it to Bug Bug, where the line is now. Coldstreams lost eighty men and a bunch that we had tea with had to be abandoned. Hasty evacuation of Hell Fire Pass described by Tank officer, Ross Downey. Our quick return is rewarded, as presence of four new sand tyres indicate, also a wire for Ginger, so the situation is greatly relaxed. Also a few letters from home: letter and polyphoto from Emily, letters from Ida Mills and Kathleen and Sheila Burrows, card from Mr Weyrns, so I had an interesting read.

30.5.41 Included in yesterday's letters was a happy one from Massey, saying he had heard a lot about our work on Front and Chaplain General had rung him up after his tour of six days up here, telling him of how much our work was appreciated. Today, Nobby got stocked and he and I set off for Front. We pushed through to the Signals and there decided to park for the night. Nobby issued socks, handkerchiefs and sweets. Had a welcome dinner and then listened most of the evening to the lads 'broadcasting' along the lines to the other signal posts. One had a fiddle, another a saxophone and improvised drum and mouth organ, playing popular tunes and all the old favourites. Talked to two chaps about life in general. One was a very keen spiritualist and a terrific sentimentalist.

I get great chances these days to study the ordinary soldier, and though it is difficult to generalise, their incurable sentimentalism is most striking. It comes out in so many ways, tattooed arms and bodies, songs, talk. Most of them believe in God, but care little about any expression of such a belief. All are browned off with the desert and long to go back to dear old Blighty. I wonder will some of the new expressions stick: so and so 'is gone for a six'; anything that surprises one is said 'to shake him'. Arabic will yet exercise the same influence on the English language as French did in the last war. Most of the lads pick up expressions very quickly.

31.5.41 In the morning several German planes flew over, but didn't bother us. Got away and up to Front troops. One CSM [Company Sergeant-Major] took me for a Fifth Columnist with the new *topi* Nobby brought me from Alex, which is like those worn by Jerries. Did a lot of small units on way back. For a long time I noticed black clouds of smoke issuing across the desert from the road and we finally came upon a lorry burning fiercely. This turned out to be one of NAAFI mobile canteens. The crew of four looked on hopelessly – lorry £1,300, £200 stock, £90 cash, all gone for a six. Corporal in charge asked me to witness that I'd seen cash box burnt out. I took a photo and lost Polaroid glasses in process. Brought back three of NAAFI staff and got a very welcome meal at the Mess.

1.6.41 We have been stocktaking. In afternoon we went to Smuggler's Cove and had a very refreshing bathe. Heat is increasing every day now. Wrote to Mother and John Pedlow. Crete has been evacuated and war in Iraq is finished after thirty days.

4.6.41 I went two miles across the desert and came upon Armoured Brigade HQ, all scattered round in a huge circle and very widely dispersed. I stopped near a staff car and got a cup of welcome tea and some bully. All were surprised to see me and were amazed when they discovered I'd come alone. I met *Padre* Rodgers, who was to be my guide and philosopher and friend for the rest of the trip. He turned out to be Harrow and Cambridge and was a most attractive person and knew his function very well. He decided that we should do one of the more convenient squadrons before dark, as there were a lot to do the next day. *Padre* turned out to be an expert navigator and indeed everyone must be in such a place, as tracks are few and very difficult. The squadron was in a great circle, with the control vehicle in the centre; flags on the wireless masts and the crews wearing black berets. We turned the lot and distributed socks, etc., and talked to the lads. They seemed a fine lot, and officers and men mix well together. All keep in touch with each other by wireless. At dusk they come in close and disperse again at dawn. These were the lads who were responsible for the great push through to Benghazi. Let's hope they go through again. They'd seen little of YM, but I told them that they'd gone so fast we could not keep up with them.

So we got clear of the squad. Dusk was falling and after a time, *Padre* said we were off course and eventually he said to go due east and, sure enough, we soon spotted a faint blue light, which was our camp. Into the officers' Mess and had a grand meal and coffee. Slept in the car and was ready for it.

5.6.41 Wakened to round of machine-gun fire, which is signal for dispersal. Quite cold and everything was covered with dew. Had a sort of shave and an excellent breakfast. Eventually we got off right into the blue, with nothing for miles and miles, not even a track in sight. Now I was in the hands of the *padre*! Good illustration for a sermon on trust. *Padre* used prismatic compass and map. Bill, the *padre*'s driver, was a good fellow and able to keep the course very well. Arrived with a unit of armoured cars, and got the now customary welcome. Drove round the lads, while the *padre* talked to the OC. One bunch gave me a mug of tea, which I managed to drink. We need a lot of literature of a decent sort. Only thing we have at moment is *Blighty*, which is a bit near the wind in its humour and I often feel we should not distribute it. Still, it's that or nothing and they all asked for reading matter. Here one is confronted with the real heroism of the war. These lads are right out in the heat of the desert sun, with no sea to relax the sand-weary body and mind, living on the minimum of rations and water, in constant danger from enemy air activity and enemy mechanised patrols. When they are travelling, they sit in the heat and dust and discomfort of a tank; and death, if it comes, is like that of a rat in a trap. And yet, seldom have I met a more cheerful crowd of lads. I really did feel that it was a privilege to serve them and to be able to give them some comforts [items such as woollen socks, pyjamas, etc].

On the day's run we did 100 miles, which in such a country is some going. The *padre* told me that at one point we were within 8 miles of the wire, with nothing between us and Jerry. Each squad warned the next one of our approach, so that if we were overdue, they could send out for us. At one stop we were told that the squad we had just left had captured an Italian lorry with two small tanks on it, one of which had escaped. Sorry we did not see the capture. Lovely view of the Escarpment and land all around, wide sweeping spaces and lovely orange sky. All was beautiful, except the immediate ground over which we moved.

8.6.41 News of British move into Syria is encouraging. Uneventful run to Alexandria, with GMC going like an aeroplane. I suppose it's the homing instinct for the garage in Alex. Arrive in about 3.30pm and find that Alex has had a real blitz. Parts of Rue des Soeurs had to be detoured. Landmine in Rue Fuad and a lot of damage all over.

9.6.41 Tried to get through to Chief, but phones out of order. The poor Arabs have been badly upset by last night and many thousands have evacuated by any means available – car, train, truck and foot. The railway station was pandemonium and you could not get within 100 yards of it. All trains to Cairo were running free [of charge]. Ginger and Scotty went through with a letter to the chief. They scrambled onto the Mail Van and slept on mailbags.

11.6.41 Had a rather unsettled night, chiefly on account of a *muezzin*, whose morning call to worship began about 3am and seemed interminable. John and I got up about 4.30am and trekked through

Alex to our respective *pensions*, meeting a lot of people returning from the shelters in the hope of snatching a few hours' proper sleep.

14.6.41 Preparing to move up to Sidi B. Lot of stuff gone up for a push forward, so we hope to be able to keep in touch with the troops.

17.6.41 All moved up in three cars with complete kit to Kilo 95, which was used as a YM in the last push. It is an old Arab Rest House with three rooms. Tent was pitched on the other side of the road. So all is set for our job here. Big push up Front is now on, but no news has come through as yet.

20.6.41 On our way up last night we met one continuous stream of traffic coming back. Action is over and apparently both sides suffered badly and we are back to the old position. Movement on road makes the boys anxious, so I go up and see staff captain of the Guards, who is most reassuring and promises at least six hours' notice if we have to move out. Still rather a strained feeling between the two lads and myself, but they have to know who is in authority and though it is unpleasant, on the long view it has to be done. Last night we had to leave the car and take shelter, as the road was machine-gunned, and one camp 60 yards from us was machine-gunned by one of our own Hurricanes. Pilot apparently lost his bearings and supposed he was over enemy lines. My feelings, strange enough, were of excitement and not fear. This is the first time I've seen this form of war. Cecil Henderson arrived in and stayed the night and we had a good *craic* about home and the people we knew. I suppose in years to come we will recall this night together.

21.6.41 A hectic day in the canteen and for the time being we have become the NAAFI and handle orders up to and beyond £20. The new fellows are now doing well and fitting in to the scheme of things. Had many long queues and all were tired at bedtime. We are on hard rations: bully beef, cheese, biscuits, jam, sausage, tea, sugar, fruit – about four tins. My poor old tummy has been a bit upset on this frugal diet, but Tiny, the genius, managed to scrounge a bag of spuds for a bottle of lime juice, so the position has been relieved considerably. I never before realised potatoes made such a difference, and me an Irishman. News these days is of Allied advance in Syria, practically unopposed.

This evening I set off on my own on mobile up to Sidi B., where I had tea with the Ulster Ack Ack and a yarn. Saw them stand-to for action when a *reconnaissance* plane went over, but they did not open fire, as they did not wish to give away their position. Then on up the Bug Bug track and stopped with our Signal friends. None too good in the morning with tummy, but carried on up and did all the troops I could locate. Had to take shelter a couple of times as planes were over. This place got a bad strafing yesterday and several of the Coldstreams were casualties. However, there was little to report today. Still a lot of artillery up on Front and poor chaps are thoroughly browned off.

25.6.41 Boys saw Hurricane shot down yesterday by two Messerschmitts 109; pilot's body was blown to pieces and nothing left of plane. Later another pilot in a Lysander tried to land nearby and broke his hip. The big event that has coloured everything else the last two days is the entry of USSR into the war, as Germany declared war on her two days ago. This event will certainly change the course of the war.

28.6.41 Getting things fixed up today when an officer of Rifle Brigade walks in and asks about stuff for forward troops in desert. As I was free and had some comforts, I offered to follow him to six-and-a-half south of Sofafi. Well, journey lasted five hours and was worst I've had so far. Down Bir Emba track, via Habata, in a sandstorm. For long bits of the run I could not see ahead at all and often could not see the dashboard. Eyes, throat and mouth were soon full and the chest wheezed like 'flu time and I was glad when we got to our destination. But here I was bitterly disappointed by my treatment by my officer escort. He left me to feed at cookhouse and did not take any more interest in my existence until I met him as I was going off the next day after lunch. This was the first time I had not been asked into the officers' Mess. I felt very angry about it, but sleeping under the stars, got less resentful.

29.6.41 Woke up to the noise of gunfire and found blankets be-dewed like Joshua's fleece. I got the comforts divided into five piles to be sent up the columns with rations, as I could not go up because of the distance and danger.

2.7.41 News mostly of German action in Russia. Heavy British bombing in Germany. Alex is very deserted, comparatively few natives about and on the whole looks much better than on our last trip. Go to YM and have a fine shower and meal. Put Ginger on to 3.45pm train and go to Comforts Store and load up with books, etc. Then I went to Scottish School, where I found a Scotch party in progress. Met all the folk who seemed to be none the worse for the blitz attacks.

3.7.41 Met two New Zealanders who had been to Crete. One was a law student at Dunedin and knows Frank Green very well and tells me Frank is in Maadi Camp, in Cairo. Poor lads had a terrible time in Crete and feel terribly resentful against the powers-that-be about it. No air support at all – Air Borne Troops dropping all day. One of them was taken prisoner for seven-and-a-half hours. Germans told them of what would be done to them in concentration camps in Berlin. Hospital was captured and Jerry made wounded walk in front as a shield for his advance, result was that many were shot by our own men. This New Zealander was walking with two chaps, one on each side, one was killed and the other seriously wounded. Dive-bomb attacks lasted all day and they prayed for the shade of night. In one dive-bomb and machine-gun attack the New Zealander threw himself down on top of another chap. The chap below was hit three times, but the New Zealander escaped untouched.

10.7.41 Had to take GMC to keep appointment with *Padre* Cuthbert Peacock and we had a blow-out, which made us very late. His camp was about 20 miles up Bug Bug track. Found it about 12 o'clock and eventually the *padre* arrived. We did HQ, but news of a direct hit on slit trench of one of forward guns altered our plans, as he had to go up immediately. I was glad enough, as GMC is not fit for desert travel. We did a lot of positions on way home and lads were indeed glad to see us, as they had no canteen stuff at all. And so, after a most useful day, we got in about 7.30pm and had some Italian stewing meat.

11.7.41 I was without a car and spent most of day in canteen and tent. In the evening I hitch-hiked up to 110 Kilo and walked across to coast about 5 kilos to discover that car would not be ready until tomorrow, and so I had to hike back. Got a lift on a Polish convoy and tried to tell them the news. Armistice signed with Vichy France in Syria. Intense British raids on Germany.

12.7.41 With car packed up to limit – 400 pairs socks, 150 tins sweets, 1 case Vaseline, 30 bundles of magazines and canteen stores – we set off and met *Padre* at 129 Kilo. Have Davie Young with me to drive and sell, as a break from the canteen routine. And he is pleased to come. Through Sidi B., where I get some oil from Ulster AA Battery and wish Lieut. McCullough a happy Twelfth. He expects ructions later on in the day. We struck into the desert and the *padre* took Track WSW, aiming for the Escarpment. It was one of the lesser-used tracks and so we had little dust and the going was good. But we had wind with us and had to stop to let the engines cool down. When we got up the Escarpment, we lunched on some Italian meat and tinned fruit and went off again past tanks, for about 12 miles, and came to HQ group. Here we had a drink in the Mess and I sold and '*buckshee'd*' [gave away] as much as possible. The *padre* had a service here and I went along and found it most helpful. He spoke very informally, hands in pockets, on his approach to religion. *James*, 'Be ye doers of the word and not hearers only.' Only about ten or twelve came along, including one officer. After this, into the Mess and the meal we had would have done credit to most hotels. Drinks, soup, meat, veg. and potatoes, savoury, water melon and coffee – all out in the depths of the desert. During the day I met Brig. Jock Campbell, MC [Military Cross], and gave him some books for his men. He is the personality of this area and one prisoner is supposed to have said of him, 'I'd follow such a man through hell'. Most in officers' Mess were Rifle Brigade men, Oxford or Cambridge, and I found them difficult to talk to. They weren't much interested in anything outside their own work and, I felt, rather bored by everything else. Only spark of interest was raised in a brief talk on Irish Question with a staff captain who claimed to be connected with Queen's County. Would that he had some of the Celtic animation still!

13.7.41 Woke up to usual sound of guns at 6.30am and found blankets covered with a heavy dew again. Had an hour's meditation and went to Communion. Anglican service is very beautiful and set prayers have a lot to commend them. But what I feel about all communions is the need of more time between each act of worship.

After the service, we bade farewell to HQ and set off for the first of the columns. The going was mixed, as usual. Some very stony bits, patches of lovely smooth sand, rough, bumpy sand hills, desert vegetation on low-lying ground and occasional *wadis* [desert valleys] that had to be circumnavigated. We saw three gazelles, the only animal of any size in these parts. It is reported that one RAF pilot recently machine-gunned them for the Mess.

Column was resting after being in action, so our arrival was timely and there was a look of great surprise as we drove up. One cannot do enough for the ordinary men living in this life, their lot is a hard one, no comfort, constant movement, danger all the time, heat, flies, and boredom when they are not digging. We gave each one a pair of socks, or a tin of sweets, tin of Vaseline and some magazines and let him buy what else he wanted. Most of them thanked us for coming out and I felt a great sense of joy in being the instrument of some little respite and change for them.

14.7.41 Yesterday we had two Jerry recce [reconnaissance] planes over and I never saw men tuck themselves out of sight more quickly. The Vaseline will be useful for those with desert sores. Off to the other column, which is located on top of the Escarpment along one of the *wadis* – certainly a change of scenery, as one can see the blue line of the Mediterranean in the distance. What a place this is, the bare rocks of the Escarpment with the sun beating mercilessly down and no natural shelter. I longed for the shadow of a great rock, but none was to be found. Hence, I frequently resorted to the lime juice bottle, with the result that I sweated more frequently. As time was short, I bulk-issued comforts to CSM and, selling what I could, I left *Padre*, following an officer's pick-up, which set too hot a pace, so we let him go his way while we went ours. Stopped at MDS [Medical Distribution Station] near Emba and gave 300 Players [cigarettes] to patients, as we act for Red Cross in such cases. On to Bir Emba track, which is in a terrible mess with dust, and as Fargo has no back cover we get a terrific cloud of sand blowing in all the time. We had to stop several times and both felt pretty miserable, especially about the eyes, which we can hardly open. After we had made about 10 miles, we noticed an officer's pick-up playing about, and as he stopped, I got out to verify our position. He said he was an Intelligence Officer and if we had not stopped, he was going to open with a Tommy gun on us. Apparently, German columns have been coming through to this track. He seemed to be a rather unintelligent officer, as he told us Sidi B. was 22 miles off.

16.7.41 Had lunch with NAAFI officers in Quasaba, where we got a first-hand account of Greek campaign from an officer who had been on the *Andes*. Many of the *Andes* officers had been left in Greece. On to Matruh, which is being bombed every night. On our way up a captain stopped us and said tropics and proper army kit had to be worn from 9 to 4 o'clock. Is the new General Auchenleck, who replaced Wavell about two weeks ago, showing his fangs?

17.7.41 Some of the lads have not been too well with unsettled insides, due, I believe, to an overdose of Jaffa oranges, and today I've been feeling a little below par myself on the same score. Oranges were always my weakness!

18.7.41 General impressions at the moment are hard to collect and write down. Entry of Russia into the war has cheered most up a lot and there are hopes of a swifter finish. Position here is very quiet. My own feelings are desire for leave soon and the hope that Massey and colleague will arrive and cars. Physically I'm fit, but I would like a mental change and look forward to seeing Palestine. Always in my mind is the desire for home and the passing months seem only to heighten that desire. Still, the spirit that made me come out here remains the same and I've no regrets.

19.7.41 Sgt. from Indian Ordnance was in and declares Fargo fit once again and promises a new engine for GMC, which has fought the good fight and finished her course. Relationship with lads is much better now. Poor old Nobby is a bit jittery these days and claims every plane that passes over is a Messerschmitt, Dornier, etc. The other day he told Ginger, while he was bathing, not to look up as Jerry could see the white of his face. I've taken over his car for the last week while he does the cooking.

20.7.41 Off to Quasaba and Matruh today. Left Ginger on his way to Daba, where he hopes to collect the renovated Crailsham and go on to

Alex. Still no news of Massey, or new secretary, or trucks. Had lunch at Q., where we found stocktaking in progress and therefore some of the lads a bit drunk.

22.7.41 Sent Scotty and Tiny off on mobile for the afternoon, while I looked after the canteen. Lads came back and car is knocking badly, so off I went to Indian Ordnance down by the sea. Have a meal there and Sgt. Young hopes to fix it up in two days. So now we have only GMC, with a big end gone, as available means of retreat.

24.7.41 Hitch-hiked to Matruh today for stoves, which I had been told were light and easily carried. Got through on an Indian truck driven by Sikhs, very fine-looking fellows with black, silky beards that have never been shaven. Got a wire from Massey: 'Expect to arrive on Sunday with Wall and truck and possibly Yorke.' So a new era is about to begin. Egyptian clerk in Telegraph took me to his house and made me tea. Apart from dirt and filth of house and smell, I enjoyed my visit. He spoke English well and told me modern history of Egypt in a concise and interesting manner. He deprecates the fact that he is not able to kill Italians and Germans. Sent a wire to Massey and went off to collect stoves, which turned out to be two immense Hydras, so with a Lance Corporal and four Libyan prisoners, I got them down to the road and after three lifts arrived at Kilo 95. When in Matruh, I saw (with my own eyes!) ten 30 cwt YMCA Toc H vans from South Africa. They can do things in a big way! I hope they are coming to take over the Western Desert. They can't come too soon.

25.7.41 Experimented with petrol stoves, which are very dangerous and caused more than one speedy evacuation of cookhouse. But Tiny seems to know how to handle them. Now we need tea, sugar and water, and all is set. Get tea and sugar from NAAFI and water arrives later on in day – 50 gallons in 25 tins. Sgt. Young brings back Fargo saying that job is hopeless. Advised me to evacuate to Cairo and Alex, with a note from him that, as front line, would gain priority. I decide to wait for the Chief on Sunday. A lot of British planes over these days.

26.7.41 Tiny has become a most valuable member of our family. He is a handyman and a very hard, steady worker, as well as a real humorist and seldom is he downhearted. Simple and childlike, he is an attractive personality and already is known up and down the highway as 'Geordie at the YM'. Really keen to serve the lads. We have had some interesting chats. Lives in South Shields, worked in a quarry before going into Regular Army about 1936, when he was told to clear out by his father. He is a diligent Roman Catholic, but not intolerant in the least. Is most delighted when he can get Confession and said to me, 'Now I am a free man', after the last one. His home life is not too happy, as his father drinks a lot and beats his mother. Large family baptised RC and Protestant turn about. In his last leave at home he beat up his father, who had been drunk and bullied his mother. He is a Regular and has been through the fight to Benghazi as a machine-gunner in Northumberland Fusiliers. His body is tattooed all over with various designs, memorials to the family and the crucifixion. He sings well, though croons everything, and is very popular in the canteen.

27.7.41 Very warm and lots of planes about. Waited about all day expecting Massey to arrive and, sure enough, about 7.30pm he steams in, though without Arthur Wall and the 3-tonne Ford. It has already given a lot of trouble. Chief was in good form and we have a long talk about all that has happened and is likely to happen. He brings a lot of equipment, which is most welcome, also a parcel from Lily of four shirts and two pairs of Viyella [stockings], just the business for me at present as my shirts are almost US [i.e., useless] and stockings are always needed here. Massey seemed satisfied with our work and told me of new mobiles that should be available soon of 5-tonne type. We are to be mobile experts and may be switched over to Syria if needed and if British troops are withdrawn from desert. Poor old Barker is still in Tobruk and is not getting much stuff through, if any. Massey brought letters, two from Mother, two from John, as well as the parcel.

31.7.41 Big event today was the arrival of a new colleague, Arthur Wall of New Zealand. He was keen to talk and we had a good yarn before sleep. Apparently the much-heralded 3-tonne truck is a white elephant.

1.8.41 Showing Arthur the run of things. Fine, quiet fellow; we should get on well together. At night I went up to speak to Major Gilmore's boys on 'Post-war Problems'. One of the boys, a Derry sergeant, tried to shake me with a poser about religion in Northern Ireland, but I came off best for once.

2.8.41 We were visited by OC of Desert Troops, General Beresford Pierce. All was in tip-top order for once and he seemed very pleased. Took a cup of tea and told me he was from Ireland also. When he asked me if there was anything I needed and I began to make various requests, he changed the subject.

3.8.41 Today I went off on leave. Went down to Bagoosh with Arthur and then hitch-hiked to Alexandria and on to Cairo by train.

YMCA Desert Headquarters in Tobruk

Chapter Four

DESERT WAR

Impressions of Palestine: memories of mountains, hills and valleys, white, flat-roofed houses in hilltop villages and towns. Cultivation, teeming life of Arab and Jew. Freshness of Jewish settlements. Compactness of old Jerusalem and small area that includes most of the sacred places. Much imagination needed to reconstruct the past, because so many religions and influences clash; sacred to three of world's greatest religions: Jew, Mohammedan and Christian. Romans, Turks, Crusaders and British – all have left their mark. It is well to remember how many definite attempts were made to wipe out every memorial of Christianity. Many things repel one, especially in the sacred spots; commercialisation of Christianity and the constant demand for *backsheesh* [Arabic term used by beggars], even by servants of the Church. One has to remember that the holy places are more than sacred sites, they are also a history of the Church and the various phases it has passed through in its desire to honour God. Today is not an age of tinsel, candles, curtains, golden lamps, icons, images and incense, and most of the recent churches are remarkable for their simplicity. We are apt to resent the tendency of the Crusaders and that prolific builder, Queen Helena, in imposing churches on the holy places – Bethesda, Nazareth, Jacob's Well and the Churches of Nativity and Holy Sepulchre – but credit is due for the preservation of these places.

I suppose after the rush of life in the desert and hurry of Jerusalem, my mind was unusually receptive to the peace and quiet of Galilee. Capernaum was refreshing and I felt I could have stayed there forever. But through it all, I felt rather detached and did not register any great emotion. Perhaps that was because of a mental weariness and spiritual flatness. In the last two days I began to come alive again and take a greater interest in it all. The whole of Galilee, Nazareth cupped among the hills, and the aspect far across the great vale of Esdraelon will be evergreen memories for me. What a playground those hills must have been for the Young Nazarene. In His time, Galilee boasted 240 towns and villages and a lakeside. And Mount Tabor conjured up stories and great men of the Bible. Gilboa, where Saul and Jonathan fell; Endor, where Samuel visited the witch the night before he died; Carmel, austere, like Elijah, who lived beside its slopes; Jordan, Hermon, Moab, Gilead, and so on. Shades of the Philistines, of David and Jonathan and their exploits, and across the centuries to another of the House of David who loved these hills and valleys and who walked by Galilee and knew every part of the community.

Other places sent my thoughts back to our Lord. The lovely little village of Bethany, built on the corner of the road and stretching up the hillside, just within easy range of Jerusalem, yet far from its noise and crush; the old road up the Mount of Olives, where I sat looking down at the city He loved and wept over; the ancient olive trees in the Garden of Gethsemane, perhaps related to those He sat under.

17-20.8.41 Back in Cairo. Heat has lessened a bit since I was here last. Sent a wire through to Arthur to send Scotty to Alexandria with the truck as soon as possible. My trip to Alexandria was child's play after the journey back from Palestine. Scotty arrived on 21st with GMC in tow, under the guidance of Tiny, and, of course, the Ford lorry was out of order. Got off with a full load of comforts, cigarettes and sweets. On the way past Fuka the engine gave a terrific backfire, but Scotty's magical touch worked the miracle and once again the dead bones sprang into life. When we got to Quasaba, it was getting late, so we decided to stay with Major Gilmore and his boys. Here I got a hearty welcome and had a most educative evening. The poor old Major did his best to camouflage some of the Mess stories, and when I left, the party got quite rowdy.

26.8.41 Got to Kilo 95, where things were busy and seemed to be going well. Arthur in good form, though he feels much the same about some of the lads as I did before I left.

28-31.8.41 Arthur is a fine companion and we live happily together. It makes a lot of difference to have company. He is married, though he is only twenty-two.

2-9.9.41 These days passed quickly and we served 1,200–1,500 cups of tea per day and handled £50–£60 in the canteen. This for three men takes some doing, when cooking has also to be seen to. YM becomes quite a *rendezvous* for some of the regular visitors, though some consume more than their quota of tea and some produce outsize mugs. Tiny asked one if he wanted to have a bath in his, as well as a drink.

It has been a week of considerable air activity in this area and a big air battle took place. About eighteen enemy planes attacked aerodromes around Sidi Barrani and some strafed the road. Our fighters managed to get up and got seven enemy planes with no loss to themselves. The Ulster Ack Ack unit saw one of the planes hit the deck about 500mph; only little bits of the pilot were left. On the road several trucks were hit and one or two men were killed. One truck was completely burnt out. The driver called in here for a cup of tea; an explosive bullet had grazed his throat and drawn blood. There he stood, a little chap with dark brown eyes, completely unconcerned and, outwardly at least, perfectly unshaken. He seemed to me to personify the spirit of England. The next day was not so good. A large force of enemy planes got in and strafed the 'dromes, damaging eighteen planes. No fighters got up after them and no Ack Ack fire was heard.

I went up, on request, to E Section and had a splendid Sunday evening with them. Service at the gun pit with about twenty men. I spoke on *Hebrews* 12:1. Then order came through that all were to stand-to in case of paratroops. Twelve Junkers 88 had been seen on Bardia 'drome by one of our recce planes. It seemed a bit rough to ask the whole camp, to a man, to stay awake and alert all night, as they have such a busy day with raids, etc. Still, it's a way they have in the Army and it'll take a lot to change it. About 2.30am the moon came up, and we heard several Jerry planes pass down the coast *en route* to Matruh.

10.9.41 Paid a call on South African YMCA, which, being part of the Army and taking the place of NAAFI, have much greater equipment and manpower than we have. They found an old Roman waterway, which they have converted into a most useful air-raid shelter – and these nights they need it. One of the men showed me the base of a 1,000-kilo bomb recently dropped.

12.9.41 Tiny has had a bout of interior decoration and has put up a

notice on the counter: Tiny Tea Bar. He has also decked the walls with
pictures of various film stars. Nobby arrived back very proud of his new
tattoo on the arm. His maiden effort – 'True love', with the name of his
wife.

14-21.9.41 I decided to go to Cairo and see the Chief, who was very
pleased I had come, as he had just sent off a cable to me asking for
someone to come down. Had a fine session with him and got a lot of
help and satisfaction. Points discussed: (1) mobiles: we are to get five
new ones; (2) orderlies: hope to get six men; (3) Siwa oasis: will do a
reconnaissance flight down there; (4) McConnell coming up to the
desert. I offered to go back to Tobruk, but he thinks it better to send
Tank back. News comes in of retreat from Kilo 95 – £180 of stock has
been lost. Things always happen when I'm away.

   We had one nasty air raid, but stayed on in YM as there was no
shelter handy. Twenty-three were killed in the native quarter and some
damage at Abyssia.

2.10.41 Three most welcome letters from home, two from Mother and
one from old Miss McAdam of Bangor, whose letter was most inspiring.
What a fine spirit some of the old folk at Bangor have. Jerry planes over
at night on way east. Sgt. Young and Staff Sgt. Duggan of Coleraine
came down on the German People's Car, an interesting job, recently
captured at Hell Fire Pass. We had a good evening yarning. Speculations
are rife about the push. Fierce fighting on Russian Front. Heavy raids
over Bardia, which we could see.

5.10.41 Sunday. We took off for the Forward Area just on sundown.
Soon the moon came up, a lovely full one, and I really enjoyed the run,
though the going was rough all the time. I felt very intimate with
nature, moon like an illuminated cheese, stars guiding our way, rushing,
cooling wind, and the desert beautiful in the evening quiet. Sometimes
we passed by lurking shadows – Italian vehicles, remnants of Mussolini's
Egyptian dreams.

6.10.41 The Escarpment looked almost attractive in the early morning,
with its light and shadow, and as we climbed we could see Hell Fire Pass
and the Egyptian barracks at Sollum. We arrived at C Company and

found men ready for the service, with a little black altar. I spoke on Elisha at Pothan, contrasting the prophet and his servant. Life depends on what we bring to it. Then we did the platoons and gave out socks, and later had lunch in a little dugout camouflaged with desert bushes and roofed with truck canopies. After lunch I did two more companies and had a hearty welcome from all ranks and was sold out about 4.30pm. And with promises of all sorts and the intention of returning soon, I set off for home. Passed through the minefield and saw a full-blooded dive-bomb and machine-gun attack on the Bug Bug track. All the lads said the plane was going to hit the deck, but it straightened up and some bombs hit the deck instead. An exciting interlude, though well away from us!

9.10.41 Very stormy and dusty. News in YM circular of old Barker, who has just recently come down from Tobruk for a rest and new work. Pretty stout effort to be on the job for nine months without a break.

12.10.41 Yesterday we had an exciting day with planes, and as orders were, 'Take cover on approach of any plane', we were kept pretty well on the hop all day. Saw quite a few enemy planes, all of which ignored us.

Germans trying to effect pincer-movement on Moscow.

14.10.41 Set off to Mersa Matruh and called in at PO [Post Office]. Got a really splendid mail – eight letters, including two from Mother. I went down to the shore and had a tin of fruit and cream to celebrate and was dead to the East for two hours. Pushed off from Matruh and got home before dark, on top of the world.

16.10.41 Weather is getting a lot colder now and we look forward to warmer clothes. Nights are shorter and work is over about 5 o'clock. Orderlies are now working very well and seem to be a lot happier, Nobby especially. I think they are beginning to realise how fortunate they are in the YM.

News from Russia is not too good and Germans are putting all into their push on Moscow. I wonder where it all will lead. Japanese government has resigned and it looks as if they'll come in to the scrap any day now.

17.10.41 Canteen work is good. It develops my patience and teaches me to judge types quickly. Each evening now about six CMPs come in to listen to the news at 8 o'clock, after which we have prayers. One of them reads the Bible and I lead in prayer. I sense in them all a feeling after God. Often a discussion develops and interesting viewpoints arise. Perhaps this is the best work of all. Sometimes I wish I could be a real *padre* and devote all my time to this work; so much of our time seems to be taken up in other things. But it is all service. Arthur arrives back very tired. I hope he'll go for a break soon, as he is not too well these days. He is a splendid fellow, so unselfish and thoughtful, and I am a trifle moody at times.

20.10.41 Sent Arthur off to Cairo today, hitch-hiking. I think a few days' change will do him good. We are on the best of terms again and both realise the strain of intimate living. Had Tiny in and had a talk with him to let him realise the new position. Life is certainly a great teacher and it needs some experience to be able to deal with these blokes. All are now in pretty good fettle, though Mack continually nags about this and that. The sandstorms are horrible, but mercifully there was none in the last few days. Lots of the fellows suffer from desert sores, a very nasty complaint caused by a tiny scratch that swells and festers. I seem to be immune from them, for which I am very thankful. The poor lads beyond Sidi Barrani have also the problem of having to drink salted water in their tea, which is not a pleasant taste. Coffee, Oxo and lime juice camouflage it fairly well.

22.10.41 A petrol lorry went on fire about 100 yards from the canteen – a convoy had stopped for tea – burned for three hours and caused a lot of excitement, as it would have been a lovely target for enemy aircraft. Finally, an Indian Labour Corps advanced on the scene and smothered the fire with sand. The car was salvaged pretty well, in spite of what our fellows managed to 'whip' in the dark.

Fierce fighting goes on for Moscow and America comes daily nearer the maelstrom, though Japan looks like another jackal act, *à la* Mussolini. We cannot but be thankful to God that He has so spared us in this part of the world.

24.10.41 Slept in the car and slept well. Had breakfast with *Padre*

Williams and driver set off forward. Passed the old familiar sights of Bug Bug salt flats, where some British Tanks are a reminder of struggle there last year. *Padre* is an unusual type, says he's the worst *padre* in the desert. He drinks, smokes and gambles and so far he's been true to his word. He drove a truck for nine years before he entered the Methodist Church. Is very much the sporting *padre* – boxer and footballer – and believes himself to be a Spencer Tracy type. This was an interesting trip right across the coastal Front. We visited four companies and got a grand reception from all ranks. One officer showed me round the company and explained the new anti-tank sticky bomb. Covered with birdlime, it sticks to the tank and blows a hole in it.

25.10.41 Camerons gave me a very nice battledress, which will be most useful. Bit of activity just now. Navy shelling Hell Fire Pass, RAF and RA [Royal Artillery] also doing their bit.

31.10.41 Took Tiny up to 13 MDS for medical inspection, as he has a nasty lump on his neck that might need the knife. The medical orderlies put poor old Tiny through it, telling him of all the things that would happen: the knife, pain, stuff that would come. But the great man, in the shape of Dr McPherson of Edinburgh, didn't cut but advised a poultice. Tiny got bad at night, and he was removed by ambulance to the CCS.

1.11.41 Went down to see about Tiny and prevent, if possible, his evacuation to base. Found him about to be evacuated to Mersa Matruh and could not stop this.

2.11.41 Once again the ubiquitous Tiny turns up, having flown the horrors of the SA [South African] hospital, which he vividly described to me.

10.11.41 On Massey's request, I set off to Alexandria with him. It's a run I'll not soon forget. Went off the road once and missed oncoming convoy of lorries several times by the thickness of a cigarette paper.

I forgot to mention the visit of Jack Tannahill (Dunmurry) of RAF. We had corresponded and I knew vaguely where he was and he, passing by, dropped in to our place by the merest fluke. Looked very well, though naturally longing to get home. Lost his Bible in the evacuation from Crete, and I was able to give him a New Testament.

16.11.41 Major got bad news today. Brother and cousin killed in England. Took him through to Mersa Matruh to send a telegram and I saw Col. Goodwin. I think we'll probably take over Sub Area's Garrison Library No. 2.

17.11.41 Had to tell Goodwin that his canteen was not attractive for the men and little variety in stock. He is pretty typical of military obscurantism, and I did some straight talking to him. Had lunch on beach near Cleopatra's Bath. Terrific traffic on the roads these days, so something seems to be brewing.

18.11.41 Preparations to move through to Matruh tomorrow were interrupted. The rains came with a vengeance last night and pretty well flooded us out and by the morning we had very definite sympathies with Noah. Mack kicked up a terrible fuss and went out and flung sandbags around, but was about as successful in stemming the flood as King Canute.

Today we've had rumours of the push being on.

19.11.41 Collected equipment for Matruh, but just as we were preparing to set off, a lorryload of civilians arrived from up the line. First, I thought they were prisoners, but someone said there were women among them: the first time I'd seen women in the desert. They turned out to be refugees from Crete. About fourteen all told: two women and a little child, and one of the women was likely to be a mother soon, and one very old man, the rest being men. They were in pretty bad condition and small wonder. They had secretly left the island at dead of night in an open motorboat, with a little food and enough petrol to get them out of sight of Crete. Then they drifted along and rigged up some sort of a sail and were picked up by British naval officers near Sidi Barrani after nineteen days at sea. The poor souls thought they had come to Nazi territory and surrendered to the officers. They all looked done in – the poor little girl, about four years of age, was almost waxen white. The men were haggard, unkempt hair, eyes terribly bloodshot, but all pathetically grateful. We gave them all we had, but most of them could only take a little and apparently most were sick when they arrived at Matruh. With their permission, we took some photos. One spoke English very well and told us some ghastly things about the Nazi occupation of their island home. The fact that they were ready to hazard their lives in such a venture is adequate commentary. We were able to warn Matruh of their arrival about an hour before they got in, so everything was ready for them.

20.11.41 Officially took over Matruh Centre from Captain Brown, who on the Colonel's orders took away most of our furniture, in spite of my remonstrations. I went to the Colonel, who said soldiers didn't need chairs but should use hard forms. He told me that I should not ask for any more or he would get angry.

Push now an established fact. Allies 50 miles into Cyrenaica. Tonight we had quite a tight little raid, some bombs dropped and a terrible lot of noise, especially when a flare was dropped. We stayed put in the building, as we hear the shelter is flea-ridden.

22.11.41 The two new Mobiles have arrived; two 5-ton Fords, presented by the Ladies of India, fitted out with tea equipment, two big ice boxes, capacity to carry 240 gallons of water, and a lot of cupboards and shelves. This is the moment we've waited for since last April.

2.12.41 Got news of Chips's tragic death in Alexandria. Seems to have died under mysterious circumstances. He was a most unusual fellow and did a splendid job in Alex, where he gave himself to the lads. He was essentially an individualist, but had a real spirit of service and was splendid in contacting the officers and brass hats [senior officers]. He was a captain in the last war, had been an actor and comic opera producer. Lately, I had come to like him very much. Among his last words to me were that the work was gradually killing him. He longed to come back to the desert.

3.12.41 Set off for Line of Communications Conference. Conference tent was crammed with brass hats and the meeting was interesting, especially *résumé* of Forward position: (1) we are now 40 miles beyond Tobruk; (2) enemy has aerial supremacy; (3) enemy has 40 tanks left. I felt a bit queer as the only civvy there, and no one else was below the rank of captain.

5.12.41 Set off with a convoy to Tobruk, which started late and crept along, stopping every mile or so. A sandstorm blew up and we found ourselves lost through the fault of truck in front, which lost truck in front of him and did not stop until he had got off-track. Convoy behind us was shorn of two vehicles behind our big Mobile, so five trucks were lost in the sand. We waited around for some time and found our company included a Major, who seemed to spot a track in every desert scrub. Eventually we stumbled on the track we had lost and put up for the night. Intensely cold sleeping in the car and my balaclava and pullover were invaluable. Next day we tacked onto a RE [Royal Engineers] convoy and made home about dusk.

Up early, we descended the Escarpment and saw the Bardia–Tobruk road once again, a sight we longed for. On all sides were signs of the battle: burnt-out Jerry tanks; loads of German petrol tins; wrecked and abandoned German vehicles; ammunition stores and hospital camps; and two beautifully kept German cemeteries, with the dead soldiers' *topis* or trinkets and bayonets laid on top of the graves and simple wooden or metal crosses. One grave was of an unknown Australian soldier. The boundaries of the little cemetery and the headstones were the tops and fins of bombs. We soon came to German trenches, and on past German detour road right round the Tobruk garrison. Lots of German ammunition here, hand grenades, anti-tank bombs and lots of other nasty work. We gave it a wide berth in case of booby-traps. On to the wire and inside the perimeter. Past the British trenches, observation posts and 'dromes, now as lively as ant hills. What a story will be told of this place, which victoriously withstood nine months' onslaught. Past the site of the Rest House, blown up so as to deprive enemy aircraft of landmarks. Past the POW cage, now full of Italians and Germans. The familiar sight of Italians working on the roads under guard of a British Tommy, some working with their hands, most looking cheerful enough.

Soon we caught a glimpse of Tobruk town across the bay. How little changed it looked from a distance. But the bay was now well filled with wrecks of all sorts of ships. As we came up into the town we saw some of the scars of battle and siege. Practically all the buildings were shrapnel-scarred and many had direct hits. We found YM in full swing under the guidance of the diminutive and dynamic New Zealander, Tank. The old Field Bakery adjoined to us had stopped a heavy one and was partially wrecked. The church in the square was battle-scarred; all the walls and tower stood, but the roof had been badly damaged. The *Madonna* was practically unscathed. Poor old Fargo No. 9 had been through the siege and was badly battered and needs new coachwork. Tank has been up since March, when I left, and was riding around in a little German Opel. New Zealand YMCA were in from the Front. We did not stay long and left Tobruk at sundown and camped about the edge of the perimeter.

24.12.41 Trying to get through to Tobruk for Christmas Day, as I carry the festivities. Very wet at first, then very dusty, and lost the way several times. Got to Chefferzen and made good time towards El Adem along tin-marked route, until I lost the tins and had to stop. Slept on the front seat and woke up on Christmas morning.

25.12.41 Watched dawn break in the East. Soon I was on the road to Tobruk and gave some SAs some Christmas fare and was thanked in a most profane though hearty manner. Bully and biscuits for Christmas did seem a bit boring. Canteen in Tobruk was busy. Met the Senior Chaplain of Tobruk, but he is as mad as a hatter. Took us out to POW camp, as he had some Italian and German books to distribute. Went through prisoners' cage with Major Bernard Ferguson, a sort of Little Father to his prisoners. He was most concerned about the prisoners and greeted them with, '*Buon Natale*'. How incongruous it seemed to be there on Christmas Day. Still, none of them seemed to bear any resentment and reciprocated our good wishes, sometimes with a Fascist salute and a broad smile. They were queuing up for food, which seemed quite savoury. Some were well shaven with hair cut; others made little effort to keep up appearances. We went into the Italian hospital, and then the German one. The Prussian doctor was the real blue-eyed Aryan. Very harsh, loud voice. They are not keen on the Italian allies and refused them accommodation in their hospital and also refused to share the water cart.

Went home with *Padre* in the dusk, down the twisting, narrow road into Tobruk, visiting some of his parishioners on the way. Arriving back, we found we had delayed the celebration of Christmas dinner, but soon laid to and cleaned up the stuff. So ended a memorable Christmas Day.

29.12.41 Some Major told Barker he could get 1,000,000 cigarettes on the hospital ship. We went to the quay and got onto the string of lifeboats filled with all sorts of wounded. One of our fellow passengers was an Irish doctor, who went out in quest of a case of gin. Passed innumerable wrecks in Tobruk Bay. The liner *Llandovery Castle* hove to, painted white with huge red crosses on her sides. A pretty strong sea was running and we made several attempts to run alongside the ship, but all proved abortive. Eventually we got aboard, but found the cigarette story was a lovely myth. So, very disgruntled, we jumped onto a lifeboat being lowered and sought comfort on the swelling bosom of the sea.

30.12.41 Set off to Derna to find out how Mack and Tank were getting on. The road was a bit the worse for wear. Bypasses at blown-up bridges were much in use. Fascists had erected a huge monument to Mussolini at their perimeter road. Roadhouses were still intact, with German notices in place of British. Derna 'drome was pretty well strewn with the wreckage of German planes. Several troop-carrying planes were smashed and a lot of smaller fry. All the area round about was strewn with huge bombs. Down the Escarpment in good order. Germans had built a new track along the east of Big Wadi, which made going much faster. Derna looked well-kept and little different from March. It was good to see the lads again.

1.1.42 New Year's Day and a real red-letter day. Our ships begin to come in: we got two splendid 3-tonne German lorries, Opel Blitz, well-equipped and one in good order; two-and-a-half tonnes of goods from Alexandria, one box of chocolate was pilfered; and NAAFI open up shop and give us huge loads for both centre and Mobiles. Splendid mail arrives.

8.1.42 Up about 6.15am and on the desert track. Very steep climb up the Escarpment and I was glad to be driving a nimble Ford pick-up. Found several deserted German camps. Most of the valuables had already been removed and the Arabs were finishing up the work. Passed through several South African camps and heard a lot of bombing. The besieged must be having a pretty hard time. Struck down off Escarpment by a track I had used in the summer and got onto the Bug Bug Road. The Italian Victory Road has now been completed and it was wonderful to spin along past places and tracks that brought back memories of many jolts, bumps and sandstorms.

9.1.42 Set off for Alexandria. Long drive, but we did look forward to some decent food, bath, haircut and wash, and also a visit to the Scottish School. On the way we passed a big Free French camp. They have come up from Syria and are going up to finish off Hell Fire. Bardia has now fallen and a lot of pressure is being put on these remaining pockets. We picked up a French officer going to Alex for 48 hours' leave. We tried out our French and he tried out his English. His English carried off the honours. We used the headlights for a time, but as we got near the city, we saw the beams of searchlights and what we thought to be flares, so we switched off and went on for some time, but it was pretty slow progress and soon we lit up again. We went to the English *pension*, but from the attitude of the hostess, I could feel that we are not *persona grata* there. George is a Private, after all! The British Army does sicken me at times.

10.1.42 My birthday, so I celebrated it with a bath. It helped to remove a little of the veneer. Did some shopping. Kosta in his usual charming form. I don't know what the YM would do without him. He is always on the spot and, like Britain these days, he 'delivers the goods'.

12.1.42 Got the car serviced and did a spot of shopping with Miss Williams. I had to buy a lot of stuff for the Tobruk Ordnance Dramatic Club and Miss W. was a great help, especially in getting stuff for female impersonation.

13.1.42 Loaded at Kosta's and got some more stuff for the Tobruk dramatists, also a hamper of Xmas fare for an Ack Ack unit in Tobruk. I hope the chickens will last the journey. I took the dark driving, as George's eyes troubled him a bit. George is a splendid fellow. A timber merchant in Hull, he is invaluable in the business and has the highest motives in the job. Worships in Liverpool cathedral. Was a staff sergeant and was reduced by a 'frame-up' by a Sergeant-Major. He hopes to take up his case again. Went to bed as soon as we got to Matruh. No sooner had we settled when Tiny came in dead drunk. What is one to do with such a fellow?

14.1.42 I took Tiny to task. We had a long talk and I decided to keep him on, on the promise that he won't touch the bottle again. He is a complete child, cannot connect his religion – he is a zealous RC – with his life, and seems to have lost his self-respect. But what's the use of sending him back to his unit, to the beer? I will take him to Tobruk and put him on the proposed Desert House on the Tobruk–Benghazi road.

16.1.42 Find from Major Lyne that Desert Route is off, so Tiny is free for Rezem. This roadhouse has done a good job.

Poor old Tim had just had an exciting night on his own. Twice he was wakened by someone trying to get in. The little 'Oasis' has been bombed several times. It is garrisoned by Poles and it looks strange to see a machine gun mounted on the steps of the lovely little mosque, which always looks so clean and white. One of the Poles keeps watch from this vantage point all day. So far, the bombing has been inaccurate.

The news from the Far East is not so good just now, though the Americans should soon get into their stride. But the Russian steamroller moves on and Mojask has been taken.

17.1.42 Decided to *reconnôitre* Agedabia. Pass through Derna and well-vegetated landscapes begin to appear. The green is a tonic to eyes tired of the bright sand. Also the farms of Mussolini's colonising scheme, all built in the same style and bearing the Fascist badge and slogan '*Ente Libya*'. Roadside is marked with cars and lorries wrecked and abandoned, evidence, surely, of the havoc of RAF machine-gunning. Many of the farmers and their families had stayed on.

Thirty miles past Giovanni Berta we came round a corner and saw Jack standing on the overturned Fargo. I had to laugh at the humour of the situation, and certainly Jack has had this coming for a long time as he takes too many risks. We left Jack Downie to look after the stuff while we went to Giovanni Berta to get Jack B.'s ear patched up and also to get a breakdown lorry. A very decent CMP gave us directions to MDS, but just as Jack was waiting to be treated, the poor CMP arrived in a terrible state. He had unwittingly picked up a hand grenade, which had exploded. His face was in a bad mess and one hand was very badly injured. When we got back to Jack D., he was in a state of nerves, imagining there were Italians in the hills round about. He had shot at several. We waited until dark, but the breakdown did not turn up, so we made preparations for the night.

18.1.42 The breakdown arrives and after a lot of towing and tugging, the Fargo is hoisted onto the road. Tank and I leave the two Jacks to it and go off for Barce. The green trees, vegetation, hills and valleys and homesteads were again refreshing. All the homes proclaimed the virtues of *Il Duce* with Fascist slogans.

21.1.42 Struck out for Giovanni Berta and found Jack B. had gone on to Benghazi, so we pushed on to Tobruk. Called in on Derna market and bought some vegetables. Lot of stuff the Germans had left behind was on sale. Derna always charms me, with its palms and the blue sea and white houses. It always seems to be a most restful place compared with Tobruk. And the Libyans do make a difference, with their eggs and vegetables.

Went off to Rezem and found the lads in a bit of a state on account of a visit from Colonel Watkins, Sub Area Commander of Derna. They felt that he had been too critical, so Tank and I decided to go and beard the lion in his den on the morrow. I'm getting good at this, but I'd better not fall foul of another SA commander, even on a matter of principle.

22.1.42 The Colonel's attitude was a mixture of hurt innocence and military 'don't care'. We parted on good terms and I'd the feeling that our lads had given us a false impression of what had taken place. At Tobruk I found old Barker had really blossomed out and had started all sorts of things – classes in German, French, Italian and Spanish, Bible study groups, and lectures, as well as service on Sunday evening.

24.1.42 Two services today. Free Church service in the Garrison Church at 10 o'clock was very well attended and about half the congregation had no seats, so I tried to make it short. *Padre* Quinn has made a good job of fixing up the church. It is a converted Fascist theatre. We had all sorts of people; a lot of coloured troops, as well as colonials. In the evening I took YM service in our own little chapel, which was packed to capacity. The singing was very hearty and filled the whole building. Barker led the singing and took devotions and I felt there was a spirit of reality in it all. I spoke on, 'To whom shall we go – Thou hast the words of eternal life', idea being that of man's desire for some authority and how so many despaired of 'religion' since the last war because it was but a caricature of the real Faith.

News from the Front is not so good, as Jerry seems to be pushing back and Benghazi is threatened. What a war this is!

25.1.42 Barker and I set off today with the idea of following Tank through to Benghazi. We set out for Derna and met a terrible lot of traffic coming back. At first we reassured ourselves by saying it was supply columns returning, but the flow continued, all sorts of stuff, RAF, guns, etc., and we realised it was a flap and didn't feel so good about it. Arrived at Rezem and were greatly relieved to find Arthur there. He had had an eventful trip beyond Benghazi, but had got through all right. Barker and I went on to Derna. The Escarpment was in a bad crush and it took us about an hour to negotiate it. Major Elmslie and his heavy Ack Ack were in process of setting up at the top in case of air attack, which we expected any time. Last news of Tank was that he was heading for Benghazi. Utterly imprudent and unnecessary to try to follow him, so we went back to Rezem. Dispersion was now becoming a major problem and we decided to keep completely mobile in view of the fluid nature of the battle. Barker and I evacuate Rezem, a rather disappointing job to do. We set off in the moonlight for Tobruk.

27.1.42 All back now but Tank. About 1am Barker and I made three urns of tea and sallied forth to docks and served the petrol convoy.

28.1.42 Little news today. Battle still very fluid. Arthur off to Derna. Did some Mobile to Ordnance and West African troops. They were happy fellows, with wonderful smiles and very limited knowledge of English. They asked for 'tum tums', which, suitably enough, indicated sweets. Tobruk Centre is breaking all records these days. Takings are stupendous. Tonight we had several raids and some stuff was dropped. It is difficult to sleep with the drone of the enemy planes above.

30.1.42 On the way to Derna I was rejoiced to find Arthur on the wayside. Then on to Rezem and I was thrilled to find Tank there, all intact. He had got out of Benghazi two hours before Jerry cut it off. He was not pleased to see Rezem closed, but responded to reason. Slept under the stars.

31.1.42 Took Tiny and some stuff and went to explore Derna situation.

Got to detour point at Martuba and consulted CMP, who said there were still plenty of British troops towards Derna, so we went on. Called in at 291 Ack Ack and had lunch at their HQ. Their Mess was in a lovely position and looked across a bay to the harbour. We had a most acceptable meal of potatoes and vegetables, which I did full justice to, and to cap all, I found that originally the regiment was recruited round Bangor and Newtownards. The young officer sent for several men, one was Sgt. McMurray, cousin of Miss McN. of 57 Dufferin Avenue, Bangor – my original digs. I knew his mother and brother in Carnalea very well. I went round all the positions and met several other Irishmen – Sgt. Smith, also of Bangor. While on the Control Tower, I saw an interesting bit of action when a bomber came in from the north and all the guns went into action, both heavy and light. The tracers of the Bofors streamed up and converged round the plane, along with the puffs of the heavies. The shooting was good, but not good enough, and we actually saw the bombs tumble out of the plane and one hit the town and clouds of smoke issued up. No sooner had the plane cleared off than two of our fighters came over – too late!

Derna Escarpment was pretty well prepared for blowing up, and blasting was going on while we were there. The REs intend to make a job of it this time.

2.2.42 This has been a day of scares and flaps. A horrible sandstorm blew all day and lashed our eyes and filled our hair. I went to *Padre* Quinn's German class. Some of the questions were interesting – how to ask for food; where do I sleep? and so on.

5.2.42 Had a long expected raid last night. I'm getting more used to them now. This has been a day of waiting and wondering. Varied accounts of the battle have come in and Jerry seems to be about Gazala and Timini. Recce plane over, so we may have music tonight. Many more of the Ordnances have left today and the place has an uncanny quiet about it.

6.2.42 Another raid towards dawn, but it did not worry us unduly, though I didn't sleep through it. Sent Wall back with big Mobile, also George Williams, Tiny Young and Geordie, just in case. Enemy are about the Gazala area. Decide to go towards Derna and do some Mobile and recce work as far up as possible. Gough Quinn wants to come also. He has a keen desire to get as near the Front as he can. Set out with him and after we got clear of the perimeter, we pretty well had the road to ourselves. We served some Bofor guns round Gazala. Further on we met some SA armoured cars, who had been through a tough spell. At Gazala we came to a roadblock and could go no further and sold out our stuff mostly to South Africans, who were very glad to get it. It was a lovely day and one seemed remote from war. I often had to rouse myself to the fact that we were only a few miles from Jerry. Quinn and I had a good yarn. He got the MC at Dunkirk and was a tutor at Oxford before war broke out.

8.2.42 Sunday. Usual raid last night. Service was once again packed. Barker took devotions and I spoke on Christ's words to the two disciples, 'What seek ye?', applying it to what youth seeks today: (1) reassurance, (2) reality, (3) freedom, (4) adventure. And how Christ answers these needs. News is brighter today and we seem to be steadying up and going to hold Gazala.

9.2.42 Another raid last night and Ack Ack in town much better. Dropped a lot of stuff, but none too near. Over about 9am and dropped a lot before making off.

Set off for Mersa. Pretty slow trip right through, as road is badly cut up now with very heavy traffic. Lot of stuff coming up. Stopped at the old YM in Bardia, which has been altered a lot during Jerry's residence. Apparently he used it as a workshop stores and a lot of useless spares were littered around. At the back there was a big Italian and German cemetery, very neatly tended. On to Fort Capuzzo, now a big cemetery for both sides. Saw a SA soldier carving names of Scottish Transvaal regiments which had fallen there. Progress down Sollum Escarpment was very slow, as six big Tank Skammel transporters were creeping along the road about 3mph. On through Sollum, full of SA troops, and on to Bug Bug. Met Tank, who tells me mail has arrived. So I beat on through to Matruh, sending Tank on to Tobruk.

Letters from home contain the tragic news about David Louden. I never thought of such a thing happening to him. He seemed to stand for life and hope. Typically, he met his death in volunteering for some dangerous task on a ship near Gibraltar. The last time I saw him, in Feb.

1940, he said the spring would see the war over. He was a fine friend, with a happy and joyous nature that knew nothing of resentment or spite. Old Dunmurry will never be the same without old David. This does bring the war home. Think of the grief at the Cedars and the loss that will always be felt, and think of it multiplied thousands and millions of times. May we who are left when it's all over be worthy of the supreme sacrifice made by the flower of our youth.

12.2.42 Last night I had my worst raid yet, lasted for three hours. We all stayed up in bed and listened to it with mixed feelings. Tonight we intend to stay nearer the deck and to sleep on the ground floor – the less to fall! We could hear the hum of a big Italian bomber and as he came into the harbour barrage box, hell was let loose and a terrific noise – bangs, cracks, thuds, whistles, screams – lasted two or three minutes. Then all became quiet and still, and we heard the ominous beat of the plane and a screaming whistle and *womph, womph, womph* as he at last let go his burden. This went on for hours, with intervals between when I sort of dozed off. He dropped some incendiaries and started three fires. The last hour before dawn certainly is a long one! The Ack Ack claimed to have shot down three planes.

In the morning I tried to write a letter to David's people and went out to see *Padre* Quinn, who plans to hold a mission beginning on Sunday week. Then things began to move as I was preparing to go on some Mobile. The sky seemed to fill with Stukas, swinging, veering and diving. Some stuff was dropped and Ack Ack went into action. Then a terrible noise and the air filled with parachutes. I thought at first paratroops were being landed, but a staff captain assured me it was a parachute gun. A casket of cylinders is launched 5,000 feet into the air, each cylinder containing a bomb on a parachute, which eventually explodes and endangers planes. Everyone became very excited as a British Hurricane dropped from the skies and hit the deck, going up in flames. Fortunately, the pilot baled out and we saw him floating down. It certainly was a thrilling sight. We learned later that we got at least five of their bombers and at least two fighters; one pilot killed. All the men who go in for this game, German or British, are brave men!

13.2.42 Well, things go on at a hectic pace, but I suppose I'll get used to it. We had quite a peaceful night. Jerry came over about 6am,

promptly dropped his load and made off. But just after breakfast fifteen
Stukas made a fierce attack on the harbour and a lot of stuff landed very
close. More parachute bombs were sent up, with their terrifying hiss. We
all hit the deck. One of our planes was shot down.

Tank and I went off to Gazala and had a lively afternoon. The road
was practically deserted and any car we saw had a 'spotter' on the back
or side. We spent some time at a RHQ [Regimental Headquarters] only
about a mile from the line. Then we went on down to locate some RA,
but we found SA Bofors guns and decided to serve them. Then seven
planes came. First we saw them flying away above the Escarpment and
we took cover in a little stone trench. Then the planes turned north and
Tank said, 'By Jove, I believe they're coming towards us.' Suddenly they
began to dive and seemed to drop from the sky. Several dropped their
stuff towards the higher escarpment, but as I was trying to photograph
them we heard a terrible whistle and bit the dust as the bombs screamed
and crashed to earth about 200 yards away, just beside the Bofors.
Looking up, we saw smoke issuing from one, but could not confirm its
fate. We went over to the Bofors and saw five craters close to each other
and one of their trucks was badly damaged with shrapnel. It was
thrilling and exhilarating, though one that might become tiresome.
Later, planes came over several times but nothing more was dropped.

Back home without further adventure. In the evening we had an
interesting yarn with a Free French soldier, who seemed most
disillusioned about it all. No wonder: his family was in Paris, he was
half-Jewish, and had escaped prison twice.

15.2.42 Sunday and another quiet night. Did some of the Bofors sites
and heavies in the afternoon. Just as I arrived back and was about to
have tea, the Ack Ack opened up and we heard an ominous whistle and
hit the deck like dead men. Eight bombs hit the Ordnance about 300
yards off. In the evening we had our service, which was packed out.
Barker took the service and I spoke on *John* 14:6, 'I am the Way', in
answer to the question, 'What is the meaning of life?'

News last week was of failure to stop the *Scharnhorst* and *Gneisenau*
[battleships] by 700 British planes. Singapore in peril; Russian successes.
Another Churchill speech, which the lads here believe is preparation for
bad news.

16.2.42 YM secretaries had a conference at Ismalia and the position of leave has been cleared up. Wall is to go when Mack returns, then Tank and Barker and I. I am debating whether I should go to Upper Egypt, or to Palestine once again.

We had two very fierce raids at lunchtime and at dusk. We heard a lot of whistles and made no bones about hitting the deck. The raids don't get more enjoyable as they become more frequent. I think one ship in the harbour was hit yesterday.

19.2.42 We took Arthur to SAYM [South African YMCA] to be transported to Alexandria on leave. I collected my stuff and got off as soon as possible. It was a very dusty day and a lot of traffic about, so the journey was not too enjoyable. Before I came in sight of Tobruk I saw a line of smoke and began to speculate about bombs. Then I saw a ring of flame near Ordnance and a thick column of smoke and also smoke near the church, which is very close to YM. Arrived in to see a lot of debris in streets and a lot of men about with tin hats on. A large bomb had dropped just on the other side of the church from our yard, which was full of trucks and men. Five men had been killed and I saw some of the lads carry away one of the bodies. The plane had come very low and had sustained a direct hit in the air and was blown to pieces. Part of it had hit the Ordnance and started a fire. One of the crew baled out and CMP were on the search for him. My lads were a bit shaken up.

20.2.42 No disturbance last night and only a few rounds today at a recce plane. Tank and George went off with big Mobiles to Forward Area. I had to straighten Tiny out, as when he was in Alexandria he saw his brother in the Northumberland Fusiliers and now wants to join him. I flatly refused to do this, as we already have given him several chances when he should have been sent back in disgrace.

21.2.42 Had another recce plane over this morning and then at lunch a pretty stiff raid of Stukas on the harbour. The Ack Ack put up a deafening barrage. Saw Major Hallam, QMG [Quartermaster-General] of Sub Area, on the subject of air raids and YMCA traffic congestion. We suggested that we stop tea in the daytime and continue canteen for a week to see if such arrangements will help to keep down concentration of traffic.

22.2.42 Today began for me like the Sundays of old, as I had to preach the Word in the Garrison Church at 11 o'clock. *Padre* Quinn took the devotionals and I did find the Anglican service most refreshing in its orderliness and the beauty of the language. Did some Mobile round Heavies and they went into action as I was there – single plane at 26,000 feet; it promptly dropped the 'friendly' signal. Then raid and 12-plus Stukas and fighters came in and we had a terrific battle, parachute bombs, etc., long trails of vapour in the sky, which after the action looked as if some amateur had been practising cloud effects.

23.2.42 A most unsettling day. Visibility was restricted by low clouds and several planes darted in, dumped their load and got off just as AA got into action. This process got us all quite jumpy. Poor old Barker had some tummy trouble and looked terrible all morning. Then Tank arrived back with his wagon in tow and peppered with shrapnel holes. He has four small pieces in his body, fortunately not serious, two in the leg, one in the seat and one in the chest. Tiny was very badly shaken. They were attacked by a Stuka, which dropped a stick of bombs across them. Both were below the car. One of the drivers in a nearby vehicle was killed outright.

At night I went to the first of the mission services. It was an experience I'll never forget – being at a mission service with a heavy air raid on. We could hear some of the bombs crunching and the tremendous noise of the harbour barrage and the beat of the enemy bombers, which seemed right above. I did admire old *Padre* Leyland, who went on unperturbed. I certainly did not feel too good. Quinn's eye was in a bad mess, as a landmine had blown up in his face. Leyland asked me to share his digs, as he says he is very lonely. It is difficult to decide, as I would like to be in YM if anything did happen.

24.2.42 It was a relief to have a pukka sandstorm, which rendered visibility very bad and hence gave us a day free from air raids. Tank, Barker and I went to the mission. Leyland spoke on Faith as a gift and was indeed most helpful.

25.2.42 Today I took Tank through to Mersa on the first leg of his leave, which he is now keen to have. He is a very plucky fellow, but has been shaken a bit. We had an uneventful trip to the YM, which had been moved to Kilo 6. Quite a good show has been erected, four tents with floors cemented. I can't see the logic in our evacuation from Matruh, especially when one compares it with Tobruk. I'm afraid the Sub Area Commander does not like the YM. Mack was in good form. Poor Jack Wilkinson was back from leave and in bed, sick – his leave had been too good! He brought a good mail and a parcel of cake and fudge from Lily!

26.2.42 I think I'm a bit short these days and must be hard to get on with, as I cut off several chaps rather quickly. I do feel a bit resentful at Sub Area's attitude to us. The Army does get me down at times. Meanwhile, the sands of time are sinking: Russia cut off German Army in Leningrad. Good old Joe [Stalin]!

1.3.42 March has come! How time moves on, but it can't move too quickly for me. Each day brings us nearer the end of all this stupidity. Packed up big Mobile for a trip to the Front with George. Got off after lunch and passed through El Adem on way to Forward Area. George rode on the side from El Adem to spot any trouble in the form of Messerschmitts or Stukas, but we were untroubled and settled down near an encampment of Arabs, with their sheep, goats and camels and tents.

4.3.42 Did another DHQ [Desert Headquarters], where powers-that-be were very much anti-litter and each batch that came up was told in pretty strong language what would happen to them if they dared to drop any paper in the desert. My sole relaxation on the job was an occasional bonfire of the cartons that kept accumulating at our feet. Heavy rain came on and we had a tiresome job navigating home, as most of the tracks were flooded. Taffy Williams has developed into a real wit and keeps the company going with his accounts of his mother-in-law and Welsh mining life in general. *Padre* Fisher was in tonight. He is a real scream and does a good job.

5.3.42 Very rainy day and seldom has rain been more welcome. Wrote to John, Beth and Mother. Mobile work curtailed on account of ground conditions. Don Gordon, one of the orderlies, has turned out to be a real crook. Lifted in Alexandria having spent £80 after he left us; forged pass; also drawing money on the Chief's name. What a thing human nature is. It shakes me sometimes.

7.3.42 Arrived in Alexandria and met Ling, the new secretary there, who is very keen on music and has started one-hour daily concerts. In civvy street he ran tours. Then *Padre* Orr and I went to the cinema to see a most enjoyable comedy about the American Army, quite the best I've seen for a long time. Stayed in the Minerva Hotel and shared a room with Tim, who is a splendid, solid chap. From the Essex Regt., he has been two years in the field – Sudan, Iraq, Iran, Syria and now Western Desert – and this is his first leave. Yet after a few days in Alexandria, he yearns for Tobruk.

8.3.42 Sunday went in and saw Miss Williams who was in splendid form, studying hieroglyphics. Spent about two hours in the hospital visiting several Ulster blokes who had been seriously wounded in the desert. Ailsa Blue was refused admission and some of the lads were very much annoyed about it.

13.3.42 Read an interesting little book by Maude Royden, *The Problem of Palestine*. I can devour anything on Palestine these days, as leave will see me there in a month or so – *yimkin*! Got back to Tobruk to find all well. Decide to send four of the lads on leave tomorrow. This announcement caused a real thrill among the lads, especially Taffy.

14.3.42 This was a big day for the ecclesiastical establishment of Tobruk, as the Bishop of Pretoria dedicated the Garrison Church and did a Confirmation service in the YM chapel. There was a large attendance and over twenty were confirmed.

22.3.42 Had prepared to go out on Mobile, but feel I'd better go to Mersa and get the four men on leave back and see Mack, also see about Tank. Took No. 13 and go cracking. Had a puncture and near Sidi Barrani petrol ran out, but two RAF blokes fixed me up. No one back at Mersa yet. According to wire, Tank is to be back tonight with the four men, but no sign of him. Had a good yarn with Mack about Palestine Question. He knows the situation very well from position of the British police, who are very anti-Jew.

These are good days and I feel a lot happier than I have for a long time. Perhaps it's the anticipation of leave. But I think it's rather that I've got life a little more disciplined and know where I am a bit better.

25.3.42 Today and yesterday blew almost continual sandstorm and with nothing to do in the morning I did get very fed-up. A great discovery has dawned on me: that I do like to be on a job. The pendulum swung with a vengeance in the afternoon – a terrific invasion of Kiwis, who took all before them. We had a NZ night and when it was about over, the delinquents arrived in force – Tank, Peter, George, Taffy and Bill – and Harry Hart, who takes Arthur's place. Mack had gone off early to convey his two NZ sisters to Fort Capuzzo, so that one should see her *fiancé*. He got back late. The sisters had caused a lot of excitement in Sollum and Capuzzo. Must be many months since those parts have seen a skirt.

26.3.42 Hart has very definite religious convictions of the conservative school and decries the modern generation with its cinemas, etc., and indicated that the Irish Presbyterian Church had lost the ancient splendour of its evangelical tradition.

Some little activity tonight. The moon is coming up again.

27.3.42 Got old Barker off on leave with the remnant of the lads. A lovely day – for the Stukas – and we had plenty of raids, some bombs quite close. Raids lasted till late at night.

28.3.42 Not the best of a night, besides the raids. Attack from within in form of fleas, which landed and took off until the early hours. Arranged an Italian class. Friends Ambulance have a very intellectual representation here and are doing lectures for next few weeks. Subjects: sociology, sculpture, painting, birds, Irish Question, German literature, music, the Amazon, amateur theatricals. We had some nasty raids today and again some stuff shook us a bit. Some of the blackouts were blown in.

29.3.42 Had to go out with tea to 115 Petrol Point, who were unloading petrol all night, and it turned out to be a highly interesting time. I got tea ready and set off about 11.30pm and found the sky red with the glow of a large fire in the Bardia direction. Went to old position of 115 and found that two of 115's dumps were on fire, burning fiercely. The geography of the place had been changed, as I soon found out when a very young subaltern rushed up to me brandishing his revolver.

'What the hell are you doing here?' he said. No answer and the same remark. 'Don't speak to me like that, lad.' He cooled off when he saw the contents of the truck and showed me to Control Tent. The fires were the result of sabotage and gangs of SA were using long spikes to comb out the blaze. AA went off several times and the men lost no time in clearing off. But no plane came near us. Tea and biscuits were much appreciated. Lot of East African lads, coal dark with lovely sparkling teeth, charming fellows. Ended up the night's work by giving my lieutenant friend a cup of tea and some biscuits, and we both saw the humour of the situation.

30.3.42 Had a surprise raid in the afternoon and a small bomb hit in the PO, right opposite. Two of the staff had a miraculous escape. Blast shook us badly and my office window was blown out. Played a bit of football with the boys – it relieves the nervous tension a lot. Went to *Padre* Louden's German class, which was mostly carried on in opposition to AA. Got a Mauritian cook on to the staff, chiefly through Mack's influence on Captain Jefferies. He speaks no English.

2.4.42 Went out to Petrol Point last night, more uneventful night this time, fortunately. Just had enough tea to go round. Lovely moonlit night, but Jerry resisted temptation. 'Johnny' the cook is going great guns and produced a four-course meal tonight.

3.4.42 Good Friday. Memories of last year float back, on boat for Greece. What a lot has happened since. We are certainly in a more favourable position. Raid in the morning. C of E [Church of England] service conducted by *Padre* Fisher. Two things that the Cross taught us – man's rebellion and God's love. Fisher is a real live wire, took a service in the docks air-raid shelter some nights ago and got a fine reception.

Went to take a photo of a grave in Tobruk cemetery. Memorial erected by Australians: 'In the morning and at the going down of the sun we will remember them.' One Aussie VC [Victoria Cross] is buried there. A great number of Poles also, must be most of a thousand there. Some graves have been neatly decorated by tiles taken from floors and walls in Tobruk.

Hart and I had a long discussion in the evening. He is a thoroughgoing fundamentalist, doesn't hold with evolution, etc.

4.4.42 Weather is a joy these days, though flies are beginning to accumulate. Tank and I set off for Sidi Rezem, very rough going on the ridge where so many perished. Primitive mosque is surrounded by many rude graves, mostly Italian unknown, with British interspersed. Many wrecked German cars in varied stages of salvage or pilferage, according as one looks at it. We went on to the aerodrome and had a look at a British Defiant, which had been abandoned, and found the 'drome ringed round with Italian fighters, most of which had been shot up while still on the deck. Our mission was not successful and we did not get any suitable tyres or spares. I was glad to see Sidi Rezem, which will always live in Desert War history as the scene of one of its fiercest battles. Saw a lot of our fighters going off on seeming business.

6.4.42 Padre Louden and I went to the cemetery and took some photos of graves for those at home. Poles have an impressive monument at the north end of the enclosure. The lads arrived back from leave – all with the usual 'after-leave' feeling. They brought some mail for me. An addition to the family is a lovely little pup of nondescript ancestry. We have named him Stuka. It's wonderful what a homely touch a pup adds to the inhospitable atmosphere of desert life. We are all growing moustaches at the moment and mine is not past the 'bad shave' stage yet. George's is doing well and Tank's looks like an anaemic toothbrush. We a really happy crowd here, no slackers or grousers, and a fine spirit prevails.

7.4.42 I'm trying to tighten up on myself these days. Up early, approximately 7 o'clock, as I have to waken the house. Off smoking completely for four weeks now. Proper devotions and some system into the work. Had plenty to do today and tried to get the book scheme into action with the new books. Gordon arrived under escort to be delivered to me, with a load of charges hanging over his head, like the sword of Damocles. I wouldn't accept him and sent him back to Reinforcement Camp. They didn't want him and sent him to CMPs. Eventually Area got him and disposed of him.

8.4.42 Tank and I have had some discussions on future plans and hope to start on Bardia roadhouse soon and probably form a separate Mobile base, so as to ease the pressure on Tobruk Centre. Major Hallam sent for me today and through Gordon's misdemeanour the whole status of all our 'attached' personnel has been called into question. Precisely what we hoped would never happen. He is very reasonable but very military in his outlook, so things seem a bit shaky.

News these days is of Russians still advancing, also Japs. Desert sees a few more patrols.

9.4.42 Taffy is in his usual form these days and the wisecracks fly round at mealtime. Jack's latest joke was about the *Führer's* reception in the next world. The Devil met him and finding out who he was, picked up some fireworks and a box of matches and said, 'Here, go and make a Hell of your own.'

On the invitation of *Padre* Louden, I attended a *padres'* conference. *Padre* Bishop, an Anglo-Catholic monk, gave a most helpful talk on meditation — Prepare, Ponder, Pray, Promise. At this little service the singing was utterly painful, few seemed to know the hymns and fewer still possessed the gift of song.

11.4.42 Tank and I did a spot of house-hunting, without much avail. Book scheme is going full blast and with the scarcer books I hope to form a reference library. Chief sent a book on diesels, which is worth its weight in gold up here. Fred Hill, the young Salvation Army bloke, is here trying to get a driver attached. It's a shame and scandal that he has to go up to the Forward troops on his own. Free French are in a lot these days, buying stuff in huge quantities.

12.4.42 Last few days' news: fierce fighting in Russia; Navy is having a stiff time; big commando raid on Saint-Nazaire submarine base last week.

14.4.42 Harold Barker came in, having walked from the NAAFI, and looking pretty tired but in fine form and we stayed up talking till the small hours. He had been to Palestine and had a fine holiday.

15.4.42 Busy handing over the reins to old Barker, who is as full of life as ever. He is a splendid bloke, inspired by the highest motives and with very definite ideas on most things. In the evening we had *Padre* Carpenter on the question of Parsons and he got it hot from our group of about twelve. Chief questions discussed were: '*Padres* – rank as officers – was this not a barrier?' Social position of Parson raised a barrier in the community? The whole position of *padres* in the war – was religion compatible with war? Parsons out of touch with people?

16.4.42 We have been having raidless days for some time now, in spite of what Lord Haw Haw said. We have distributed over 200 technical books, apart from lighter stuff, both French and English. *Padre* Lacoin, French Foreign Legion, in for stores today. We hope to do a Mobile run to the French.

I'm glad leave has come, as I'm beginning to be very forgetful and let things slip easily, though I'm perfectly fit physically.

17.4.42 Set off with Jimmy Young after usual *adieus* for Mersa, with a rotten *khamsin* blowing most of the time. I was indeed glad to get away. Mack is in usual good form and Mersa at present is a sort of YM rest camp, well equipped and wired off like a convict settlement. Had a talk with him about new place at Axis–Bardia road junction. On the way down saw Tank and his boys at Bardia and called in at Area 8 and saw Major Roberts, who promised to provide two men for Axis house.

18.4.42 Mack took me down to Bagoosh aerodrome in the hope of getting a lift to Cairo. Saw the Duty Pilot, who told us to stand by at 3 o'clock. A nasty *khamsin* was still blowing and the heat was oppressive. Waiting for the crew, I expected three or four begoggled officers to whiz up in a staff car, but, lo and behold, three young lads, sergeants and corporals, wandered up. And we all piled in, sitting face-to-face on long seats running from top to tail. Soon the old kite, a Bombay Bomber, burst into life and her engines fairly roared. We taxied for quite a bit and then with the best of the engines trembling, we took off from the 'drome, leaving behind a blinding cloud of dust. We hopped over the little escarpment and Bagoosh 'drome faded into desert and sand. There was little to see, except the contours of sand formations chequered here and there by cloud shadows. Soon the fun began. We had been warned that it would be pretty rough and it was – rising and dropping most of the time, and it did go for the sensitive parts after a bit. Two fellows became sick and moved back, where one of the crew provided the necessary 3-gallon petrol tin, and I took up a strategic position in case of emergency, which I'm glad to say did not arise.

It was a great thrill to see the Half Way House (between Alexandria and Cairo) far below and the Wadi Natrun stretching out like huge pieces of linoleum on the desert. Everything looked so small, it made me wonder how bombing could be accurate at all. We veered from here and soon came to the Delta, and how wonderful it looked. The fields seemed to be divided up by some magical mathematician and presented the appearance of a slice of select chocolate cake, with various shades of yellow and brown and green. We landed at the 'drome near Heliopolis and got a truck to Cairo, where I arranged to go to Alexandria with Massey in the morning to pick up my passport, camera and cheque book at Scottish School.

21.4.42 Set off on the 2.55pm train for Ismalia, where I found the YMCA club – a big show that must have cost a lot. I hitch-hiked to El Quantara and caught the train to Lydda. Didn't sleep at all during the night – my companions were two lusty South Africans and a Kiwi and some of their conversation was pretty sickening. Changed at Lydda for the train to Jerusalem.

22.4.42 The city was really a joy to look at in the bright spring sunshine and much fresher than August last. Lovely YM hostel and canteen, where we had a splendid lunch. Had an early night, getting passes, etc., for Syria.

23.4.42 The coast run through Jaffa to Tel Aviv was interesting – oranges everywhere, lovely, big, juicy Jaffas. What wouldn't they do with them at home these days! Palestine is a friendly country and everyone, especially the Arabs, shows a kindly interest in one's welfare.

Passing the border into Syria was a complicated affair for my fellow travellers, who were civilian, though I had practically no trouble. The railway between Haifa and Beyrouth [Beirut] and Tripoli is being made by SAREs [South African Royal Engineers] and it was fascinating to watch the preparations all along. The approach to Beyrouth was picturesque; huge hills slanting down to the coast covered with lightly coloured houses and villas; place very thick with olive groves. Soon sped on into the town itself, with its narrow streets, French *gendarmes* with little batons and shrill whistles, small trams, men in baggy Turkish trousers and sophisticated French women, and plenty of Aussies.

27.4.42 I was glad to get away from Beyrouth, which had rather a depressing effect on me and seemed to represent something that had seen its best days. Hotel was mouldy, just as most of the town was. Of course, the university was a splendid exception. Drove up over the Lebanons and had a grand view of the seaboard and the surrounding mountain chain and hillsides, dotted with villas.

In Baalbeck we visited the six Corinthian columns of the main Temple to Zeus. Underneath was a network of passages for sacrificial victims. Now they make admirable air-raid shelters. Then off to Damascus. Passed some lovely villages and an Armenian colony, rather like a poultry farm, which had been established by those who had fled from the Turks. Up again over the Anti Lebanons and down past running streams, bare sandy mountain passes and long caravan trains. Damascus is impressive, with its houses sweeping right up the hillsides. Motored in along the Phaphar valley, whose course we had followed for several miles. So we entered what is probably the oldest city in the world. Mentioned in *Genesis* 14:15. Got fixed up at Church Army Hostel. Head *Padre* Smith was here and also Rev. Maurice Sigil of Jewish Mission.

28.4.42 Mr Sigil took me round the city, out to city wall, place where Paul escaped, Great Mosque Street called Straight and all the wonderful markets along it. I was more impressed by the antiquity of it all than Cairo or Jerusalem.

30.5.42 From Haifa, I boarded an express bus for Jerusalem. Got a seat beside a girl who was reading Hebrew and turned out to be Spanish. I found the occupants of the bus, all Jewish, most friendly. I discussed the Palestine problem with one from Berlin and he said he was disillusioned about it and Palestine had not been the proposition they'd hoped for. Another friendly fellow talked to me about the Jewish settlement in which he lived. Parents were in Germany. He had been in the settlement for seven years and was very keen about it. He seemed to be a very ready fellow and I could see from his face that he'd passed through some tough experiences.

1.5.42 Started out from Jerusalem for Gaza, so as to be on our way for tomorrow. Lovely drive in moonlight.

2.5.42 Long run through south Palestine, land of camels and donkeys, sheep and goats, country with distant horizons and sweeping low hills, Bedouin tents. Land of Abraham and Lot, Hebron, Beersheba, the focal points of Arab terrorism. Then on into the Sinai Desert. We took the ferry at El Cantara; the Customs did not trouble us. On to Ismalia and across the Delta to Cairo.

4.5.42 Heat in Cairo is insufferable and after a few purchases I got off to Alexandria, which had a bad raid last night and Church of Scotland had a miraculous escape; direct hit on both sides. Miss Williams and fifty others in hall under the church. I haven't seen anything closer for a long time.

5.5.42 Padre Orr has been doing a lot of inquiry about chaplaincy. Rev. Potts, SCF [Senior Chaplain Forces] RAF in Cairo was keen that I should apply to London to get a chaplaincy here in Middle East. Problems are (1) will it be possible to be ordained in Middle East? (2) will RAF Chaplain General allow me to become a chaplain without going home? I've weighed up the pros and cons and feel that the change to this form of life is now desirable. It will be a new experience in which I will be more definitely on my life's work. I will see the RAF and get another angle on service life. I will be attached to a definite unit. There is a great shortage of *padres* in RAF. The case against is strong also, but the decision final can rest until I get further news in regard to (1) and (2). Anyway, I sent off a letter-telegram asking Father to get the General Assembly to ask Church of Scotland to allow Presbytery of Jerusalem to ordain me.

12.5.42 Up at Area today, which is now established in Italian Caves, well out of Tobruk. They want us to open a centre there, which we may do if they help us on the staff question. Each day now we slip round to a little cove on the harbour shore and have a quick, refreshing swim.

13.5.42 A letter arrived today, bearing the grievous news of Jack Boyd's death somewhere in the region of Burma. My heart feels very, very sore, for Jack's loss leaves a very big gap in the home circle. What a blow to Aunt Annie and Uncle Rob. I remember Jack especially because of his loving and generous nature. His passing changes forever the old world of home, especially Ballycastle. Wrote to John and the Boyds. Also a long letter to Mother.

19.5.42 An AA officer, 2nd Lieut. Millar, was in and he turned out to be from Derry. He was a teacher and knew many of my friends. Paddy from Lurgan left in some weekly *Belfast Telegraph*s, which made good reading.

20.5.42 The first meeting of the Tobruk Fellowship was held after an English class with the Mauritians. It was quite a success and I do hope something worthwhile may come of it. About fifteen fellows turned up and most of them said something. Points that came out: no Bible study, as there is a Bible study on Tuesday already. Discussion to be for a definite object and not for the sake of discussion alone. One suggestion was to discuss the sermon. It will be good for the preacher, anyway. Chap called Lewis waited behind and told me his story. His difficulty was that of reconciling God and the fact of war being allowed.

24.5.42 Harry Hart back again. We had a long talk about staff problems, which worry him at present. He is settling down well and we begin to hit it off now, having come to theological understandings on some points. Several planes over, one last night. The moon will be full in a few days' time and they are making use of it. Blair Mayne was in tonight. He is in this area recruiting for his mob and an ideal man for the job. Andy Mitchell of Lurgan was thrilled to see him again and said he'd follow him anywhere. Andy is a splendid wee bloke, brother of Billy Mitchell of Chelsea FC and himself a star in the same sphere. He is a fine Christian and radiates it in his life. Such contacts make life rich up here.

25.5.42 Set off for Bardia on the old Italian ambulance with Jimmy. It roared, rattled and fumed but covered the ground and got us there. Had a yarn with Tank and his boys, all of whom were in good form. Tank is very handy and has fixed up all sorts of gadgets, water pump, etc. His notices, done with the complete professional touch, are a scream. This at the side of the building – 'Whatever you've come to do here, don't do it here, but go out into the Desert and do it.' Letter from *Padre* Orr, indicating that he has written to the Deputy Chaplain General about the possibility of an emergency commission as a chaplain.

26.5.42 Last night was one of intermittent air activity, though I didn't hear any bombs fall. Reached the stage now of staying on the first floor for better or worse. Raids with fleas made the night's sleep more restive than usual. Wrote to DCG [Deputy Chaplin General] Colonel Ross about chaplaincy.

Mexico now joined the Allies. Russian advance on Khakov. Rumours and precautions and speculations today.

27.5.42 Push began today by the Jerries. All sorts of rumours came through and in the afternoon a *padre* arrived who had run into a German column. All they took was his watch and let him go free. Raids started pretty early and we went to bed to the music of Bofors and Bredas.

28.5.42 Quite a bit of stuff went up during the night and some stuff was dropped. Big battles on outside perimeter in Bir Hackhim and Sidi Rezem area. I had promised to do the rounds with *Padre* Gilchrist, so I piled on the stuff and went out, not feeling too sure of things. Felt my way out to the perimeter and there pondered a bit, but decided to go on. Terrific lot of air activity. Guns in El Adem in action continuously. Did an AA crowd on the move from Front and they were glad to get the stuff. Sky filled up with planes, weaving to and fro, mostly our fighters. Three Messerschmitts raided El Adem and scampered off. Saw a pukka Stuka raid on the Escarpment. It is a thrilling sight, especially when our fighters pursued them. On the way back passed two of our fighters which had made failed landings. Stories today have been amazing, mostly of escaped prisoners. And Jerry is being favourably contrasted with the Italians. Captain Cassor, who gave us lectures and took Italian class, was killed by air strafing yesterday.

29.5.42 About 10 o'clock last night they started to come in and it was an hour and a half of the real dive-bombing stuff. We all came down, even Jack and Barker. Some of the stuff was quite close and the barrage noise was terrific. All the time there was a sort of brooding noise over the town. Then suddenly a distinctive whine could be heard and the Stuka was on his way and then, 'here they come', another harsher whine and the dirt would drop. In the morning, Jack and I went off with big Mobile to El Adem and did all sorts of people: escaped prisoners, lost odds and sods, and various bits of armoured troops. We covered a lot of men, and one crowd, as they were on the move, asked us to go with them to their next position. However, I was turned back by an officer in a pick-up, who said they were probably going into action.

Another noisy night, so slept downstairs. The morale of the troops here has never been greater. Message from General Ritchie to all ranks:

'I send you this message because we have now commenced a great battle. Much depends on us all. Great trials lie before us till this battle is won, as won it will be. But to win is not enough; nothing short of bitter defeat of the enemy is sufficient and this we and our sister services will achieve. Great calls will be made on your strength, but I know you will meet them as before, with utter disregard of self in the common cause of achieving victory.'

Chapter Five

THE FALL OF TOBRUK
AND POW LIFE IN ITALY

Tobruk fell on 20 June 1942 and, with it, my part as an active member of the British war effort ended. I became a prisoner-of-war, first captured by the Germans, to become shortly a prisoner of the Italians, in whose hands we remain, now in Lucca Campo in Italy. However, let me start from the beginning and set down the events as fairly and correctly as four months' memory will allow. I recorded the previous experiences and events of my wartime life as a YMCA secretary in two notebooks, both of which I hope are safe in Alexandria. The record of the second volume extended to within five days of the fall of Tobruk, so it is from that point I will take up the story.

The long-expected German push took place on 27 May 1942 and for several weeks the battle raged back and forward not far from the Tobruk perimeter, and for some time all seemed to be going well with our efforts. These days were very busy ones for us in Tobruk and, towards the end, most anxious ones, as the 'griff' [news] was increasingly startling. But all through we never visualised the possibility of capitulation. Our time was spent on Mobile trips up to the line, mostly to El Adem and towards Knightsbridge and in the Gazala area of Acroma. We had one memorable visit to the Worchesters, about nine days before zero. It was an exciting run and, looking back, there was a definitely unsettled atmosphere – several Stuka raids and a lot of our transport shelled. Things were getting quite 'warm' and we were glad to gain the security of the perimeter in the evening.

On other trips we noted swift movement and changes of our Tank units. Many blokes were captured and escaped. A typical sight at this period was landscape covered with transport ready to move, planes overhead, and huge clouds of dust and sand hanging in the air. Planes made off with bursts of AA on their tails and sometimes fighters. Away to the north, a terrific tank battle was being waged and we could catch an occasional rumble. Most of the troops at the wire, out of battle for a rest, were invariably in good heart.

As the days passed, news of battle varied and often was beclouded by ill-founded rumours. The Bardia–Tobruk road was crowded with traffic, new staff going up and old staff coming back for a refit. Travelling on the narrow road was very unpleasant and transport of all sorts was lined along it: convoys of tank transporters, which took up three-quarters of the road; Bren gun-carriers, in which drivers could hear nothing; damaged planes being taken back for repairs; not to mention the dozens of ordinary convoys going both ways.

Tobruk YM had a very busy time as Mobile HQ and also serving the troops that were in the perimeter. All the usual programme continued during the last days. The first news that things were not all they should be was on Monday, 14 June and it came in a drastic way. Many units were evacuated and others told to cut down staff to the minimum and put everything on a 'siege basis'. Major Hallam of 88 Area called up and eventually allowed two secretaries and two men to stay. So we got all the rest of the staff together and sent them off to Bardia. Jack Crossan and Harry Hart were loath to go, but we all believed that confidence would be restored in a few days, or perhaps at most there would be a short siege. The official version was a siege of three days or three months. So with light hearts we sent the others off, feeling that it was a good precautionary measure, though not really necessary.

A few nights earlier we had our first taste of shelling, when Jerry opened up from the direction of Gazala, and some of them lit near enough to be quite unpleasant. Shelling is very different from bombing – it is so persistent and no one knows just when the shells are arriving after the report. Bombing during this last period was not terribly fierce, except for two or three nights when he did let us have it with really heavy stuff. Everyone came down to the ground floor and the fun did start. We could hear the 'Stuka Parade' buzzing about like a swarm of bees above the town, then suddenly the sound would grow louder and nearer. Barker would say, 'Look out, boys!', and the famous Tobruk harbour barrage would go full out, the dive would reach its maximum and we would hear the ominous whistles and then a tremendous crash and the building would rock and dust rise and some loose glass blow in and everyone would breathe again as the building still stood.

This performance, repeated at greater and lesser intervals, with explosions near or farther away, constituted a night's blitz at Tobruk. When dawn did come, we were amazed to see that all was quite normal and it was only from the early callers that we would learn what wounds the town had suffered during the night. But the damage done had to be looked for, it seldom was very great and comparatively few casualties were incurred, even during the siege.

When Tobruk was cleared of unnecessary personnel on 14 June, we made preparations for the siege. We kept Ford No. 77 and Lt. Hill of the Salvation Army also stayed with his 3-tonne Ford Mobile. The next few days were days of expectation and we were not surprised when the road to Bardia, our last means of land communication with Egypt, was cut and the real siege was on. Things in the town were fairly quiet then and little news came through. The hospital ship stayed on until 17 June.

I spent a lot of time in the canteen, as we were now short-handed and the four of us had to share duties. Our policy was to sell out all we could and not to restock. Trade was very brisk when the NAAFI shut its doors, and we had all sorts of visitors. Soon all we had left were odds and ends, like boot polish, very little edible stuff. As usual, about 4.30pm we went to Anzac cove for a swim, and we had our regular religious discussion, though I remember little about it now. The temporal had more possession of my mind than the eternal. By this time it was fairly evident to us all that the action had, from our point of view, been unsuccessful. Tanks were retreating down to the frontier. One BBC News commentary shook me: it suggested that 'the loss of Tobruk would not be so very serious', as it had served its day. This will always take a lot of explanation to those who were in the Tobruk perimeter on the succeeding days. It certainly did not stiffen the morale of the garrison.

On Saturday, 20 June we were wakened very early by shellfire. We knew that the attack had started. The shelling was heavy on the town, heavier than I had ever experienced it before and very few people came to the YM, as the going in the streets was very precarious and shells were landing quite near from time to time. We carried on much as usual, opening the canteen and the rooms, but only one or two came in. During the morning, Bentley of the brigadiers' Mess advised us to be ready to evacuate by boat in the evening, so I put on what clothes I thought suitable and collected together some other odds and ends that I wished to take with me. As the day went on we got little news. Barker went down to Area HQ and was told that all was under control. He was given an optimistic account of the operations. Towards lunch the shelling dropped off a bit, only to be recommenced in the afternoon with increased intensity.

In order to put the day in, we started to whitewash the kitchen. Talk about Nero fiddling while Rome burned! We went upstairs and had a look over the town and out towards the perimeter and there we saw an amazing sight − several columns of thick, black smoke down by the Derna and Bardia roads and dozens of lorries on fire all round the area. It was impossible to say what was happening and none of us was unduly worried. The feeling was rather one of complete mystification, but still Area sent no message up to us. Stragglers began to arrive into the YM and they were equally in the dark as to what was going on. About 4 o'clock the entire staff of the NAAFI arrived in and told us that they had been shelled out of their place about 4 kilos along the Bardia Road. Jerry was on the other side of Tobruk Bay. The NAAFI's main shed was completely gutted and some of the staff had had a miraculous escape. A scratch meal of bully and biscuits was put on for them.

We were in a very dirty state after the house decorating and decided to risk a swim at Anzac cove. I shall not forget that trip. The town and its environs were completely deserted and there was an uncanny feeling in the air. We felt almost as if we were intruders, as I suppose we were. When we got down to the cove and began to undress, we felt that something very queer was happening. All over the other side of the bay − it must have been about half-a-mile across − lorries and staff cars were ablaze and shells were falling into the sea. The idea seemed to be a sort of obliteration, step by step, at least that was the thought that struck me at the time. Then along the horizon and the *wadis* on the other side huge explosions went off from time to time and huge columns of thick, black smoke pillared up to the sky, and I was very much reminded of pictures I had seen of the evacuation from Dunkirk. Some of the shells did the long hop across the bay and lit in the town. We carried on with the swim, nevertheless, and we came out feeling much the better for it. As we dressed we noticed a gunboat do a swift about-turn and make for the open sea; also several lighters were moving that way. On seeing all this, we were not relishing our trip back, though still we had not grasped the facts. When we reached the top of the hill, where we had parked the car, we were welcomed by the terrific report of an anti-personnel bomb. We scrambled for cover and after a few moments bolted for it in the car and were much relieved to get back to the YM without any harm.

We found the NAAFI boys setting off for the transit camp on the Derna Road. We set to and got the tea ready for the evening session and the stragglers who were now in the building, and decided to load up the Mobile with cigarettes, etc., ready for a big evacuation from the Beach Hospital area. Just then a lot of anti-personnel shells came over the town and we wondered what was on. Barker suggested that I go down and see what was doing at Area HQ. No sooner did I get to the door, than I got the answer. As I was about to pass the blast wall, I saw six German soldiers walking straight for YM with Tommy guns blazing away. I went back to Barker and Jack and said that I thought there were Jerry paratroops, as I didn't see yet how the German forces could otherwise be in the town. We walked out just in time to join the line of Tommies who were filing out with hands raised. We were too amazed and surprised to do anything and I remember one of the Jerries taking Peter's watch, so I had time to stow mine out of sight.

The German infantry looked very dusty and tired and unshaven, as if they'd been on the job for a long time without a break. We were collected in a group on a street corner and a miniature street battle commenced between the Germans and the Ordnance Corps. Some of the Panzer troops arrived up on an armoured car and snapped into action. Soon the air was streaming with tracers and the noise was terrific. Some of the German soldiers were systematically going round the houses and billets, shouting to the occupants. They sprayed the buildings with the Tommy guns and, if they were in doubt, they threw in a hand grenade. We waited with a little anxiety and considerably more fascination as the battle went on. The Ordnance fought well and put one or two tanks out of action.

We were hustled off down the street, still too much astounded to register any emotion. As a parting jest, one young Nazi shouted in guttural English, 'Now it's a long way to Tipperary!' Fred H. of Salvation Army asked to be allowed to go back to the YM for his accordion and a German took him back. We were conducted onto the waste ground beside Area HQ and there we found hundreds of other prisoners collected from other parts of the town, which had capitulated about an hour before. It is difficult to recall all my feelings now that I had time to realise our position. Dusk had come and we could see a lot of German armoured vehicles lined up in the square. One or two places that had offered resistance were dealt with by tanks. The prisoners poured in and among them we greeted many old friends. I helped to carry the body of a British officer across the square. He had a very nasty wound on the temple and must have been killed instantly. Several explosions went off, which we located as the Power House, the Water Point and the Petrol Dump, and new columns of flame and smoke filled the sky.

We had been taken so unexpectedly that we had nothing with us except the clothes we had on. No food, no kit, no blankets. It was now dark and after about two hours sitting in the open square, we, a melancholy crowd, were conducted out of the town and up to the Italian hospital. And that was the last we saw of Tobruk and the YM that had been open since January 1941 after the British entry into the town. It did not cheer us up to pass by places of happy associations – the *Padre*'s house, turns on the road we knew so well, now to walk past for the last time as a prisoner! Everything was in the hands of the Germans and it was interesting to see them in the flesh, having heard so much about them. They struck me as being very much like ourselves and, I should say, very tired of the whole business. I did admire their organisation, and certainly they were not wasting any time on the job. Their equipment was very practical and all were armed with Tommy guns, pistols and hand grenades.

We were massed in the middle of the hospital compound, on the huge Red Cross sign, which protected the hospital from the aircraft. We sat there, huddled together, at sixes and sevens, and by now getting a bit hungry. A *padre* came out with an ambulance and distributed blankets, which were most welcome. The German officer requested that all cigarettes be put out, and on being asked why, he said in case we became a target for the *Luftwaffe*.

I don't think many slept very well that night and we were glad when morning came and we were able to stretch ourselves. We walked around feeling very hungry. *Padre* Naylor gave us a cup of tea, some bread, a piece of Lifebuoy soap, a New Testament and several other Gospels, all of which proved most useful. He had been in Ireland when he'd first joined the Army and it seemed odd to be discussing home at such a time. He suggested that we come to the Mess, but we had the two lads with us and didn't want to leave them. Indeed, we were not sure what to do at this point. We'd never thought of being in such a position and what our standing would be. Anyway, most of the men were lined up and marched off to a POW pen up on El Gobi aerodrome and we stayed behind on the advice of some officers with Red Cross personnel. All day we sat opposite the Medical Inspection Room and no one took the slightest interest in us. The boys went along to the Field Bakery and got half-a-dozen loaves, which kept us going in food, with a few other bits and pieces we were able to raise. The food and water position was becoming bad now. The Germans had commandeered all that was available and I did not like to think of what it would be like in a few days. We discovered a 44-gallon drum of water and that kept us going.

It was depressing to sit and watch all sorts of wounded being brought in by ambulance to the Medical Inspection Room and the theatre, and as I witnessed the orgy of pain and suffering, I was thankful that I had got off with body and limbs intact. All day long German traffic flowed in and British and South African captured transport mounted. It was a very hot day and from time to time we had to change our position to get out of the heat of the sun. I was amazed to see the amount of kit some of the officers had with them. Several must have had all their possessions. Someone found the way into the Hospital QM [Quartermaster] Stores and we got a lot of useful stuff. Complete small kit, Indian flannel shirts, some books, game of chess, pillow, and several odds and ends. Later, I picked up a little valise and a sticky bomb case, which constituted my luggage. *Padre* Louden turned up after having twice tried to escape. No one was very clear about the eventual position of a POW, though many ideas were advanced. We had evening prayers together and lay down where we were and got some sleep during the night.

Next day we were greatly relieved when the order went round that all non-medical personnel were to be removed to the POW cage. Two big buses came up and we soon piled in. There was a terrific lot of transport on the road – a lot of it was ours being rounded up, I suppose. The bus was full of officers and manned by two Jerries, who certainly were not worried about us, as both had their revolvers slung up on the side of the vehicle. We did not know where the cage was and apparently the driver didn't know either. We passed the NAAFI and the cemetery and forked right at El Adem turn and on and on we went until we were outside the perimeter. In retrospect, this was our best chance of escape, but even then it would have been a slender one. Apparently we were on the wrong way and made back for the town again. I noticed at the roadblock and roundabout several German tanks were gutted, though there was no other sign of any conflict, except at the NAAFI, where two more tanks were gutted. It was a very nasty and dusty day, one of the days that one likes to forget: *khamsin* storm blowing amidst a terrible heat.

At El Gobi 'drome we saw our fate – about 15,000–20,000 men were amassed together about 1,000 yards from the road behind the NAAFI. I suppose we had missed it on the way up on account of the sandstorm. We were dumped down here and found things in a pretty miserable state, especially in regard to water, though some sort of organisation was now afoot. Units were lined out in squares and supplies of water in 44-gallon drums were being issued to the men, a half-mug of water for all purposes. This may have been improved later. We attached ourselves to 88 Area and tried to fix up a sort of shelter as protection against the sandstorm, but, inside, the heat was almost intolerable. At this point we were separated from the boys and put in with the officers, where we got some welcome food: two tins of British bully and Italian tins of meat and vegetables, and some water. Then we saw the poor NAAFI boys who had been through a terrible ordeal after they had left us the day before. Going up the Derna Road, about twenty-five of them in all, they had run into several German tanks that shelled and machine-gunned them. Ten were killed and several severely injured. The remainder had to leave the wounded behind and go off to the cage, and were in a pretty bad way.

We heard of many other different experiences. Some had made valiant efforts to escape, but had not got beyond the perimeter; some had gone to the beach and waited all night for ships that never came; some had hidden in caves and *wadis*, but had been rounded up that morning. Perhaps the most pitiable of all were the Camerons, who had been last to lay down arms, fighting on until 3am.

Everyone was in a pretty downcast mood. The inevitable reaction had set in and people had had time to think things out and realise that the impossible had actually happened. And we were no exception.

Meanwhile, the *Luftwaffe* loomed overhead, gloating, as it seemed, over our misery. I suppose the German pilots were interested to see the number of prisoners taken. It was strange to see the big white-crossed planes and not to hear the Ack Ack barking defiance from the ground.

Fortune favoured us: we were selected to go in the first draft of officers to the next halting place *en route* for Italy or Germany. We were keen to get clear of Tobruk now, as every sight we saw or place we passed gave us a twinge, like the opening of a wound. The twelve Opel trucks in our convoy reminded us of the two we had used for our YM transport in the Christmas push to Benghazi and beyond. About twenty of us were packed in and the German guard, a very young bloke, was quite friendly. This indeed is one of the points that lingers in my mind and that has since been corroborated by practically everyone else, though a variety of different motives have been suggested as inspiring this friendly attitude: 'Propaganda'; 'Conviction of their own inevitable defeat'; 'Respect of one soldier for another'. Anyway, their behaviour was most considerate. I was glad when we got clear of Tobruk and as we left, the dust storm cleared up. We passed a terrific amount of traffic: guns, very large calibre, like Bardia Bill; some tanks and a lot of Italian troops. I had not seen any Italian troops in Tobruk the night it fell. Now, masses of them passed us in their big Lancias in high fettle and letting us know their feelings. It was some comfort to recall the convoys of captured Italians I'd seen in the early days of 1941, when Wavell's Army took about 250,000 prisoners. Taking a sporting view, we could not complain at the change of fortune, for we had had our hour and now the boot was on the other foot.

We hoped we were going to Derna, but instead turned off at Timini and rumbled over the desert for about two miles and came to a sort of encampment, recognisable by the large congregation of troops and conspicuous by the absence of tents. Here we were dumped and given our space of desert for all purposes. It was a primitive show: go-as-you-please latrines, a bed under the stars, a tin of Italian bully and biscuit. After a vain attempt on both of these, we settled down for the night. As yet we were fastidious about food, but that soon wore off. During the night the RAF arrived and gave Timini 'drome a real pasting and a lot of anti-aircraft shells went up. It was a strange experience to be the victims of one of our own RAF raids and their efforts seemed to be quite effective, as we saw from one or two burnt-out lorries on the road next day. We could not see what damage had been done on the 'drome.

Next morning we awoke with the dew covering us. We tried the biscuit and bully again with better success and also got a drink of water. Batches of officers were being sent off in big lorries and trailers, and after a long wait, we got off about lunchtime. The heat was very great and there was no shelter and the water problem was being looked after in the usual Italian way. We did not have Army water bottles and had to drink our supply on the spot. From this point on we were in the hands of the Italians and indeed saw very few Germans, most of whom were at Tobruk and beyond. Pioneer Corps of Italians were working on the roads, bridges and minefields as we passed along.

The trip from Timini cage and the road was a severe trial. Now fifty officers and baggage were in bigger trucks and we set off for Derna, very glad to be on the move again and wondering what was in store for us. South African and British officers were together and one of our party was Bill Bowes, the famous English cricketer. We sped along the road, which was in a bad state of repair and the going was far from comfortable. There were a lot of planes passing along the coast, to join in the battle, I suppose. Stukas, Messerschmitts and Savoia Machetti bombers, all flying very low, as they were now in their own territory. Everything told us that Jerry was making a mighty big push to follow up the Tobruk calamity. This did not cheer us, especially as we could do nothing about it. One of the biggest hardships of a POW's life, we realised, was lack of reliable news. From now on we were subjected to two sources of news: rumour, usually fantastic; and enemy news.

Ulm Rezem, the little oasis and first sign of vegetation on the way to Derna, was now transformed into a hospital. The old water tank in itself recorded the history of the Desert War in three words – *Acqua*, Water, *Wasser* – and now the circle of tenure was recommencing. It was interesting to see the Derna aerodrome in action, the graveyard of so many Axis planes, most of which were now cleared away. All these aerodromes were in the hands of the *Luftwaffe* and the first sign of Italian planes was at Barce. (Derna 'drome saw the end of six German troop-carriers in December 1941when they, believing the 'drome to be in their hands, landed and were given a very warm reception by the 4th Indian Division.) Soon we were wending our way down the Escarpment and looking down at Derna with its palms, white houses and beaches. I looked forward to 'visiting' Derna again, but we passed right through the town until no buildings remained except a very mouldy-looking outhouse on a hillside. As we got nearer, I saw that this was our appointed place, as it was very thickly surrounded with barbed wire.

The water supply here was mercifully good, but we were lined up in a courtyard for a body search and saw that the guards were not altogether Anglophiles. Apparently they were Senussi and anxious to show their 'soldierly' qualities. Dressed with red fezes, with long tassels and ancient rifles and cartridge bandoliers, they seemed to be very pleased with themselves and lost no chance in exerting their power over the captives. The search began in front of the camp Commandant's door. I noticed the guard's hungry look at my watch, so I took it off and put in my pocket. However, another Senussi spotted this and told the Italian corporal who was doing the search and he decided to make an example of me. I should like to say that I refused to give the watch to the guard, as he had not the right to take it, but what were rights here when no one understood the other? I was led out of the line and the corporal went through my kit and hit me two wallops on the face. I managed to keep my temper and not hit him back. My two companions were also handed out the same medicine, though neither of them did anything to merit such treatment. Then I was separated from the others and put into a sort of henhouse with wire across the door. There I found a lot of officers who had already been through the fire. The other members of our party soon joined us.

I don't think we'll forget this Black Hole. As we sat on the dirty floor, miserable, with flies everywhere, more and more officers crowded in. The part of the floor we took over was under a large hole in the roof. At night it was reassuring to see the stars, but a shower came on and I caught a bit of a cold from it, which did not improve things.

Two days later we were awakened early and packed onto a long convoy of lorries. I think everyone was glad to see the last of Derna. On the way to Benghazi, over a really lovely bit of country, especially the climb up the west escarpment, the view of the sea did make me homesick. It was a very long run to Barce, where we eventually halted, with practically no stops along the way and uncomfortably packed in the trucks. This was a propaganda tour, showing us off to bolster the flagging enthusiasm of the colonists of Cyrenaica. Most of the people seemed to know that we were coming and any stops were near colonial settlements. Their only discernible reaction was one of curiosity. We went by the north coastal road after we had passed through Giovanni Berta, with the lovely passes and trees and lots of Roman remains along the way. This would be an archaeologist's paradise, but a POW's interest was much more confined to the present and future than the past, especially the Roman past. The Tocra escarpment was very fine and the coastal plain below is very like Devon and Cornwall with its red clay. Down onto the coast that leads on across flat country to Barce, passing a big Italian aerodrome, where all the staff congregated and looked at us with great interest. I don't think they'd ever seen a British soldier before.

We ran the gauntlet of curiosity and some minor demonstrations in Barce on our way to the transit cage, about 4 kilos beyond the town. This was quite respectable as a camp; most of the men were indoors and the rest were in tents, which was no hardship as the weather was fine. We were issued with brand new aluminium dixies [cooking pots] and forms to be filled in with all our particulars; also printed postcards to be sent home stating without any qualification, 'I am a prisoner of the Italians and am being well treated'. As letting our people know of our safety was now our chief concern, we didn't care about how the news was expressed. We got a warm meal of thin rice that went down amazingly well and life took on a much brighter complexion.

The next day we had a hot spray and soap that made us all feel very fit and refreshed. We were selected for movement to Benghazi and it was quite late in the day when we found ourselves in the trucks. The cage at Benghazi turned out to be a huge building in an Italian FSD [Field Service Depot], with very little space behind for exercise. About 400 men were packed into this building, with its rows of double-decked bunks very close together. But we were glad to get into cover and also to bed. We spent about three days in this place before flying to Italy. During that time, there was little to do except lie on our bunks and read and wait. There was a good supply of water and the ration of a loaf and a tin of Italian bully was enough. We did, however, long to be on the move again and be quit of the desert. It is tolerable enough for the free man, but no place for the captive.

Eventually, after a lot of false alarms, we arrived at the 'drome and found fourteen Savoia Machetti, troop-carriers, like huge black moths. We were divided into groups of fourteen and marched to our allocated plane and guards. It was a very warm day, a typical day, you might say, to leave the desert and certainly this was a spectacular way to leave. We were all immensely relieved that we would not have to go by sea, as we knew of the power of the Royal Navy and did not wish to feel its teeth. We climbed in with the crew of five Italians and four guards, and the engines started up. Through the dusty window we saw the others taxi into position. We all went forward to help the tail-lift of the plane as she left the deck, and with a bump and jolt we were in the air. Up, up we went and we looked out on Benghazi harbour below, and the much-bombed Juliana and Cathedral Moles and a lot of wrecks in the harbour itself. I wondered what fate had in store for it, as it had already changed hands five times in the eighteen months of my desert life. We flew along the coast in the direction of Tripoli and then took to the sea and lost sight of land. Occasionally another plane would loom into sight, gently riding on the atmosphere, and once or twice a fighter pulled into view.

The crew struck us as efficient, but not a little jittery. I suppose it was an unusual trip for them. By now I was feeling very hungry and I did envy the pilot as he ate some peaches. Then we got a shock when the pilot left his seat, sat on the floor of the plane and soon dropped off to sleep. We were considerably comforted to find that the controls were dual and that the other pilot had taken over in the side of the plane hidden from our sight. Various thoughts came into my mind – the fantastic possibility of escape; what they'd be doing in Alexandria now; Sunday at home – and then I dozed off for a while. One point in favour of this trip was that all the time I was going nearer home and this was a comfort. And the idea of seeing Italy, even as a POW, did help – a new experience, and experience is cheap at practically any price.

Coast at last and a thrill of expectation ran through the passengers. No sooner had we sighted land than we lost altitude and flew quite low over fields and the ox-drawn carts going along the roads. We crossed what turned out to be the heel of Italy and saw the 'drome looming up. Then *bump-bump-bump* and we had arrived. An ancient Lancia lorry rumbled up and we were taken to the hangars and aerodrome HQ, where all the other prisoners were lined up in their lorries. A South African brigadier told us that a hot meal had been promised for us in the town of Lecce.

It was good to be among green fields and olive trees and country roads after the sand and monotony of Libya. There was no traffic, except for an occasional Army lorry and one or two high-wheeled farm wagons. Several villages turned out *en masse* to see us pass by. Most people seemed completely apathetic, except for a few schoolchildren who cheered us as we passed, and no one betrayed the slightest emotion of hostility – a consequence, I felt, of their absolute weariness of war and longing for the end. In Lecce, a fair-sized provincial town with a considerable population, we stopped at a big square building and dismounted before a large and undemonstrative crowd. The billet turned out to be a disused hospital and we were ushered upstairs, where there were about 60 mattresses for 200 men, and of course we were among the 'also-rans' and parked ourselves on the floor for the night. After a long delay the much-anticipated meal turned up, not hot, but a slice of meat roll. However, we were very hungry and soon accounted for it.

A comic turn was provided by one of the guards, who, overcome by his enthusiasm for music, joined wholeheartedly in an improvised concert among the prisoners. Music knows no barriers and we discovered that the easiest way to an Italian's heart was through music. The water in this place was by far the best I'd had since I left home and so we discovered that our new way of living had its compensations. Now at least we were in a country not unlike our own, and with better weather. We slept as well as could be expected and after a meal of 'coffee' (a mixture we gradually got used to) and bread, we went out on to the flat roof for some exercise. Lecce looked to be a fairly ancient town, the centre of an agricultural district. What impressed us was a sort of listlessness about the streets. Almost no traffic at all, except old farm trucks. Any civilians were old or very young; everyone else was in uniform. The only sign of life was in the playground of a nearby convent, where the children were having their play hour.

About midday we learnt that we were soon to be on the move again, and the town once more turned out to see us off. Our guards, from the Alpine Regiment, were now a much smarter type. At Lecce railway station we were put into first-class coaches. We were in with a friendly bunch of South Africans and British officers and speculation about the future formed most of the conversation. The newspapers were full of the fall of Mersa Matruh, which we didn't quite believe as it seemed an incredibly speedy advance. We stopped at Brindisi and one of the South Africans got into conversation with a German in a train alongside ours. They shouted across to each other in German, in full hearing of a platform full of Italians. The German was bound for Libya. He asked who had taken Tobruk and was not surprised when we told him, in spite of all the Italian press claims that the victory had been won by the Italian Fascists. He thought the war would continue another two years, and on being asked who'd win, he shrugged his shoulders and laughed. The South African asked him what they thought of the Italians and he said, 'Just the same as you do.' Just then we drew out.

We kept near the coast and saw the sea from time to time. One officer cheered us up when he told how one of his friends who'd been a POW in Italy sent home for his evening clothes so that he could attend the opera! At each station bartering went on for anything edible and *bambinos* supplied the necessary liaison between the carriage and the refreshment bar. Mostly we were able to get fruit, lovely plums and a few sweets. One notable feature was the honesty of the *bambinos*, though I was stung for 10 *lire* when the train went off too soon.

After about a three-hour run we came to Bari, a big city port on the east coast. Soon we were marching along the street with full kit, singing 'There'll always be an England', which struck me as quite amusing. We walked on and on and left the town and the kit got heavier and heavier as we marched. At last we turned up a dusty little country lane and into an avenue of huts, mostly under construction. We came to some that were quite decent, made of brick, with wooden bunks and a well-watered bathroom. We got an issue of coffee and went to bed believing that we would be there for two or three weeks in transit to a permanent camp.

We were wakened early and 200 of us were lined up with all our kit for a thorough search. We four, Barker and Ray and Fred and me, were called first and our notebooks, papers, photos, enamel mugs, forks and several other things were confiscated and our tins of Italian bully punched, so that we had to eat them on the spot. Next we were marched to a fumigator, our clothes were removed, and while they were being steamed, we had a shower. Clothed again, we were marched off under a separate guard – apparently we were not considered officers by the Italians. We were put into a mouldy pen, like a chicken-run, and given ground space in a very primitive tent without bed boards. An English major of the Scots Guards was sympathetic and tried to help, but in spite of all the arguments that followed, the Italians were adamant – we were just ordinary soldiers to them. Barker, who spoke fluent French, discussed and argued with several Italian officers; some understood and some didn't; all said, 'Si, si', and did nothing.

We began to realise that we were in a pretty unenviable position. British POW officers were financed at the same rate as their Italian counterparts. There were no YMCA secretaries in the Italian Army, hence our position was not recognised and we were considered as private soldiers. Our status reminded me of the Aryan controversy – we were 'like officers but not of the same substance'. We felt let down by our HQs that our position in such an eventuality had not been clearly established. It was difficult to blame the Italians, and they treated us as special soldiers; we had not to work and got double rations. We were told that our position would be finally decided in Rome, and we wrote there and to the Red Cross, but none of our letters was answered. We were in Bari from 29 June until 30 July and all that time we lived in uncertainty and unfulfilled expectation.

After a few days, all the officers were cleared out of our pen and we were left with all the odds and ends of the camp: a bunch of Cypriots who never kept quiet, day or night; some Arabs and Jews from Palestine, who were as bad; a few Yugoslavs; about twenty Greek officers who had been living as civilians in Corfu, their home, but in case they'd be tempted to go back to Egypt and join the Allies, they had been interned in Italy. Later we were joined by some Kiwis and Aussies, who'd been at large in Greece since the evacuation in April 1941 and had only been caught in the spring.

The routine here was a rude awakening between 6 and 7 o'clock and coffee issue, no sugar or milk, but it did wake us up. Then the work party was assembled of almost Pentecostal variety, with a similar variety of tongues. The Cypriots had no desire to work and usually half of them reported sick and most of the remainder played a game of hide-and-seek with the most tolerant Italian Corporal. There was a parade several times a day and the counting of the prisoners often took over an hour, though there were only about sixty in our pen. Then we were 'free' for the day. Now and again we got the loan of a novel and we played a lot of chess. At times I could have gone mad with the heat. The tent got terribly warm inside and the olive trees didn't afford much shelter. Food proper came any time from 12.30 to 2pm and it consisted of one-and-a-half loaves (400 grams) and half a dixie of cooked rice and vegetables, with a lot of water. Also a small piece of cheese, except on Wednesdays and Sundays, which were meat days and each of us was handed a small piece of meat, the cheese and rice missing from the rest. The rice and vegetables were repeated about 5.30pm. It did seem a long time from 12.30pm until 5.30pm and from 5.30pm until 12.30pm the next day, but these were to be our palmy days. I don't think we're likely to forget Bari, with its olive trees, its lizards, its fleas, which gave us several entirely sleepless nights and bodies that looked like strawberries; and the hocking of the Cypriots, who cleared their throats on every possible occasion.

We realised now that we were truly 'in the bag' and had plenty of time to digest this unsavoury truth. We were shoved about a bit, and every other day the very officious Italian Captain, who certainly did not love the prisoner (apparently he'd been a prisoner of the Greeks in Albania), would demand a roll call of the whole camp. By the time all the Cypriots were marshalled, an hour or so would have passed.

It was here that we first got Red Cross parcels and what a rumpus they caused. I think we had three issues. All the tins had to be punctured before delivery and so the issue took most part of a day. One parcel between five men – one-fifth part of a quarter-pound bar of chocolate, three biscuits, one-fifth meat roll, etc. But the tea was divine after five weeks on the ersatz coffee.

We gradually settled down and our great philosophy was: each day finished is a day less, and that the war wouldn't last beyond Christmas. On occasion I did have fits of depression, always in the daytime, but I found the evening very soothing, especially after the heat of the day. I would look out at a track through the grass, amid the shadows of the olive trees, and long to walk along it as a free man.

After we'd been there about two weeks, about 3,000 men arrived and were put into the next pen to ours. South Africans and Tommies together. The going was pretty hard, as they were on four-fifths of a loaf, cheese and two by half-dixie of rice and vegetables. Our two lads turned up, Peter and Jack, after a very nasty trip across from Benghazi to Brindisi and two nights spent in the open in a dried-up canal bed. We heard all sorts of weird and wonderful rumours – Dakar taken by joint American and British action and a five-point landing on Europe, being the two most persistent. They added some colour of speculation to an otherwise tedious existence. When the boys arrived, all sorts of trading started and over the wire went many a fine pair of socks, belts and pullovers for bread and cigarettes. Many of the fellows readily sacrificed their bread ration for a few fags.

One incident concerning the shooting of a sapper [engineer] in the pen next to ours should be recorded. A group of Royal Engineers had just arrived, suffering, like so many, from dysentery, and had not had time to get to know the geography of the camp. About 2am one of them got up for the obvious purpose and walked towards the wire separating his pen from ours and was shot through the head by an Italian sentry. British officers near to the incident claimed that he was not challenged. I think the simple explanation for the shooting was fear, which characterised the actions of the Italian sentries all along. Not so much fear of us, though I suppose the British still have certain fear value, but more of their own officers. This and an incident at Derna, when one prisoner was shot dead and another injured because they stepped over the line, are hard to forget. Life is a very precious thing, especially when one has already escaped the dangers of battle.

After the third week we went into the wooden hut, which housed the Greek officers. Here at least we had a wooden bunk and straw-filled palliasse, though for several nights the fleas were active. During the day a ceaseless attack was kept up by flies, which were just as bad as in Egypt, only now we'd plenty of time to think of them. The Greek officers were a decent bunch, pathetic in their optimism. Only one of them could speak a little English. The Greek tongue is most unmusical to listen to at any time, but when you have to listen to it all day, it becomes tedious. The senior officer would harangue the others at intervals, hitting great heights of eloquence and rage. The place was wonderfully quiet when they did eventually leave.

About sixty fellows came in from Campo 65 and the cadaverous appearance of many of them did not cheer us up. Conditions they told us of were pretty grim – new camp, small rations, cold, scarcity of Red Cross parcels. Eventually the Cypriots were sent off to this camp. Then the Italian Captain decided that we should all be cleared out. We were given two days' rations, about 3,000 of us, and as we marched to Bari I thought of the day yet to dawn when we would be walking out as free men.

In the station, after a half-hour's wait, a goods train pulled in with some third-class carriages. We were in luck and our batch got into the carriages; the others were put in the goods wagons. Off we went, via the coast, through Brindisi and right across and up Italy; we slept through

Rome. We arrived in the lovely Tuscan town of Lucca around 1pm.

As we marched from the station the whole populace seemed to be there, gazing at us with friendly curiosity. Eagerly we scanned the horizon for sight of our new home and eventually we saw the barbed wire, sentry boxes mounted on platforms and arc lights, several wooden Army huts and a great mass of bivvy tents. We were put into an unoccupied pen and in the heat of the sun our kit was searched by *carabinieri* and soldiers. This done, we were marched into the other pen, already occupied by about 1,000 men. We were sorted into tents, South Africans and British together, and we found ourselves in with the Springboks. It was the first of August.

We soon got into the routine of the camp. We were on half-rations, as at Bari, but three Red Cross issues (still one between five) did help us to get acclimatised to the new conditions. No one but a POW will ever realise what these parcels meant to us. After each issue, a market would be established and cigarettes were accepted as the market currency: 40 cigs for tin of biscuits, according to the market fluctuations, which, of course, depended on the last cigarette issue. A typical English parcel contained about 15-18 articles:

    tin of biscuits
    half tin of margarine
    2oz tea
    quarter-lb chocolate
    1 meat roll
    1 tin meat and veg.
    1 tin tomatoes
    quarter-lb sugar
    half-lb cheese
    1 tin Nestlès milk
    1 tin jam
    Yorkshire pudding
    quarter-lb cocoa
    sweets
    ordinary pudding

The last four items varied. Canadian parcels were very popular, especially the powdered milk, biscuits and bully beef. We always made a beeline for the chocolate and polished it off on the spot. Parcels issued, the brewing up would commence and all sorts of ingenious fuel-saving stoves were produced, made from tins. Wood for this was always a problem and much of the camp criminology could be related to this, as the Italians did not provide adequate cooking facilities. Wooden shelters for reading and writing, latrine boards, trip-wire posts, were surreptitiously annexed for this purpose and the culprit, if discovered by the camp police, was put in the 'pen', where he forfeited a parcel and cigarette issue.

The camp was on a gentle slope, divided into two sectors, about 4 acres each, and each sector was intersected by several ditches running down the slope. The first sector, in which we spent the first part of our time there, was better than the second, being higher; the second was like a typical piece of Irish bogland. All was surrounded by a high fence, trip wires and floodlights, and about fifty sentries watched from mounted platform sentry boxes. The camp was over 3,000 strong. At first the atmosphere was strained, but later it crystallised into one of cordial goodwill and many lasting friendships were formed. I found the Springboks very friendly and courteous on all occasions. They had a sort of boyishness and openness of manner and readiness to talk, and included lawyers, advocates, teachers, farmers, diamond- and gold-miners and others from all sorts of business, all with a refreshing newness of outlook, typical of the Dominion soldier. They were all dazed by the turn of events in Tobruk and I always had the opinion that any blame could not be thrust upon them. We were altogether in No. II pen for about three weeks. When more Tommies arrived and all the British were put together in our pen, Barker and I decided to stay with them.

Barker soon got a Welfare Committee going that did a splendid job: concerts, education, lectures, talks, services and discussions. A most popular item was the News Commentary, given by Staff Sergeant Lloyds (SA). A staff member of a South African newspaper, he gave a commentary on the news each Sunday, drawn from the Italian paper and any other available source, and some of his efforts and forecasts were brilliant. Sober optimism was his policy. Barker's knowledge of French was most useful and he made friends with Carlo, the interpreter, and through him with one of the camp Colonels, who turned out to be a good friend. The senior British officer in charge of camp was a Cameron RSM [Regimental Sergeant-Major], who didn't know French or Italian and naturally it was a delicate task to communicate through interpreters.

We went through a period of seven weeks without any Red Cross issue and most of us were starving. Fortunately, the weather was perfectly fine and that kept down our appetites. But it did shake me to see men rummaging through the garbage dump for bits of cabbage stalks, and others bartering with the Italian guards. The cigarette scarcity was even worse and it remained a shock to realise that, for many, tobacco was more vital than food. The Italians were supposed to issue five cigarettes a day, but this was seldom done, and when a Red Cross parcel was issued, cigarettes became the camp currency.

The second sector became all British and the first became Springbok, but we were allowed to go and come as we liked. The Sunday services on both sides were splendidly attended and we must have had 400 men at each service. Singing was a bit of a problem, until we got the men to print hymn sheets. Usually Barker or Hill took the service, while I took the sermon. It was a grand experience speaking in the open air. In the South African pen there was a bunch of fellows who helped and two of them took the morning service and one joined me in the service at night.

Sleeping conditions were far from ideal, as we were herded together in Bedouin-like tents made up of sections of Italian groundsheets; forty men in each tent, with five sections of four along each side. Each tent had a leader and every set of 100 made up a group under a commander, who dished out rations and circulated camp instructions, or griff, each day. The camp was run by officers who did a fine job under the most difficult circumstances, having to liaise with the Italians and to run the camp, which was made up of a pretty diverse cross-section of the British Army.

Both sectors had hospital huts and Royal Army Medical Corps staff had Italian doctors in attendance. Medical supplies were practically nil and about two or three rolls of dressings were issued each day, if at all. There was a lot of dysentery, and malaria increased alarmingly, as the drains were stagnant and fly-infested. Jaundice also became very common and diphtheria cases became frequent. Serious cases were moved to Lucca hospital, where treatment was good. There were many lesser complaints, practically every sore went septic, and owing to lack of dressings, they took a very long time to heal. Cellophane from Red Cross cigarette issue was used for dressing. Lice bred in abundance and the first routine of the morning was to go through the seams of our clothes to seek out and destroy the night's crop. Scabies also increased and a big percentage of the camp was isolated before treatment was secured. The sanitary system was primitive – a long trench in the ground with wooden planks across and a bamboo enclosure around constituted the latrine. The smell in the evening when the wind turned towards the tents was indescribable. The washing system was a long pipe with holes at intervals and a wooden trough underneath. This was passable enough until about the end of September, when it ceased to function. Otherwise there was a makeshift shower-bath with about ten vents to wash 3,000 men. There were also four other taps in the camp for all purposes.

The beginning of September saw the start of grim days. Still no parcels, cigarettes non-existent and the camp began to get restive. Two South Africans had attempted escape during our stay in the first pen. They crawled, *ventre à terre*, for 100 yards along a shallow drain that went under the wire. They got under the trip wire and through the first main wire and then the sentry saw them. Both made for the camp and the sentry shot three times. One was hit near the base of the spine; the other in the leg. Both recovered after some weeks in dock. This escape attempt caused tremendous excitement among the guards and Italian staff, and bugles sounded, cars buzzed off, floodlights swept the camp, soldiers shouted and brandished their rifles. It was, in a sense, highly amusing.

In September many escapes were planned, but the only one attempted ended in tragedy. Two Coldstream Guards climbed over the wire; one damaged his shoulder jumping down and the guard fired. One escaped, but the other was shot dead and his mate came back looking for him and was captured. The next day they had a funeral and the Italians paid their respects and the man was buried in Lucca. This stirred up the camp, but things got a bit better and cigarettes more frequent. The fruit, sold to the camp, came in regularly – peaches, grapes, figs, tomatoes, apples and chestnuts – and these made a tremendous difference in helping to eke out the frugal Italian rations. We made all sorts of mixtures with the tomatoes and made tomato dogs by scooping out the loaves. Usual order of meals was:

coffee: 8am
skilly [soup]: 10am
loaf and cheese: 12 noon
coffee: 1pm
skilly: 5pm

The skilly was made of rice or macaroni, vegetables and water. Issues varied from one-quarter to one-half a dixie, according to the amount of water.

In mid-September the arrival of an English medical officer and *Padre* was a considerable help to the morale of the men. A few days later a Red Cross representative arrived and made a thorough tour of the camps and was disgusted with conditions. He promised that parcels would be sent through as soon as possible. Most of the camp slept on palliasses with no groundsheets and so many of them were rotten. A couple of weeks later parcels arrived and the whole tone of the camp was transformed, and dozens of little fires sprung up and the brewing up began again. Red Cross issue of clothing was also made and we got greatcoats, woollen underwear, battle slacks, etc. – a splendid effort for which I will never cease to appreciate. The Italians issued slacks, etc., to those who were left out of British issue.

I shall always be thankful for the really lovely country round about, the nearby hills and the little village with its church standing like some fairy castle among the clouds, and away in the distance the lofty ridges of the Apennines. Each day the colours and perspective was transformed and the light and shade brought out the contour of the hills. Picturesque red tiled roofs and the white-walled cottages and houses glistened in the sun and from the distance gave the impression of newness and freshness that was dispelled on closer acquaintance. The little mountain near us was terraced with groves of olive trees and we later learnt that Lucca olive oil is celebrated. The fields round the camp were full of maize, which we often coveted as we watched the Italian maidens and old men reap the harvest. A tremendous amount of the farmwork was done by women and the sole means of transport was an ox wagon. There were a lot of vineyards in the district; and it was grand to taste a few ripe figs from the abundant fig trees. So our surroundings did help to lift our minds.

Barker's friend, the Italian Colonel, took us out for several walks. He was a lawyer and most friendly and considerate. When I feel vindictive against the country, I will always remember such men. The Colonel was obsessed with a desire to learn English. He had an inordinate love for proverbs – 'All roads lead to Rome' – and he was delighted when he eventually grasped the meaning of 'When in Rome, do as the Romans do'. It took most of a walk and the help of an Italian sentry – who was a doctor of economics from Rome University with a good knowledge of English – to explain. It was a great thrill getting away from the camp for an hour and during the walks we saw some of the peasants in their little villages. I was impressed by the beauty of some of the peasant women – black hair, dark eyes, red lips and fresh complexions. On the few occasions when the opportunity was given they decked us with figs, tomatoes and anything they had and were very friendly and ready to help in any way they could. They were very poor, though we were told that they were much better off than the townspeople. Certainly I never felt any hate for them, but rather hate and resentment against a society that makes war possible.

The days at Lucca passed: September, October, November, and the Italians kept putting off our move into winter quarters. The weather got very bad, with days of torrential rain and thunder and lightning. The nights became very cold, and as we slept with the front of the tent open, we thanked God for the greatcoats the Red Cross had provided. When it seemed that we were unlikely to move, we felt almost desperate. Parts of the camp were in a state of quagmire and the waterline rose with each shower of rain. Eventually we were swamped out and moved to the only bit of high ground left, along the side of a stagnant drain that the men were now allowed to use as a urinal at night.

As each day ended our philosophy was still to say, 'Well, another day gone and another nearer home', or 'It won't be long now'. Barker maintained through all rumour and truth that it would be over by Christmas, and he was usually asked, 'What Christmas?' Many believed March 1943 would see the end and I think it will come between March and June 1943. So it remains to be seen.

The author, looking gaunt, as a prisoner-of-war

Chapter Six

CAMPO 70

Campo 70 had a prepossessing entrance, with a huge arch inscribed with the words 'CAMPO CONCENTRAMENTO PRIZIONERI DE GUERRA' across the top. It was mid-November and we thought that at last we had 'arrived' this time as we marched into an imposing courtyard with well-cultivated flowerbeds and a fine block of buildings along the side. After all the mud and water of Lucca, with its little tents, the solidity and permanence of this place were very reassuring. Here at least we would have a roof over our heads, and that was a good start. The camp lay in a valley and several villages were scattered around the hills. Fermo and Monturano were nearest to the camp, which was about 10 miles from the Adriatic coastal town of Porto San Giorgio.

It did not take long to discover that the flowerbeds, the courtyard and the fine buildings were not for us. We quickly saw the familiar khaki figures crowded round the barbed wire, clamouring to have a first look at the new arrivals. No sooner did we approach the wire, than they began to quiz us – where were we captured? Whence had we come? Had we any news of the war and any Red Cross parcel information?

Beyond the barbed wire we found ourselves in the premises of a canning factory that had since been transformed into a POW camp, its high grey walls and huge barrack-like sheds ideal for the purpose. Our quarters consisted of six sheds, like barns with high roofs, three along each side, and a lower building in the middle with considerably more ground space. Below the sheds was a 3-acre stretch of open ground planted with fruit trees, which we came to call the Orchard. Here, we were allowed to walk around a rectangular path, about 600 yards long. The whole area, apart from the lower end of the camp, was surrounded by a wall, 12 feet high, with 5 feet of barbed wire on the top. Sentry boxes were located at 60-yard intervals on platforms on a level with the top of the wall. The absence of the wall at the lower end of the camp was fully compensated for by two very solid barbed-wire entanglements and a greater density of guards per yard. Indeed, one would not approach within 40 yards of this lower defence without endangering one's life.

Our reception was in no sense impressive. We were taken into the middle building – almost large enough for a football match – and were sorted out once again and assigned to one of the barns. There was no furniture whatever, just bare walls and concrete floor. We had arrived unexpectedly, and would have to take potluck until the wood arrived for the bunks. In the meantime, we received palliasses, and by filling them with straw we managed to arrange ourselves in tolerable comfort. More alarming was the discovery that we did not come on to ration strength until the next day. We had been issued with hard rations for the journey – bread and cheese – but we were hungry now and had been looking forward to a cooked meal. But it was not so decreed.

We found that there was already a considerable number of men in the camp, of such vintage as El Agheila, Sidi Rezegh, Greece, and many of our fellows from Tobruk. There must have been about 3,000 in all, but every month or two a new batch would arrive and upset the organisation and all would have to begin over again. In the end it became like a geological section with its various strata: at the bottom would be the originals and so on to the top stratum of the newest arrivals. These groups tended to stick together and not mix very much with the others.

With the ever-increasing numbers new problems arose. There were only two wash places for the whole camp and the conditions were unimaginable. The water pressure was very low and we had to queue for an interminable length of time when we wanted even a little water. It did develop our communal spirit as we learnt to share the trickling water vent with half-a-dozen others at various stages in their ablutions. Exercise was even more problematic. The Italian war effort demanded that the Orchard be ploughed up, so we had to confine ourselves to the narrow path round the rectangle. In this, one had to be sure to walk with the tide, otherwise the going was very difficult. And one had to keep in step with the hundreds of others, as there was nothing to be gained from cutting out and passing those immediately in front.

Camp routine was: *reveille*, coffee, 7 hrs; parade, 8 hrs; soup, bread, cheese, 12 hrs; parade, 14 hrs; soup, 15 hrs; bed, 21 hrs. The parades were most tedious. We formed batches of 40–50 and an Italian Lieutenant and two Corporals counted us, each group coming to attention as they arrived. They never did shine at mathematics and, of course, we had to stay on parade until they had accounted for every living soul, checking round all the barns, the cookhouses and the hospital for those who could not come on parade. Anyone coming late on parade was put straight into the cooler for a few days.

It is amazing to realise that within ten months in this camp we must have been on parade for at least twenty-five days. It was wonderful how we spent that time. There was always someone interesting to talk to and the inevitable comedian would sublimate his pent-up feelings by giving a running commentary on the proceedings. 'Here comes a model of Italian manhood', as through the gate came the Adjutant with his bent back and round shoulders and spotted face.

Cooking facilities were primitive. The Detaining Power provided a cookhouse and wood for cooking the soup and later on for issuing a pint of hot water each morning. Otherwise we had to improvise. As a result, most of the early weeks in the camp were spent in manufacturing small stoves from Red Cross tins. This took a considerable amount of patience and skill, as the only available tools were a borrowed knife (also home-made), a nail and a piece of stone. This revealed a wonderful amount of ingenuity and resourcefulness in all the barracks, which were for weeks just like a tinsmith's shop and a deafening hammering continued throughout the day. The tumult and the clamour died about 8 o'clock, when most went to bed. One night, however, this unwritten law was broken by one enthusiast who decided to go into action while the others slept. There was dead silence for a few moments, save for the strokes of his hammer, then a cockney voice piped up, 'Hey, cock, is this a rushed job?'

The Colonel Commandant allocated the upper part of the Orchard, next to the huts, as the brewing-up ground – what an amazing sight to see 200 or 300 men stooped over their little stoves, some fanning with pieces of cardboard and others puffing and blowing. Thick clouds of smoke hung over it all. Like Lucca, there was a shortage of fuel and all sorts of things were sacrificed for a cup of tea. When you went down to the brew patch, you never thought of wasting a match, but looked for someone who was nearly finished and asked, 'Hey, chum, got any embers?' Duly you would inherit his embers and, with such a flying start, would soon have the tea boiled and then bequeath your embers to those who came after, with a loud bawl, 'Anyone want embers?' You didn't have to wait long.

After a few days, we were fixed up with wooden bunks. These were three-storey efforts and if you were lucky enough to live on the top, you had to be very careful in climbing down, especially at night, so that you did not tramp on the face of either of your lower neighbours. These beds were built in blocks of six and through much usage they became rather shaky. As a result, each of the six occupants was kept very much aware of the movements of the other five. Each block was about 3 feet from the next, so that every group of six had about 18 square feet to live in. Undressing was usually done in relays of two, and with a bit of a crush, all six could find accommodation at mealtimes.

The early months in Campo 70 were not very comfortable. Parcels were irregular and from November until May we considered ourselves very lucky if we got a parcel each fortnight. We were fortunate in getting the greatcoats before we left Lucca, but many of the new arrivals had still nothing to wear but the shirts and shorts in which they had been captured, and quite a few had no boots. It was pathetic to see them come on parade with blankets wrapped round their bodies and feet clad in home-made shoes. The Italians simply had nothing to give them. The most tragic time of all was when those who had been kept in the hellish North African camps began to arrive in the months of December 1942 and January 1943. They had been kept there since June and most of them were in a deplorable state of malnutrition, their bodies were emaciated and they had little or no reserve of strength left. In our camp alone in the first two months of 1943 at least forty men died.

In the early days the *magazzino*, where the stocks of Red Cross supplies were housed, was a sort of barometer of camp morale. When it was filled, everyone was in good spirits and camp life was animated and cheerful. But when supplies got low and came to a halt, morale dropped accordingly. In those days of precarious supplies the most important man in the camp was RSM Davis, who was camp Red Cross representative. His job was to go to Porto San Giorgio when the parcels arrived and superintend their transfer to the camp. No suspected criminal was ever more closely shadowed by any official of Scotland Yard than the RSM. If he chanced to clean his boots in the evening, the rumour would buzz round that he was getting ready to go off to the 'Port' the next day. Every action of his was interpreted as indicating some Red Cross development. There were several individuals who did nothing but watch Davis. In a real heroic manner he stuck to the job for several months and then asked to be relieved, as he had had enough of being 'a marked man'.

Before the parcels became regular, the food problem loomed very large on the horizon and we had every opportunity to demonstrate the power of the mind over the body. We never felt really satisfied and the worst time was when we had just finished what little food was provided. Somehow, that just served to whet our appetite and that was danger time for the few precious Red Cross tins we had managed to keep and ration out at the rate of one between four each day. The strain of this was too much for some and they resorted to any means to get food. One chap struck on an original, if unscrupulous, method of increasing his larder. He would go into another barrack and chat casually with one of the inmates, whom he had never seen before, and then ask for the loan of a tin of condensed milk until the next Tuesday, when he drew his parcel. He would be pleased to return it with interest in the form of cigarettes, as he himself was not a very enthusiastic smoker. The other obliged and off went our friend to conquer new fields. At length his bluff was called and the whole trickery revealed. One of his creditors was heard to utter dire threats against him. He went missing from the next parade and the Detaining Power suspected the worst and put us all on an extra parade, which lasted for several hours while they ransacked the place in the hope of unearthing a body. But their efforts yielded no results and at last they allowed us to dismiss.

Next morning the mystery was solved and tragedy turned into comedy. He was found quite happy and fit in the *magazzino*, among the parcels. Unwittingly the Italians had locked him in the day before, when he had been on fatigue duty. At least, that was his story. During the night, needing rations, he had accounted for two Red Cross parcels. It was rumoured that the Italian Colonel was so relieved to find him alive that he gave him extra food rations, put him in the hospital for a few days, and then sent him off to a new camp.

This offender was very fortunate, as other 'food criminals' got a very rough handling if they happened to be caught. There were only two cases of this and both were dealt with by the men and had to be admitted to the hospital. Another man was made to wear on his back a notice with 'THIEF' writ large upon it. There was a terrific division of opinion in the camp about the crudity of these methods, but they certainly stopped any further stealing.

Theoretically we were supposed to be able to buy from the Italian *cantina*, but this turned out to be rather a generous description of that institution. All we were able to procure with any degree of regularity were onions. However, these were most acceptable and they certainly helped us through the winter cold, most of us without any serious illness. We came to enjoy our piece of raw onion and bread at breakfast time. Well can I remember how we celebrated the fall of Tripoli and, holding up our pieces of onion like the Jews of the Exile, exclaimed, 'Next year in Blighty!'

The accommodation for the sick was better than at Lucca, although the food problem was especially difficult in the case of those who were ill. It made the work of the medical officers much harder, since the patients had no reserve of strength to fall back on and recovery was a much longer process than normally it should have been. One of my jobs was to go into the hospital each evening and read aloud to the patients for an hour or so. It was difficult to find a suitable book. I think the one that was most enjoyed was Agatha Christie's *Ten Little Nigger Boys*, an enthralling detective story in which the reader is kept in doubt right to the last line as to which of the ten suspects is the murderer. I heard later that some of the patients ran a little side bet on the result of the story. I had never realised before how frequently most authors mention food, some seemed to take delight in painting pictures of stacked tables and brimming cups. I had to censor ruthlessly all such passages, as it was just unadulterated torture to read vivid descriptions of Yorkshire pudding and roast beef to those who hadn't seen a good meal for years.

The sociologist would have found Campo 70 a happy hunting ground, for here one had every opportunity of watching how communal life grows from the most primitive beginnings and how, by organisation, life is gradually made reasonably tolerable and even interesting. Here was a group of some thousands of men suddenly flung together into conditions that were completely new to them, facing problems of mind and spirit that they had believed to exist only in the realm of psychological fiction. But order grew from chaos and authority came into being and the basic necessities were distributed and everyone had his share of food and his 6 feet by 3 feet of bed space. Standing orders were issued, discipline was enforced and a new society had come into existence.

Many saw in the enforced leisure a great opportunity for self-improvement and one of the first organisations to come into being was a school. Plenty of teachers were available and the enthusiasm was very great for the first few days, but then many fell out as they found the pace too hot for them. Others stuck to it and some very valuable work was done. Musicians gathered together and in a few weeks, with the help of instruments bought from the Italians and three piano accordions presented by the Pope, the camp had quite a respectable orchestra.

It took the theatre somewhat longer to become organised. The first venture was a version of *A Christmas Carol* written by the *Padre*, for of course we had no copies of the original by Dickens. I played the part of Marley's Ghost and we performed the play for the hospital on Christmas Eve and everyone was very enthusiastic. The only criticism made was that it was too short (only three-quarters of an hour), in spite of all our efforts to spin it out. Later some excellent shows were produced, including *The Desert Song* and *Pygmalion*.

When the weather began to settle in the spring and the food increased, football and boxing claimed their thousands of fans and some very fine international matches were staged. In the summer a regular epidemic of cricket raged and the Orchard was a mass of pitches, all intermingled. And after an early harvest, which made the Orchard free ground again, the camp became a miniature metropolis, especially at night. Great crowds of men would slowly saunter round the rectangle and stop here and there to watch what was going on. We'd wander down from the billet, past the ever busy barber's tent with its long queue, then carefully negotiate the brew patch, to avoid knocking over somebody's porridge. A large crowd would be enjoying an open-air variety show, or a general knowledge bee. A smaller group would be gathered round to hear what the camp Communists had to say. Further on, many would stop and admire the agility and suppleness of the Tumbling Club. A big gathering under the trees would be listening to a lecture on 'The Tunisian Campaign' by a newly arrived prisoner, or 'Ten Days' Freedom' by the latest escapee, who had just been recaptured and now basked in the kudos given to one who 'had a try at least'. On the walls of one of the barns, the latest edition of *The 70 Times* could be read. With the combined efforts of trained journalists, artists and cartoonists, it was really a splendid publication. Also, a staff sergeant in the Engineers managed to rig up a wireless set and we began to get regular news. And not far away was the *Padre's* tent, where evening prayers had just been said and various groups were collected to discuss 'Christianity and Post-War Problems'.

Here in these few acres was the concentrated life and energy of a goodly sized town, with men drawn from every walk of life. It was revealing to see what a vital force life is and how, when it is dammed and blocked in one direction, it will eventually find outlet and expression in another. Nearly everyone found some mysterious little ploy to keep himself going. Living was three times faster than normal. Here one had all the problems of communal life. It was an ideal laboratory for the psychologist, the moralist, the philosopher and the theologian. As one prisoner said: 'If one could settle the problems of a prisoner-of-war camp, he would settle the problems of the world.'

Padre Thompson was '*l'homme qu'il faut à la place qu'il faut*' in Campo 70. I met many *padres* before and a few after, but never one had so clear a conception of his job as *Padre* Thompson. He was Chaplain of an Essex battalion and had been wounded and captured in the battle of El Alamein with many of his regiment. Often the *padre* is apt to look on the organisation of services as his chief job and beyond that does not attempt very much. However, such work was only a small part of *Padre* Thompson's programme. He produced a course of thirty talks on the 'Christian Way', a modern presentation of the faith, written in terms that the ordinary soldier could understand. Many groups were put through this course and quite a few became members of the Church. (These lectures were later published by the Epworth Press in a book called *The Wisdom of the Way*.) He started another course on 'Christian Marriage', which had a broader appeal and all sorts of men attended. As a result, many back home again today bless the words of wisdom and instruction first heard in captivity.

Few men knew the mind of the soldier better. I always felt in his services that he had his finger on the pulse of the camp and knew just what the feeling was. No one could ever accuse him of being 'too heavenly minded to be of any earthly use', for all his talks and sermons were completely relevant to the prevailing conditions. The church in Campo 70 met a very real need and few who came to the services went away without a feeling of new courage and cheer. He had the great quality of taking men where they stood. His religion was of a very practical nature. In the early days, when things were very bad, many of the men began to let themselves go and just lay down in their bunks and gradually lost interest in everything and endangered their own self-respect. Subsequently, many got into a morbid state of mind and their health became greatly affected, some few even coming to the point when they didn't want to live anymore. The *Padre* tackled the problem in one of his services and asked everybody to do what they could to help these unfortunate men. He asked all present to enlist in the Anti-Bed-liers Club; each member was to seek out any 'bed-liers' he knew and report them to the *Padre* or the MO [Medical Officer], who would do what they could for them. I do not think it is an overstatement to say that many men today owe their health, self-respect and some even their lives to this practical Christian service.

Just after *reveille* on Sunday morning, the men would collect in the spacious Central Hall. Each one usually brought a blanket to kneel on. When all had collected, the Communion service would begin. The only furniture was a table covered with a blanket, on which there was a simple wooden cross and the elements laid ready. What a motley collection of garments the men wore! A few were still clad in the khaki drill of the desert, now sadly the worse for wear, others wore ill-fitting Serbian trousers, some others more fortunate had been able to get part of a British battledress, but this made an odd combination with the Italian breeches that only reached halfway down the leg. Only a very few had shirts with collars and many had no stockings. Looking down the rows and rows of uplifted faces, I could sense how 'the comfortable words', 'Come unto me all that travail and are heavy laden and I will refresh you', found a response in every heart. The bread – part of someone's small Italian issue – was brought round in a plate wrought from a butter tin. Then the wine, Italian *vino*, in a cup also made in the camp, brought home to each that it is not the place nor the form of the service that matter, but the spirit of the worshipper.

Campo 70 also had its incidents to punctuate the monotony of the days. Several escapes were planned and caused the usual flutter among the Italians, who liked the wanderlust of the prisoners no more here than at Lucca and could not understand why we wanted to leave such a camp. One very simple escape was made by two men in the early spring.

Our camp was right on the railway line, with a sidetrack built into the camp grounds. Each week a truck stood in the camp for the purpose of collecting disused tins (rumour said for the Italian war effort) and when the truck was filled, it was moved off. This usually happened once a week. These two men struck on the bright idea of getting into the truck the night before it was due to leave the camp and bury themselves among the tins. They were able to climb in easily enough and spent there a very meaty and fishy night. Sure enough, the train stopped next morning and linked up the truck and off they went. They arrived at Porto San Giorgio and there they waited to find out what was going to happen. Nothing happened, so they began to climb out. Apparently they made rather much noise in this operation and were spotted by some children playing around, who reported their presence to the station authorities and they were soon rounded up.

A few weeks later another attempt was made by two commandos. They managed to escape by joining a working party that was operating on the banks of a very shallow, stony river which ran past the back of the camp. Here they persuaded the others to cover them up with stones and when the guard came to check up on the numbers, he found that he was two short. He immediately marched them back to the camp and the escapees were able to get clear of the area. At first they walked by night and slept by day. They struck for the north and hoped to cross the Swiss border. After travelling for several nights, they decided to try walking by day and this worked very well. They asked for food and shelter each night at a farm and said they were Germans. They were given plenty of food and both had the impression that the people knew they were English and were more willing to help them because of this. But their travels were ended in a very simple way. They had to cross a road patrolled by *carabinieri*, who were usually of a more intelligent type than the ordinary soldier. They managed to pass themselves and were walking away when one of the patrol noticed that they were wearing English boots and called them back for an explanation. Of course they were not able to stand up to a close interrogation and once again they were prisoners.

Prisoner-of-war life had, of course, its grim moments and the strain proved too great for some. One afternoon we were all greatly shocked and shaken to learn that a man had committed suicide. It had been done in broad daylight under one of the trees in the Orchard. The whole camp was hushed and silenced. It brought home to us what some of the men were going through in the depths of their own minds; those, who through no fault of their own, were inadequate for this life; those whose home lives had been too soft; those who could endure endless physical discomfort, but found the mental strain too much; those who could not meet the adversities of captivity with a united front, being already inwardly torn apart by 'trouble at home'.

No sooner did the Italians hear of this tragic occurrence than they put us all on parade, while they examined the scene of the death. I cannot describe our indignation and disgust when they proceeded to walk through our ranks and examine our hands to see if there was any blood on them. Their attempts to track down the supposed murderer were just as infantile as their inference that such a person existed in our ranks, and after a futile investigation of several hours, they let us go, having come to the conclusion that it was suicide after all.

As the year of 1943 advanced, so the tempo of events beyond the confines of the camp speeded up and finally came to a head in the autumn. It was an expectant spring and a nerve-wracking summer. First Tripoli fell and soon the whole of North Africa followed. Lampadousa and Pantellaria were the stepping-stones across the Mediterranean to Italy and they were taken with little resistance. Sicily was invaded in the greatest action the war had seen and soon after Mussolini decamped. Hopes ran very high with us, as we all felt that anything could happen. Units were secretly organised in case of sudden need. But still the war continued and it took forty days to finish Sicily. A wild rumour, which was later confirmed, was the first news we had of the [Allied] landing in Reggio Calabria. Now at last we felt that the big day was at hand. What a thrill it was to know that our own forces were no longer separated from us by thousands of miles of sea and desert, but were on the same mainland as ourselves and quickly advancing towards us. Excitement became very great and everyone had visions of home in a few weeks and we began to take each other's addresses. Here are a few notes that I wrote at the time:

12.9.43 What a tremendous week we have just passed through! News worked up to crescendo pitch on Wednesday when the wonderful announcement came through that Italy had 'packed in' and was actually fighting with us. In spite of the fact that we knew of the invasion, it was a great surprise when the confirmation of capitulation did come. Word came through over the loudspeakers and we all set off to see our friends and celebrate as best we could. Everywhere we went we had to partake of celebrating brews, even though it was only a mouthful. The place all filled up with happy, chattering, cheering men. All began to sing as the band started up and every now and then there would be a rendering of the national anthem. Some wandered round the Orchard in the moonlight, thinking of the folk at home and of the new future so suddenly opened. Quite a number of the men visited the church tent and there was many a prayer of thanksgiving said in its quietness. So it seemed that a long journey (nearly fifteen months) was drawing near its end.

On Thursday we woke up to a completely new atmosphere. The camp was taken over by the British officers and the Medical Officer conducted the parade. He was not too sure of procedure, but with the help of an infantry Sergeant-Major, he completed it without incident.

We had a Thanksgiving Service today and there was a great turn-out of the camp. The orchestra played the hymns, *Padre* Willis and myself conducted the service and *Padre* Thompson gave us a sermon on thanksgiving, but in spite of all our super-optimism, there was a note of warning in his talk. He said that we must not build up too much on our release, as we were 'not out of the wood yet'.

14.9.43 Yesterday was a mixed day of reassurance and alarms. News was broadcast to the camp from time to time. Some German columns are touring north through Porto San Giorgio. There is talk of evacuating the camp to the surrounding countryside and dividing up into small parties and hiding until our troops get through. Last night we heard the BBC after some fifteen months. It was grand to listen to the chimes of Big Ben ringing through the camp and to hear the clear voice of the announcer.

17.9.43 This has been our third day of suspended anxiety, on account of the peculiar position of the fighting in Italy. The British have advanced and have a line from Brindisi to Naples. In the north the country is in complete chaos; the Germans and Italians being mixed up and fighting everywhere. The Germans have occupied some of the large northern towns and are also in Rome. Our district so far has been very quiet and we hope it will continue so.

I do not think any of us will ever forget the days that followed. In them we passed through the whole range of human emotions. After the first tremendous outburst of enthusiasm, with visions of repatriation and home almost within grasp, a sobering sense of caution settled down upon everyone. Each day a crowd would take off with all they had of food and that was the last we saw of them. The Senior British Officer and *Padre* spoke several times over the loudspeaker and everyone was told to remain 'calm, cool and collected'. This was later parodied as 'calm, cool and your kit collected'. They told us that everything was under control and that we had sent out patrols to keep an eye on German movements in our district.

Meanwhile, all the Italian guards had vanished and only a few of the officers remained and we could come and go more or less as we pleased. On the whole, the men kept reasonable discipline and the vast majority were satisfied to have a good ramble over the countryside, returning and sleeping in the camp in the evening. We had one lovely walk and it does stand out in my memory in view of what was to follow. What a thrill it was to go out without being shadowed; to wander along the lanes and over the hills and stop and rest wherever you fancied and to come back just when you felt tired! It was in the harvest season and the trees were crammed with ripe fruit and grapevines dangled enticingly. When we tired of the vine, there were always peaches and apples to fall back on. It was a perfect day and it was amazing to think that over the quiet countryside some 10,000 men were wandering around just as we were. A lot of bartering going on. Often as we wandered past some farmstead we would see one of the ex-captives trying to strike a deal with an Italian. The soldier would hold up a woollen vest (these were very much in demand among the peasants) and ask for so many loaves or so much *vino* in return. We visited several farms and were given a very hearty welcome, although I had the feeling that the people were afraid. However, as far as I was able to judge, the prisoners all behaved with consideration and friendliness. We did what we could to put the people at their ease. Language was difficult, as few of us knew more than a few words of Italian, but I tried out the few Latin words I could remember, and by adding an 'i' or an 'o', the results were considerable. My chief reaction to the farmers was sympathy: they struck me as a very simple, hard-working people, who had little time or mind for politics. As we returned to the camp we met many who had been entertained too well and the billet that night was more like an overcrowded bar than a dormitory.

This period of suspense lasted nine days and all sorts of stories came to us as to what was happening in the country. We were told that the Germans were retreating and that we were safely situated between two Italian divisions, which would see that we did not fall into German hands – rather a mental somersault for most of the Italians. We occupied ourselves as best we could, trying to carry on with the old programme. All the time we reasoned and argued and hoped for the best. The 8th Army was surely bound to get through very soon now. Even if the Germans did think of moving us, they could not get the transport, and if they tried, the RAF would see to it that some of the viaducts and bridges were put out of action. Perhaps they might take the officers and warrant officers, but they would never think of the rank-and-file. And so it went on endlessly, but every moment, at the back of our minds, was the big query as to what would really happen.

The answer came swift and sudden. On 18 September we all ambled out to morning parade as usual. In the course of the check-up some pointed to the back wire and said, 'Who is that?' We turned and saw an unusual type of sentry, far smarter-looking than the usual Italian, with long peaked cap covered by a camouflaged steel hat and a cocked Tommy gun under his arm. He was striding along behind the barbed wire and soon he was followed by another and another. It didn't take long to come to the awful truth. We were surrounded and recaptured. Soon all the sentry boxes were filled and the front entrances manned. They sent for the camp Sergeant-Major and told him that they were only Military Police, here for security, as a division was passing through and that they would be moving off after thirty-six hours. They did go off after thirty-six hours, but not before another crowd had taken over from them.

Even with the Germans around us, we still dared to hope. True they had recaptured us, but they hadn't got us out of the country yet. If only our troops would hurry up, and we vividly imagined the hasty flight of the Germans! The awful rumour began to circulate that railway wagons were being assembled to take us away. We listened in agonised suspense for any metallic ring that might be shunting. One night we had a great scare when a lot of wagons did arrive, but they had come merely for the transport of stolen livestock to Germany, so we breathed again. The days passed and the next unsettling story came from the bakers who went to Monturano each day. They reported that they had been ordered to bake a lot of extra bread. What could that mean? The optimists said that it was what the Germans would leave with us as they evacuated and beat a hurried retreat northwards. The pessimists maintained that they were travelling rations for the camp on its way north. The pessimists were right. To our bitter disappointment trucks began to arrive and with great reluctance and heavy hearts we began to adjust ourselves for the worst.

During the last days, the camp was in a state of intrigue. In the darkness of night many made their way over the wire. The Germans were very understaffed and had to guard the camp with only a fraction of the men the Italians had used. Realising this, they would fire flares over the camp at night and rattle off a few rounds of machine-gun fire, just to let us know they were still there. However, this did not deter those who had planned escape and, picking the least well-guarded spot, they slipped over in dozens. Others found more ingenious methods of escape. Several members of the Dramatic Society who had played female parts mustered together their costumes. They managed to find entry into the administrative block at the front and, stepping through the window in full costume, they minced their way past unsuspecting guards to freedom. Legend has it that 'The Lady in Red' from the pantomime made a most devastating getaway in this fashion.

One delightful incident took place about this time. It concerned one of my fellow countrymen, called McNally. He often came to visit me in my barn, and as there were few Ulstermen in the camp, it was almost like a day's leave home to talk about Belfast. He was a great Orangeman with a massive tattoo across his expansive chest of King William on his white horse crossing the River Boyne. He would regale me with Ulster wit and song. His morale was irrepressible and it was impossible to resist his infectious good humour. Now that we were rounded up by the Germans, McNally told me that he had decided to escape, make his way to Rome and claim sanctuary in the Vatican. In an unconscious *double entendre* I replied, 'You'll be all right as long as you keep your shirt on!'

On 24 September the first party moved off, to be followed every day by another, each about 2,000 strong. Meanwhile, the plotting went on fast and furious. Many were transferred from one party to the next in order to 'postpone the evil hour'. One crowd dug furiously night and day at a tunnel right under a German sentry box; others planned to hide under the weighbridge; and some others hid themselves in the rafters of the administrative block. Our party was third and in the end we were glad to get away, as every turn in Campo 70 reminded us of disappointed hopes and of friends who were already on their way across the Alps. Better to get on the move than to mope round this place of shadows and memories. It was remarkable how well everyone disguised their inner feelings, for all were bitterly disappointed and now it seemed that we had to begin just as new prisoners all over again. One of the boys plastered a message to the 8th Army on the wall: 'We waited for you as long as we could. Now you will find us in Stalag XX in Germany and don't be long.' And that went for us all.

Hohnstein, where the author was interned as a prisoner-of-war of the Germans

Chapter Seven

STALAG IN SAXONY

3.12.43 In Deutschland since beginning of October and it certainly has been a remarkable time. The events in Italy and ensuing journey to Germany shook me a bit, but we soon became adjusted to the new environment. The journey from Porto San Giorgio to Zeithan (Saxony) needs no record on paper as it is indelibly recorded on the tablets of memory. Practically six days in hell, in a wagon for forty men or eight horses; we had forty-nine and kit and closed doors. Long waits of listless hours, sanitary improvisions, little wired-in windows.

Stay at Jakobstahl. First impressions: primitive arrangements, bloodhounds, flatness, barbed wire, sentry boxes, captured Russian men and women. Bungalows, complete chaos in dark. Italians. Flogging of Red Cross winter stuff for cigarettes. Scale of rations from noticeboard [per man, per week]:

meat: 250g
lard: 68g
potatoes: 5,250g
dried vegetables: 220g
fresh vegetables: 1,600g
margarine: 150g
cheese: 46g
bread: 2,325g
sugar: 175g
tea (ersatz): 14g
jam: 175g
salt: 140g

8.12.43 Two lettercards dispatched home today. No news of home yet.

The main street of the camp is like some Far East international settlement – swarthy Russians; French, mostly in their fourth year as *Kriegsgefangeners* [prisoners-of-war]; tall, fair Dutchmen, with their old-fashioned, high-necked tunics and side caps; Poles and Yugoslavs with their peculiar 'sliced' caps; not to mention the mixed vintage of our hosts. I have already spoken to one Czech sentry. The Russians are in a very bad way and hover round our buckets like vultures, the hunger looking out of their clay-coloured faces. All have SU [i.e., Soviet Union] carelessly daubed on their backs and almost all wear clogs. Then there are many of our new allies, the Italians, whose lot now is not an enviable one. They look in a pretty bad state. News is very hopeful these days and all hope the agony will soon conclude. The bombing of Germany is reaching tremendous proportions and one whole week we had warnings regularly from 7am to 8pm and lights were extinguished until 10–11pm. Berlin seems to be finished.

The Teheran Conference has just taken place and there should be big moves soon. This camp, Stalag IV B, is in Mühlburg in Saxony, somewhere near the River Elbe, between Dresden and Leipzig. Surrounding country is completely flat, the only variety being several pine forests. Very primitive latrine system. Huge supply of parcels, 80,000. Splendid Red Cross clothes issue. Interesting hut now, several Dunkirk POWs. Irish Guardsman, Paddy Shields of Larne, three years in Poland, twenty-one days' march. Some have eighteen months done. Harold Barker now 'Man of Confidence' [prisoners' representative to Germans] for British Army here. Much more settled now after jittery summer in Italy. Dentists here, two French and one Dutch, very good service. Wonderful de-lousing, bath, vaccination, inoculation system all in one.

14.12.43 Busy for Christmas. Boys have made splendid show here with labels, boxes, coloured paper, from Red Cross boxes. Lecture tonight on 'Military Parachutes'. Reading *Lust for Life*, the story of Van Gogh by Irving Stone, as well as usual study stuff. Hard to concentrate with noise. News tonight that four powers at Teheran issue ultimatum to Germany – or else invasion from north, south, east and west. Refused by Von Ribbentrop. Stalin to be in Germany within a month. No mail from home still. Made a potato-and-meat roll pie for supper. Snow on the ground all the time now, but cold is exhilaratingly dry. Working hard at German. Boys are at present discussing 'latrines we have used'; they are mostly Dunkirk *Kriegsgefangeners* and have considerable experience! Canadian parcels are coming in and are splendid for winter. Collection for the Russians was disappointing here, though some huts did splendidly.

19.12.43 Busy on Food for the Russians committee. I don't think I've ever seen men in a much lower state. They scrape every morsel of food and potato peel from our buckets. They wear rags and clogs, with strips of rag for stockings. They are indeed most pathetic, with their starving eyes.

I asked to be moved over into the RAF compound after Christmas, as I think I will be of more use there. My parody of 'The Mountains of Mourne':

O Mary this Stalag's a wonderful sight
In Deutschland it snows now by day and by night.
They give us *Kartoffeln* and barley and wheat
With *trockin Gemüse* and sugar of beet.
Their ersatz cheese ration oft goes for a walk
In fact it can stand on its feet and can talk.
But for all their great rations I'd much rather be
Where the women and children can laugh and be free.

O Mary these Jerries are cads
With their 'heel clicks' and 'eyes right' and endless fads.
The *Feldwebel*'s a terror, all buttons and braid
And harangues us each Sunday with a tiresome tirade.
He says he's a soldier and all will be well
If we knuckle under and stay in our shell.
But for all his great promise I'd much rather hear
The howl of the east wind on old Bangor's pier.

O Mary I'm longin' for old Ireland's shore
And when I get back there I'll wander no more.
I've been to the Orient, I've lived on the Nile,
I've been to Sakahra and seen the Sphinx smile.
I've camped by Vesuvius and seen Pisa's tower

And now by the Elbe I languish my power.
But for all this great travelling there's nothing so dear
As the mist over Ireland as its coastline draws near.

27.12.43 Amazing days! So much happening and a sense of experiencing life, seeing people and studying character and reaction. Christmas was an international festival and we had the freedom of the camp and were visited by South Africa, Russia, Holland, India, France, etc. Jim Taggart was here and we had a reminiscent Christmas meal. We got two parcels during the week and 150 English cigarettes.

We had a big drive for the Russians, whose condition now is indescribable. Quite good results, though some people seem to forget that they were ever hungry themselves. In the end the Russians got most of our Christmas rations and a considerable amount of Red Cross food. Made friends with some Russian medicos, and though it is a great mental strain to talk for hours in German, still it is worthwhile. They are an interesting bunch and all out for their country.

The news has come that we are appointed as Assistant Chaplains and will go to different camps. Mine is Stalag IV A. I look forward to the change and I'll get some different work there, I hope. I hear it is a *Kommando* camp and I might have facilities to visit the attached camps. This has been a valuable period, but a most restless one for me. I seem to be very unsettled at times and have little reserve of temper with some people, though I feel that I've learnt more practical psychology in the last three months than before. I feel unsettled chiefly because of inactivity. I do desire to express myself in the way for which I've been trained. These eighteen months have been intensive training and now I feel the whole experience would be well completed by a few months' actual work, on my own, without *padres*, and with some sort of a definite status. I think this change to IV A will provide the opportunity. I often feel here that there is so much to be done and yet so little chance to do it. The whole system of camp life militates against it: fatigues, rumours of moves, lack of accommodation.

Jack Wilkinson, our old Tobruk orderly, turned up in a pretty bad way after a week *'in Freien'*, though he is better now. He got within range of our artillery and was caught on crossing a road. Hard luck! The Italians look in very bad condition.

1.1.44 New Year has come and we are still in isolation. I was supposed to leave today, but that has been postponed. Jim Taggart brought round the rest of our plum duff, shades of Christmas, and finished it off tonight. Meet endless number of interesting people in here. Several blokes who fought in Yugoslavia and were rounded up after two months. Welsh lad, musician with long hair. Also some of the boys from Cos, who had a most exciting time in a 'second Crete'. The deciding factor seems to be our lack of air support and the whole attempt seems to have been undertaken with too few troops. Others have been *Kriegsgefangeners* since Crete. Paddy Shields is the life of the party and two-and-a-half years has not quenched his spirit. He worked in Berlin until the RAF made it too hot! Sgt. Tiller and Paddy Flynn are Dunkirkers. Flynn speaks fluent German and seems to have educated himself in his three-and-a-half years, mostly in Poland. He gives a pretty fair and reasonable account of his life and treatment.

We were wakened the other night by the drone of planes and all lights out. News from Russia is now very good and the new '*Bei Nachten*' [by night] offensive seems to be going ahead. All the plans for the invasion seem to be cut and dried now. We have waited for this for two years and hence we are rather unmoved until we actually know it as a *fait accompli*. Still no news of home, last news was August! I speculate a lot these days on the future, what I'll do and how things will turn out in the post-war world. The Italians in here are looking very poorly now. They are badly equipped for this climate, though it still persists in being mild. Another three months will see spring here again and, let's hope, near the end of this.

14.1.44 Fairly well dug in now in Hohnstein, a lovely district and I can well imagine that it is a most popular locality in peacetime. Yesterday we went for a walk down the river valley, with its deep gorge and high forested spurs all round. It was lovely to see the children with their toboggans on the hill. Life here is cushy in the extreme. I share a room with Sgt. 'Smudger' Smith (Man of Confidence), with a spring bed and sheets (so comfortable I could hardly sleep), shaded light and the library at my disposal. We had a cinema show the other night and an egg for breakfast on the tenth, my twenty-ninth birthday.

16.1.44 Worked in the post yesterday, as a huge assignment of mail came in, mostly for the prisoners captured in Italy. I've not had any myself as yet. Plenty of gramophone records now and so we get a lot of music. One record called 'Solitude' and 'Flamingo' will soon be worn out. News is *immer gut* and it looks like curtains soon. Three hundred divisions in England and also Russia. I feel very optimistic these days and worry little about the future, though I do long for news of home and also the power to do some more positive work. It takes some imagination now to think back on our conditions this time last year. My hair seems to be growing very grey.

18.1.44 Time moves luxuriously along. Last night Smudge Smith gave me a pair of pyjamas and a new towel. All the washing is done by Russians. Mass on Sunday was attended by nine different nations: French, Poles, Germans, Belgians, Italians, Dutch, Russians, English, Yugoslavs. The singing of '*Gloria in Excelsis*' nearly brought tears to my eyes. Old wheezy organ and strange language. Fine walk in the afternoon. Little *Dorf* [village] we stopped at was 8 kilos from Hohnstein. Stopped in a little inn and had some light beer and then retraced our steps across country.

22.1.44 I have been up twice to see *Hauptmann* [Captain] Schultz and he has recommended that I go round the *Kommandos* as *padre*. It will be good to get round the boys and help to cheer them up and to hold services with them. There is a *Padre* Frazer here who is Scottish Episcopal. I hope to get some griff from him on the work. In the meantime I am pretty much at a loose end here, living better than ever before. Cooked meals, table, cups, plates, knives, forks, regular walks. But comfort is a danger to one's ideals and has to be carefully watched. Think much of the future, whatever that is to be. What part is Christianity to play? Is it to be merely an individual thing, or are its claims to be everything? My life vacillates between confidence and a complete lack of it, but I feel that is due to the present lack of responsibility and work.

24.1.44 Mind today filled with a great variety of thoughts. Read some poetry and wrote some out in my *Common Peace Book*. I do feel that I am accomplishing something really worthwhile in developing my love for it. I think Shelley's lines, 'Life like a dome of many coloured glass/Stains the white radiance of Eternity', are surely the most beautiful in our language. I find it is difficult to settle down to one book or one subject. I am absolutely unable to settle down to read a novel. I think the one thing I will value most when I get back is quietness and the possibility of being alone and of having a room to myself. News is in the air today: (1) Anglo-American landing in Italy, cutting the Germans off from north; (2) peace proposals muted between Berlin and London.

26.1.44 Had a walk down into the valley and along to the guesthouse by the mill. Drank two stiff milks and trudged back to our fortress home. Boys playing, 'I'm Dreaming of a White Christmas'. Go into the theatre occasionally and listen to the French orchestra play.

27.1.44 Feet restless today and found it hard to settle down. Wrote to Kathleen. Sometimes I find living with these men difficult, e.g., table manners are pretty well dispensed with and it is a case of each man for himself, which is difficult in a 'combine', but it makes up part of the whole mosaic of my experience since 27.9.40 and I would not change it for anything else. Another problem living with these blokes is how to be one of them and yet not become too familiar. One's spirit becomes like Moira O'Neill in 'Corrymeela':

> 'Over here in England, I'm helping wi' the hay
> An' I wisht I was in Ireland the livelong day;
> Weary on the English hay, an' sorra' take the wheal
> Och! Corrymeela an' the blue sky over it.'

7.2.44 Yesterday was a day to be remembered. In the morning I went to the French Mass, once again an international gathering, at which three men were confirmed by a priest. One realises at such times that the value of service is as much the atmosphere and the purpose, as the actual spoken word. In the afternoon we went for a walk in the snow to Waltersdorf, along a road that Napoleon built called the Camel's Back. Lot of snow and boys enjoyed themselves in snow fights. Lovely country. This is Saxony Switzerland and well deserves the title. Concert at night given by the French orchestra was most enjoyable: half of it was classical and half jazz.

No mail yet. Think an awful lot of Kathleen these days. I often wonder if I'm not building a lot on imagination. Three-and-a-half years is a long time away from home, but I believe I can leave all that to the future and to God.

9.2.44 Well, events came to a head yesterday as *Padre* Gordon Frazer arrived and we had various conferences with the German *Hauptmann* and *Oberst* [Colonel]. New order has come out forbidding *Geistlichers* [clergymen] with officer's rank to visit the *Arbeit Kommandos* [work commands], but others like myself are free. Frazer fought tenaciously, but the *Oberst* could not go against the order. My course seems to be clear now and soon I should be on the job. Frazer is a very friendly bloke and gets on well with the men. I wait now to see the Swedish YMCA secretary, Christiansen, who should be helpful.

13.2.44 Deep snow today. In the afternoon the *Stamm leute*, all spit and polish, went out and had some photos taken. Apart from this we relaxed and did some snow plastering and had a most enjoyable *Spaziergang* [walk]. Eventually we arrived at the Mahle Gasthof [guesthouse] and had hot milk and Helles beer. Sächsische Schweiz was in full swing and it was good to see so many children and grown-ups out enjoying themselves on the slopes. The ground lends itself very well as a toboggan run and the children know how to handle the sleighs. In the evening we had a service in the billet and it seemed to be most acceptable to all. It is the start of things for me.

19.2.44 Yesterday was a real big day, as ten letters arrived, including three from Mother, one Father, one Emily, one Beth, two Kathleen. Good news all round. Now I feel re-equipped for the future, whatever it may bring. Ready to redouble my efforts. Kathleen's letters were splendid. I begin to dream dreams of the future. Very cold now, but the country is indescribably beautiful.

5.3.44 Back to stalag after my first tour of Freital, where I visited all nine *Kommandos*. The work varies and is mostly heavy – cement works, timber, loading and unloading. I had eight services in all and usually gave them a general talk beforehand, greetings from YM, etc. Mostly old prisoners captured in Italy. Variety of billets, treatment, etc.

Letters flow. So does the tide of events in my life. Thoughts very much on Kathleen. Four letters from her in fourteen days, so I do feel hopeful. News from home is good. Emily unofficially engaged. John & Co. perhaps home by the end of the year. Father would not stand as Moderator, thank goodness too!

Terrific raids on the Reich now. *Fliege* alarms most days in Dresden. Russians advance! Italy stands still. All eyes on the Atlantic wall and the *Kanal* [i.e., English Channel]. Vast troops in England. How long now? How long when it comes?

Saw the sights of Dresden – several beautiful churches: Dom, Kreuzkirche, Hochkirche. Also the Semperoper and Platz where the *Führer* usually speaks, and the Beredice Hotel in which he stays. Also the castle and palace and wonderful mural of Saxony's history. Elbe with five bridges and its pleasure steamers and notable art buildings. This life does indeed contrast with the Italian days. Now I've most of the things I want and my life is filled with work.

Chapter Eight

WAITING FOR THE INVASION

22.4.44 Looks now as if the mail from home and England is finished. All points to the imminence of the invasion. May it be soon!

23.4.44 Slipped into morbid state. Often those things solve themselves, patience is the answer to this and the blessed ability to smile and laugh. Thoughts: group challenge, sense of need here. Much I might have done. Fear of position, personal considerations, daydreaming, get to know the men. Afraid of hurting people's feelings, compromise, lack of prayer.

24.4.44 Frustration at curtailment of my work. Will see the *Oberst*. Don't let it get me down. Things have been easy so far and way will open. So much to be thankful for – liberties here. Pray for guidance in the interview with the Colonel.

Really lovely day, clear blue sky. My favourite seat: what a view from the top of the valley as I look across to the spurs covered with evergreens and seasonal trees. Sun shimmers and a pleasant spring wind blows. Overhead an occasional plane passes just to remind one that the war is still on. Away in the distance I can see the hills of Czechoslovakia. Many birds are singing and the air is filled with the warm, sweet smell of spring.

26.4.44 Much better day yesterday. Seemed to get somewhere, task now is to maintain a sense of purpose in all of my life. Big thing is caring. Don't read too much of self into attitudes of others. Realise other people have their off-days also.

27.4.44 The true man is the man in whom the life force has complete outlet and expression. The life force is the driving force of life; it can be the source of evil and destruction, or the power of creative good. The problem of life is to free this life force and give it adequate expression. Mental and spiritual health therefore lies in disclosure of inhibitions, complexes and frustrations of the past, which cast their shadow on the present. It is mentally healthy to face one's life and one's environment and not avoid it or suppress it. 'The truth shall make us free.' Now let the creative, open life flow, develop a real power of self. Basis is thoughtfulness and readiness. Confidence and self-expression will be won, 'A true son of God', free from fear of anything.

29.4.44 Yesterday was a day of reassurance and encouragement. Mr Christiansen of World Association of YMCAs arrived, and though I had but a short talk with him, it was useful and I did realise the extent of YMCA work as never before. Gave in requests and he is to make a report of my work to Adam Scott in London HQ. Also, the issue of my visits has been well and truly decided. Now I must get ready for another big effort of 'total war' on the *Kommandos*. Realise the importance of spiritual weapons these days. Ideas: Why not organise some form of a real YMCA here between the nations, to promote a better understanding?

'Unto Thee shall all flesh come [...]
O God of our salvation;
Who art the confidence of all the ends of the earth
And of them that are afar upon the sea.' (*Psalm* 65, Vs. 2, 5)

2.5.44 Bit of a tiff last night over the question of food and its allocation. Need for guidance and objectivity in these things. The things that finally harm a man are the things of the inner spirit: greed, hate, envy, rivalry, dishonesty, impurity. Realise God in these experiences. Full expression of emotion and feeling in proper direction. Realise the larger horizon. Real job is to be the real thing, 100 per cent, and not worry about outside status, respect, etc. Put all energy into being and not waiting or expecting. Value of discipline, tidiness. See others in their need; see the other's point of view.

4.5.44 Up at the usual unearthly hour and on my way to Dresden

Links. Countryside looks so vibrant with new life, as all the trees are in bloom. We found the work camp (it is entirely Cypriot) and had breakfast with Bill Adams and then got plans together. Arranged the trip after an opposition saga with the German sergeant in charge, but the problem was overcome. Bill Adams has gone on business to Pirna, and in the interim I sit and think in silence with Thucydides or Aristophones from Farmagusta bringing in odd cups of tea. Memories of their fellow countrymen in Lecce come to mind. Deep thoughts today on human nature. Is our work a lost hope, or is it the hope of the world? Depends on how real that hope is to Ray Davey. 'O God, help me more and more to be the servant of truth as it reveals itself. May I translate all my dreams, plans and prayers into action as I meet these men.' Pray for a really settled purpose of mind and spirit now. Family, Kathleen, new pals. Tact, caution, honesty, love, friendship.

6.5.44 I am in Schlachthof, which is just as it is called: Slaughter House. Bill Hill and seventy blokes. Trying to start Toc H and service. Preparation for two *Kommando* visits. Services if possible. Need for more poise and grip.

9.5.44 This tour is the best yet and really worthwhile. Power to see it out in top gear. Joy of activity, some really fine blokes in the area. Many requests of all sorts. Constructive work with Bill Adams.

11.5.44 Spent the night here in Weiznitz Ufer – a really splendid *Kommando*. Many of the Campo 70 boys here. Expectation of the Invasion Army, tense now. German papers are full of it. Morale of boys 100 per cent everywhere. Today last *Kommando*. Position of a Bulgarian girl: Britisher wishes to bring her to England after the war.

13.5.44 Back at Hohnstein again and getting ready for the next trip. Still no mail since 28 March and it looks as if something is nearly at hand. Letters from home make me realise that great changes are afoot there and I will go back into a changed world.

Later, out in the woods, trying to sort things out. Prayer for all the *Kommandos* – those who haven't the opportunity of quiet that I have here. Really delectable to be on the hillside and able to look down the river valley. Trees have made rapid growth since I was last out. Birds in full song. Promise and hope of spring fills the air. Difficult to remember the war rages so close at hand. Thinking of *Padre* Thompson. Feel that the process of self-analysis has been most helpful, real sense of power and confidence in the last tour. 'Man know yourself.' Awareness that I should get back to the heart of the Gospel message in my talks. My great task is to be a herald who proclaims the truth about life's meaning and to have the courage, confidence and ability to fulfil my calling and commission. Put aside lesser standards. Diligence and patience in all I try to do.

14.5.44 Sunday. Back in the same spot for a bit of peace. Church bell tolling – 9 o'clock. Down below in the valley the Hitler *Jugend* pass by, singing their marching songs. I wonder what is in their minds and what the clang of the church bell says to them at such a time? For whom the bell tolls, indeed!

15.5.44 Service yesterday in Big Hall. We had competition, as the Russians sitting on the wall outside keep on singing 'The Volga Boat Song'.

Prayer and Bible reading and study. Pray for real emancipation from my old world: rugger, newspaper reports, Blue interpros, tours, running, cups, with all the waste of energy and thought. Now concentrate on people, purpose in life, wider, deeper things. Poetry, music, comradeship. Psychology, theology, economics. Explode the old sense of values, think of the utter valuelessness of it all in itself. Surrender it and its desires. Aim at self-assurance and confidence built on deepest values – love, interest and humility. My life to be a challenge. Cut out softness. Try to interpret these two great themes in a modern way. *Acts* tell us of the impinging of the Gospel on the larger world and describe the Ascension and then the Coming of the Spirit.

The Ascension: how are we to interpret this? It's useful to think of three stages in the education of the disciples. (1) The actual physical presence of Christ recorded in the Gospel story and ending on the Cross. (2) The Resurrection appearances were a further stage in their education. He is still the same person, the same Christ, but He is clothed in a more celestial body. He is not bound down to physical limitations as an ordinary body is. Truth that is in ectoplasm can help us here. (3) Third and last stage is when He has finally shed the celestial body and is launched into the world free from all limitation of time and space. The Lord of all the Earth, whose spirit is as near to the Eskimo in his igloo as the Indian in his tepee; to the English textile worker as the carpenter who still works in Nazareth. Spirit whom the diver in the coral seas can experience just as the high-altitude flyer.

'Immortal Love, for ever full
For ever flowing free,
For ever shared, for ever whole,
A never-ebbing sea!'

Realise the Ascended Lord is here now with me as a POW, wanting to be more and more part of my life. Fight for personal release these days: know myself, make unconscious conscious. Create in me a new heart: new sentiments, new dispositions, release all the power wasted in hidden conflict into the mainstream of my life. Bring up all the complexes. Different way that truth comes out. Outward symptoms: irritability, bad temper, excessive love for sport as compensation, lack of deep interest in study. Self-consciousness in certain groups. Results: sport, life built all and all in rugger. What if this were to cave in? Reactions in desert. Not sure of men and how to take them – 'Chips' Cummings, orderlies, Massey. Constructive side: shape my sense of my own worth apart from family – experience, gifts, mind can be developed. Develop personality, willingness to learn from everyone. Real determination to help myself with power of God. Rooted and grounded in God. Kathleen: pray for guidance here.

Picture of life as a race. *Corinthians.* Life as a marathon, cross-country. Start, easygoing, nasty bit until second wind comes, through woodlands, up hills, down through valleys, across ploughed fields, through rivers, through swamps, over hedges and ditches, then a long, open patch and finally the spring home. Brings out every quality a man has. Stamina, courage, endurance, patience, intelligence, experience, speed, both physical and moral. Runner who always stays on the flat never becomes much good. I have patience, staying power.

20.5.44 So glad to get letters yesterday from Mother, Sheela and Kathleen. Think a tremendous lot about K. these days and seem to be very far gone. I guess this is the real thing now.

23.5.44 Yesterday five old letters from John and also one from Mrs Kerr. All seem to be well. Mrs Kerr is a splendid person, full of life and spirits. She really does live an integrated life. A huge chunk of her letter was cut out. Gratitude for the prayers and thoughts of so many. Release in this life tension.

24.5.44 Today realise God and bring His spirit into the life of camp. Reading Fosdick's *On Being a Real Person* with great interest. So much to learn, to do, to grasp, to achieve. Talk on Whitsuntide. Prayer. *Genesis* 21–23. Story of Abraham and Sarah, Hagar and Ishmael, sacrifice of Isaac. This was a revelation to Abraham of the nature of God. It was the end of the old hateful custom and a step towards the knowledge of the 'Father of all'. How real Abraham's faith was! How would I act if I were confronted with the loss of the dearest things and people in life?

25.5.44 Faith of Abraham in the guidance of God. May God bless and be in my life and marriage, if such a thing comes off.

> *O God I thank Thee for the gift of life with all its possibilities, with all its interests, with all its urge and drive. Help 'the many' of my life to become 'one'; help me to find the central true way that leads to complete, integrated, adequate life. Suffer no fear, no wrong choice, no carelessness to drive me from the way. I thank Thee for the adaptability of life, the ability to settle down to POW life and see in it the way to truer and fuller life. Still Thou dost create good from evil. Help me as the days pass to step from the little smallness of myself into the limitless largeness of God and His love and purpose. Teach me to rise from a self-related life to a God-related life; from pleasure to reality, which finally ends in Thee. Amen.*

26.5.44 Why are we religious? 150 ways of defining religion. Difficult to define because life itself is difficult. Root of religion is the urge after fuller life. Religious urge is for the highest, fullest life – God. It is the urge for qualitative life not quantitative. Religion is not a cloak: it is identified with life itself. We are incurably religious.

27.5.44 Sense of unrest and dissatisfaction today. Pray for peace. Thoughts of my people at home. Thoughts on Whitsun. Spiritual forces in life. Different Churches today. Coming of the Holy Spirit. Divine energy. But I feel that just at present it is not as real as it might be to me. Feel a bit sick of myself. Not getting around the boys the way I should. Pray to be shown the fears that block the way. Pray for Christ's spirit to flow right in and through my life. Too much self-pity. Blaming circumstances for so much. Is there a real scepticism in my own heart re. Church, re. Christianity and society? I believe in Christianity, but not very hopeful about it as applied to society. Do I really want to make people better? For instance, Christianity in this camp, little world on its own, all the problems of the world. My job here is to present Christ to individuals. To work for a real change of spirit. It is only the Spirit of God that can do anything here.

> *O God, give me a deeper faith in the 'Good News'. Give me a vision of the possibility of redeemed human nature, a vision of what may come to pass in this world. May all the barriers which loom so large – the seeming evil and unchangeability of human nature – ever be seen against a background of the love and power of the One High God. O Lord, increase my faith, help me to commit myself more and more definitely to Thy cause and to seek Thy will more and more. Amen.*

28.5.44 Whitsuntide. Feel flat today. Realise that these depressions are largely of my own creation. Prayer. Father, Mother, nearly four years since I left them!

29.5.44 The last few days have caused me to ask myself an ultimate question – the question of ultimate belief. Shall we call it the Kingdom of God? Do I really believe in it, or is it not rather hidden in this mistiness on the edge of my thoughts? I do believe in the 'ultimate rightness of things'. As to the Kingdom of God, in its obvious sense of a God-ruled society in time and space, modern theology gives two divergent lines of belief. Firstly, there is the line that the Kingdom of God will never come on Earth. God and Man are far apart. We know God only by His sheer Grace – the 'bolt from the blue'. There is no ascent from Man's side. Second, there is the belief of the evolving nature of Man, moving towards God, and God at the same time meeting Man. Distinct possibility of Kingdom of God on Earth. The first seems to be despair, a retreat from life, and is significantly the work of a German Christian and I do not think I can accept it. Tendency to encourage fatalism, *laissez-faire*, perhaps even spiritual pride. Note today the world religions, -isms, etc., and what they have done. Christianity and God must take its place with them, and it is deeper because it can change human nature. Isn't it true that much of the evil, twisted human nature, thwarted lives, frauds, liars, warmongers, etc., are the product of bad conditions, past mistakes? Hence one of the big jobs of the Christian is to change social conditions. So it is vital to take a bird's-eye view of ends, so that we may be stronger in applying the means.

Stanley Jones says that he believes that the Kingdom of God is written not merely in books but in the very structure and make-up of the universe and of ourselves and of society, i.e., it is embedded in our own mental, moral and physical being.

30.5.44 The weather has now turned and is really glorious, almost too warm in the middle hours of the day. Yesterday we had a fine day's outing to Lilienstein, which commands a splendid view of the Elbeland and away to Czechoslovakia.

Further to general thoughts of yesterday, when I pondered on the ends and my own conviction about them. Now for me, in this particular time, what is the task? We see the end now and believe in it. How can it be created in the world? First of all we must realise that this is no man-made institution; though there is much labour, perspiration and sacrifice involved, yet it lies in the end with God. The Kingdom is God's gift, we are but the channels, the instruments. Our part, therefore, is to keep alive to God, to let Him work through us, not to hinder Him. What does this mean for me? It means the ability and willingness to lie loose to other conventions and to know God for myself. To realise His will for my life. To realise I'm not spiritually 'mass-produced', but am, in my own way, unique to God and in this world. Our job is to create character and so remake society.

1.6.44 Today I seem to be right on the ball again. Perhaps it is the prospect of another trip round *Kommandos*. Gordon – old POW, many natural gifts, conscientious and thoughtful and efficient. Kept a very good attitude to life considering his POW life. Very popular all round. Got a healthy outlook. Very happily married. Life focuses on his home, wife and child. On the whole, must have had a good background. Comes out in many ways and compares very well with other blokes, but much more is demanded of such a person. Higher integration on an even higher level. Interests must be widened far beyond home. For in a sense home is just the extension of a man's self. Perhaps he needs to develop a little more independence. Also some fears there: fear of being thought unmanly; fear of piety; sensitive to criticism. Now is time of preparation for the future. Get ideals, beliefs, convictions clear. Aim very high. Every real man must have an ideal that is beyond himself, his family, and the power at least to move ever towards that ideal. 'To whom much is given, much is expected.'

3.6.44 Off today. The way to learn to love men is to work for them, out into their lives. Deeper, deeper dedication of self here in Hohnstein. Much to be done. Each man is an uncharted country. Remember the value and worth of courtesy to all people at all times – in dealing with other nations, absolutely vital.

5.6.44 Have had two splendid days. Had three services and at least 75–80 per cent turnout in all three. Good spirit. News that Rome has fallen. Somewhat distressing letter from Kathleen, who is having a tough time at her youth club in Edinburgh.

7.6.44 Rare and memorable day yesterday. Left Pillnitz at 6am and went to Company HQ and from there was conveyed by narrow-gauge line under the care of a *Feldwebel* [Sergeant]. Arrived in Radeburg and found the POWs all there – from '70'. Then prisoners began to filter in – 'The invasion has begun' – until it was confirmed from many sources. Two-point landing so far, Cherbourg and south of France. What a tremendous thing it all is and what it means to the world and how much there is involved in it! Had a service at 6.30am. Up today at 4am and back with a most unusual guard – Klinger. Wait now at Radebeul for transport to Hohnstein. Grateful for this trip. Most enjoyable and interesting. Perhaps it will be the last. Finding Jones's book, *Victorious Living*, most useful.

8.6.44 Back to port – to routine after the excitement. Get things cleared up and ready for the next tour. Now a new spirit of hope begins to creep into everything, as news from the Western Front begins to flood in. Last night 35 kilos push was the news. Also good news from Italy.

Last analysis of religion – what controls my actions, self-interest or Christian interest? These days I believe I have made a little progress in realising what growing up means and what the source of life is. The insistent demand to lose self-interest, self-relatedness and awake to the outer life, other people, outside ideals. This is the secret of self-forgetting. I have seen this so many times in the last two years. I must ever hold myself to this, even though it is painful. I must avoid the recoil–pleasure principle, fear of life. At my best when on *Kommandos*, as I was also in First Bangor. (1) Face facts; (2) make an effort; (3) surrender. Get a complete grip on life. Develop independence of thought and judgement. Develop initiative. Talks – realism all the way. Own experience of religion. One of the great secrets of Drummond's power was the fact that he preached nothing except what had personally come home to him and entered into his heart of hearts.

9.6.44 These are big days. Things seem to be going well in France now. Thank God! Yesterday I went down to *Hauptmann* Zumpfe and found that the position is now easier and I'm off on *Sonnabend* [Saturday] to Königstein area. Also Königswartha and Schmorkau come into my parish now. Things are looking up and I must really try to end on a high note.

12.6.44 Have been to Dohna, all Campo 70 veterans in a paper factory. Quite happy. On eleventh I visited Königstein 234, which was supposed to be a Jewish *Kommando*. Spent the night there. In afternoon I saw them play a football match, in which two Jerries took part, and then both *Kommandos* joined in a service, in which Jews, RCs and all took part, and the Germans brought in fresh flowers, in a *Kommando* originally built by Russians.

Implications for us at this stage of the war. Love is at the root of things, not force and hate. That means we have to live consistently. Life is a complete whole. Attitude to others, to the enemy.

O Father, Thou hast taught us that love is at the heart of life. This great truth often blinds and amazes us. We but feebly grasp it. It is too big for us. Still we seek to live on the level of might or of law. We are afraid to commit ourselves to anything more. Teach us to commit ourselves to the way of love, love to others, those whose way of life and point of view are different from ours. May love which is potentially in every one of us leap across the borders of race; may it burn away the barriers of creed; may it recreate the destruction of war. Help me to express and practise that great belief in my daily intercourse with people; with all my friends; deeper interest and desire to help; with all the lads I meet and work with; may the Spirit of Love run through others, with those who detain us. May the commandments of humanity transcend all the lesser barriers. Amen.

13.6.44 Back to Hohnstein. Tragedy last night when a Russian POW threw himself from an upper window. I did realise the horror of all this business. Speculations on the end now, three to six months. How we all long for it.

14.6.44 'When you go to bed at night, have for your pillow these three things – love, hope and forgiveness and you will waken in the morning with a song in your heart' (Victor Hugo). First lesson in living is 'to acquire the ability to distinguish the important from the unimportant and to act accordingly.' Reading *Genesis*. How God directed Jacob and how he developed as a character, finds himself and is a leader of the people. Deep sense these days that God does guide and lead still. Often He takes life out of our own hands. POW experience. How I needed it!

18.6.44 Yesterday many German-inspired rumours were in circulation about some new weapon. However, the King has been to France and progress is still being made, so why worry?

21.6.44 Interesting time in Königswartha hospital. Held a service and celebrated the Sacrament on the twentieth. Today must concentrate especially on the bed cases and the maimed. Idea for a talk: casting out the seven devils but puts nothing in its place. That is what war does. Nature abhors a vacuum and it will soon be filled. Healing power of Christianity.

27.6.44 Days passing pleasantly. Sunday, 25 June travelled to Lohsa and had a service. South African camp of about 150 men working on road construction. S.M. Botha, a most affable South African policeman, in charge and camp was in a happy state. Travelled with interpreter, a German teacher who speaks very good English. At night went to a sort of Fraternal in Erika and had a very enjoyable evening with Wally, Cecil and Bert. Big stir on among the Jerries at night. Visit of General! Yesterday I went to Weidnitz and had about three hours there. About 47 men, all from Crete, who had been there two-and-a-half years. Quite a lively camp. Felt deeply the tragedy of all this business, as one sees the German life go on all around, worry, strain, anxiety, sorrow, hardship. Love of home and family. Pray for guard and *Dolmetscher* [interpreter].

28.6.44 Spend the day in Erika. Yesterday I travelled to Ostfeld Grube and must have walked most of 20 kilos. Service in *Kommando*; hymns led by violin. Jack Gilbert has run regular services there since the start; he is known as the 'Vicar'. Walk there was nearly too much for my guard and interpreter, as his ticker is very bad. Coming back we intercepted a thunderstorm and were fairly well soaked.

Seems now that Cherbourg has fallen. Today I must recollect myself. Remember the different people involved. Prayers, invasion, peace, Church, friends, future. More and more adjustment to life. May I never become a time-server, nor lose spirit of adventure, nor 'lie down spiritually and mentally'. Pray that I may get a job to which I can give all I've got.

4.7.44 Out on the bulwarks of the castle. Lovely day. Hohnstein below in a delightful summer haze. Sharpen focus in my religious practices. Getting into a rut. Keep spiritually alive and tuned. Ever keep my responsibility before me. Keep alive the moral and spiritual issues of life roundabout.

9.7.44 Awake early yesterday and off on the 5.30am train to Dresden. Arrived there and found no *Posten* [guard], so I waited in the Russian *lager* in Friedrichstrasse until 4pm. Then I travelled on to Heidenau, where Sonder Midder picked me up, and came on to Barenstein, a lovely little village in a wooded valley. Thirty-seven boys, including Edward McKee of Newtownards, working on a derelict mill. Several of the old Campo 70 boys. Spent a fine evening with them, very hearty welcome and boys were clamouring for knowledge of the other *Kommandos*. Service went down very well. Gave a talk on 'Suspense'.

10.7.44 Up at 6am and walked to Naundorf, nearly 20 kilos away. It was a lovely walk, up through wooded hills, fields full of crops, lovely little villages in the freshness of Sunday morning. It became very warm. German and English swapped by the way. Spent a very happy one-and-a-half hours with the 'Mutineers' and eventually arrived back at Hohnstein, tired but satisfied.

Travelling is becoming an ever-increasing problem here. Trains and trams are crammed to capacity. I've never seen anything like it before. It's amusing to work out the distance and the actual time taken to travel. Dresden to Hohnstein, about 25–30 kilos, takes from 4.51am to 7.15pm, and includes two changes. The return trip from Naundorf, which lies about 40 kilos from Hohnstein, took from 12.15am to 7.15am and included five changes and four hours' wait. Yesterday was the start of blackberry picking and apparently the trains could not cope with the crowds. Lots of holiday-makers on the Elbe banks. Paddle boats are very popular. Hitler *Jugend* [Youth] everywhere.

11.7.44 Yesterday came five letters, including two from Mother, and one from Beth. Poor Mrs Wright! The pride of our country seem to be taken. John was one of the gentlemen of younger Dunmurry, quiet, intelligent, courteous, friendly, splendid athlete. What a blow to my own circle of close friends – Jack Boyd, David Louden, Joe Unwin, John Wright, Marshall McComb, John Esler.

12.7.44 At last the letter from Kathleen has come and it has made life different for me. What a wonderful girl she is. The letter reads like a poem; its restraint, beauty and feeling make me realise just what a person she is. I do pray that I will be worthy of her love. Now I can understand why men have sung, 'I wish that the stars/Were a million guitars!' My heart is very, very full! I pray our whole relationship may be 'rooted and grounded' in God. I feel that He has given very much to me and I hope I'll be able to return a little. This is the biggest event of my life and I believe it will be the most significant. I feel my life touches Kathleen's at so many places – background, education, sport, interests, people, religion. I feel I can call it total love and that I can bring God into every part of it. I think of her with great joy: her vivacity, charm, wonderful eyes, sincerity, humour, depth, mind, modesty, humility, naturalness. I always remember the flashing smile, the eagerness for anything, indeed the real woman – there is a woman! I do not fear the future now. It will be tremendous seeing her again after four years away from each other. But this love of ours, which has blown into life, has been there all the time. Surely it will live always, especially when we see each other again and have the physical presence to add to the unity of mind and spirit. Now I must settle down and radiate that love and affection out into the lives of the people around.

14.7.44 Thoughts almost continually of Kathleen and the letter. Now I feel another stage of life is approaching, or what Hadfield would say, 'another rebirth'. How wonderfully God has prepared me for it. Mental outlook in 1939 and 1940 compared with now. The limitless largeness of life, as C.S. Lewis says; we are creatures that never die. Life is like a great adventure ever filling out and expanding. Old things are cast aside, old ideas, old interests, old recreations fall for new. What a tremendous explanation the Faith is of life! How it transforms life through and through. I believe God comes very especially in such experiences as mine now. I pray He'll be very much with Kathleen these days.

> *O Father, life is calling me to a new level of living; from irresponsibility to responsibility, from a wandering to a steady way; for all the wonder, joy and zest of life now, I thank Thee; for all the loving care, teaching, patience and devotion of my parents, I praise Thee. For the love of a girl, I glorify Thee. May the future be a time of growth, service, deeper and deeper knowledge and sense of Thee. May life grow richer and fuller as I learn to step out from my own dingy littleness, fears, inhibitions, prejudices, compromises, to the larger limitlessness and freedom of God. Amen.*

In the meantime, between these big events, life flows on here. Thank God I've got a fascinating job to do which takes up all my energy or I would go crackers waiting in Hohnstein for the Big End.

22.7.44 These are days of suspense and rumour. Russians have now penetrated the border of east Prussia, and France and Italy move on slowly but surely. Many of us hope for September as the big month. History shows that this part of the year brings decisions and I think the idea of another winter will shake most of the Germans. And for POWs, winter will mean death to thousands, if not millions, of Russians and Italians.

Yesterday an attempt was made on the *Führer*'s life and it looks as if the 'brew' is due to boil over any time now.

Es geht alles vorüber, es geht alles vorbei –
Nach jeden Dezember, koummt wieder Mai.

[*Everything passes, everything comes to an end –*
After every December, there follows a May.]

And what a May it will be for the suffering world.

This period of POW life has been of immense human interest. To be able to travel continually through one of the big cities of the Reich; to see the enemy on the job; to see the ammunition trains, the hospital trains, the battered planes; to hear *Flieger* alarms raised to warn the people against our own countrymen; all such experience is only given to a few and often one lives through it with bewildered feelings. Humanity is the big thing. The anxiety on thousands of faces; wives and husbands on tearful farewells as soldiers go back to the '*Ost*' Front; schoolchildren baffled at the *Hauptbahnhof* [central train station] in Dresden being evacuated from bombed-out areas. Overcrowded trains and trams, tired *chafferins* [lady conductors or stewardesses]; hungry, overworked people munching away at their 'black bread' in the packed compartments. Never a sight of a few people enjoying themselves. Looks of interested curiosity at the POW. Seldom any hatred. Civilians make up with my *Posten* and ask about his charge: '*Engländer oder Franzose oder Polen?*' Lingering eyes gaze at me from head to sole – pressed battle jacket, oiled locks, creased slacks, polished boots. And what a sight to see 100 *Engländer* marching through the streets of Dresden. Whistling, heads high, spick and span, uniformly dressed, in step, boots shining like the stars. People stop and stare. Imprisoned in body, but not in spirit.

24.7.44 Sense of peace today. Study of *Acts*: 'The creation of the new humanity.' Today we stand at the birth of a new world order and I stand at a critical point in life, one phase about to end and another to begin. Today is our opportunity. Pray for guidance and willingness re. my future work. May this study make me realise the power of the Spirit as never before. We know God's purpose for Mankind and have in His Spirit the power to create it. This book is not Church history: but news of the dynamic power of the Spirit of Christ to save the world; to create, out of a multitude of nations, a new and united humanity that will make Earth more like Heaven and bring every man to a realisation of his true destiny.

26.7.44 Walked with an Italian fellow prisoner to Porschdorf, then travelled through slowly to Zittau and on to Kleinschonau, a hive of industry. Long hours and boys a bit weary. Service at night. Glad to be out on *Kommandos* again. Best work of all. Put all into it now, for the home stretch. Get out of self and give all the way.

27.7.44 In the *Kommando Zweiglei Ziltan*. Happy inter-imperial group of nineteen men, SA, NZ, Canada, England, Scotland, etc., working on bricks. Angus Campbell, a very interesting Man of Confidence, has been a professional lion-hunter, professional soldier, hopes to be a market gardener, then on to Parliament and Secretary of Dominions!

Today: 'Be of good cheer.' Real secret of joy is nothing superficial: it is the harmonised, integrated life, the life lived above internal friction, fear, stress and anxiety. The life that has found its end and is able to rejoice because it has found the complete outlet – self-expression. It has become in tune with life and can do no other than sing. It is not mere pleasure nor is it happiness. My job here is to convey that experience to these men.

28.7.44 Another small, new *Kommando* and one of the best I've been to. Lovely clean billet, easy work, sixteen men, good food, considerate administration. Never-to-be-forgotten meal. Steady atmosphere here, very good Man of Confidence – Chap Davis, knows Bunting, H.E. Barker's friend who has been missing for a long time. Off from here at 2 o'clock to Neustadt – rather cheerless *Kommando*, where L/Cpl. Herbert Damms was killed last week in a railway shunting accident.

30.7.44 Arrived back in Hohnstein. Wrote to Mrs Damms.

31.7.44 These are tense days for our guardians. The whole *stalag* staff, men and women, were called up to the *Kommandhat* today and a big pep talk was delivered. News for us is good. Things seem to be moving in France and Russians are about Warsaw. Many thoughts stray to the future now and going home. What a feeling it will be after four years' wandering in so many places to go back to the old environment – Ulster, Belfast, Dunmurry, Manse. How vivid the summer of 1940 is in my mind. But I know I'll have to expect great changes – the age of people and how they will look, gaps in the circle. I do believe I've learnt a great deal this time abroad and I will appreciate home in all its aspects so much more as a result. No parades. My own room, solitude, hearth with a coal fire, wireless, civilian clothes, baths, fresh food. Quiet voices, piano, singing and church, family, fellowship of Dunmurry people, etc., etc. I hope I'll bring back a better discipline to my life, rising, devotions, habits, time, planning.

Today I do feel a tremendous urge to read. Psychology, history, theology, economics, physical science. One valuable way to use the experience of sport in the past will be in boys' clubs, Scouts, etc. I do relish the thought of such a job. My one concern about the future is to get a job that I can do well and that will pull out all my energy. I don't want an easy job. The next period in my life is going to be a vital one for me. In a real sense, these four years and Bangor are linked with college and preparation. Now comes the time of responsibility, steady, consistent work, and growth of character.

1.8.44 Got a letter from Mother of the splendid date 17 July, which brings news up-to-date again. All good news. Will is distinguishing himself in the RAF. Beth is back in Scotland. George and Margaret's son is to be called Peter Raymond. Mother and Father will be on their way to Portrush today, and Emily, too. I wonder what we'll be doing next year. Lovely to get out and imbibe nature. It seems to bring a real sense of peace and restoration to my mind. All the valley is in the glory of advanced summer. Apples are abundant. Cherries are everywhere. Some flaps on here these days. They have about had it, as Western allies and Russia move to meet together.

7.8.44 Yesterday a real Wesley day. Did three *Kommandos*. Walked with a rather taciturn guard to Goppeln. Lovely morning, reminiscent of August among the harvest at home, though rather hot for a weighty pack of gramophone records, books, etc. Approaching Dresden from the Nieder Sedlitz hills, whence Napoleon bombarded the city, gives one a splendid idea of the layout of the town. Bounded on both sides of the Elbe by hills, the city lies in between.

Today: battle of ideas. Way of Life. Religion and life separate, *cf.* use of religion here in Germany. Religion of the East. The only way to conquer one way of life is to use a better one. The only way to overcome one ideal is to use a better one. Points in our ideal: (1) value of men, (2) universality, (3) freedom, (4) purpose of life – destiny.

8.8.44 Travelled from Sportsplatz to Cossebaude with very old, fat guard who'd lost his wife in June. Once again a very warm day. Thoughts of August at home in Ballycastle and Portrush. Service last night in the open was most disappointing as far as attendance was concerned – about 20 out of 110 men. Last time it was considerably more. Round the billets today and talk with everybody. Realise the faith, hope, strength, patience of God in my life. 'Each act of ours leaves upon the world a fainter or a deeper impress of God.'

9.8.44 News of movement in France comes through. Very warm weather now, recalls the desert days. Mixed thoughts at present, both morbid and pleasant. Keep my eye on the job in hand. Need for stricter self-discipline. So easy to slide along aimlessly. Think much of the idea of 'forgiveness' these days. Think out what one should say to the enemy on positive lines. Distinguish the sin from the sinner. Practical: attitude after war. Last time: enemy physically defeated, but not won.

11.8.44 Spent an enjoyable night with the South Africans of Hainsberg 6, a most sociable and friendly crowd of men. All recently arrived from Stalag IV B. One old boy of sixty-one, about the strongest man in the camp. Very well looked after, although I spent a rather sleepless night with many midges!

Re-read Kathleen's letters. Some passages are lyrical and reveal a real sincerity and depth of soul. May I be truly worthy of her love! Pray for the end soon!

14.8.44 Still here in Hohnstein. Should have gone off today but as the Company has no guards, I wait until tomorrow morning. Very pleasant day and I'm sitting out on the football field, sunbathing and thinking happy thoughts. Had service last night, singing very good: Ron Standfield (professional guitarist from Ravens Band) and Ted Murray at piano. Sang 'Jerusalem' and 'Praise My Soul'. Spoke on 'Love Your Enemy', and certainly everybody listened. All finished by Christmas – how often we've said that! 1941, Tobruk; 1942, desert; 1943, Italy; 1944, Germany. Still, I believe it will come off this time.

15.8.44 News of a landing at Toulon just come in. Won't be long now!

16.8.44 Tonight I wonder about the future. What is it to be? The mission field, or home, or even YMCA? Pray for guidance, willingness to go where I'm needed. Think a lot about the field in China.

19.8.44 Long day's travelling yesterday, but worth it. Boys here in Lobau in good heart. News that Paris has fallen and Russians are in Germany.

Feeling much more on the mark today. Thoughts on the theme of Power of Love and how it must be incarnate in our lives these days. So many ways in which it can be manifested. Spirit, good cheer, thoughtfulness, little things one can do about the *Kommandos* to help.

24.8.44 Today, all out for a '*Freital* alarm' – down into the bunker for ten minutes. All clear and then we heard the hum of planes and planes; what a sight, away up-up in the clear blue, scintillating like fireflies as their wings caught the sun. Three bombs dropped on Freital. News is that Romania has packed in and that Paris is really fallen. Most speculators give September as the likely finale, and what a day that will be!

25.8.44 Still keeps intensely warm and close. Harvest fields look splendid and the whole landscape is lovely now. Events in the outside world move on, rumours are a daily feature of life and it looks like a repetition of September 1943, with a difference. Speculation now as to whether we will go home by air or boat! These are naturally restless days and the thought of going back home after four years is a thrilling and startling thought.

Father of all, keep my spirit alive in these days of waiting. Make me more and more sensitive to the needs of others, to their hardships, problems and fears. Help me to turn my sensitivity inside out, from myself to others. Waken me up more and more to my responsibilities and the challenges of life. Help me to throw off all the inhibitions, fears and compromises of childhood and adolescence. May the light of Thy truth lighten the shadows of my personality and show me what is hindering, just as the X-ray reveals the fractures and diseases of the physical body. May Thy transforming power create an ever-increasing unity, purpose and harmony in my life. Help me to realise that my unique contribution to everybody and everything is myself. That is my sole responsibility. Amen.

30.8.44 Got back yesterday after a short but very strenuous tour and the last three days will certainly live in my memory for a long time. Saturday we foolishly lost the way to Rathen and tried our hand at mountaineering. Our guard, Johny Schartz, came off worst, as he fell about 50 feet and lost his rifle. We walked round by the usual path and arrived below some two hours later. As we'd already missed the train, we went back to look for the rifle, but the guard could not find the right valley, so we had to give it up and go on to Rathen, where we arrived an hour too early and sat on the Elbe bank and ate windfall apples. The train was packed and stiflingly warm, and we had to stand whole way to Riesa. Got in about 8 o'clock, in time for a brew of tea, then spent a terrible night with the fleas. Sunday, visited *Kron Prinz Kommando* and back to Groba. Held services at both places, then heard that I had to depart in the morning for Dresden, for a funeral. Set off with the old Riesa *Posten* and was tapped as usual without success, as all my cigarettes had followed the other guard over the cliff. Arrived in Dresden and was taken to the garrison Friedhof, where Donaldson of Schlacthof had been buried. The air raid at Freital had killed up to 300 people, including one of our boys, Alec Bellamy. About fifteen boys from Freital arrived smartly dressed. Germans also provided a military guard of honour and the funeral went off with dignity and respect. At the graveside, while the service was in progress, the air filled with planes, which most believed to be British. Boys filled in the grave themselves and put on two wreaths. I travelled back with the boys to Freital. I was glad I did this, as everyone there had been upset by the raid and especially at the loss of such a splendid, cheerful little chap as Bellamy. I saw some evidence of the raid – several craters, smashed windows, buildings, rubble. Our boys have been working pretty well non-stop on sorting out the bodies, digging the graves and tidying up the graveyard.

1.9.44 I'm in Schmorkau for a funeral, which is long overdue, as the death took place on Monday. Military funeral went off without any problems. Eight nations with wreaths, gun carriage.

2.9.44 Travelled back yesterday with my *Dolmetscher*, with whom I had a most interesting and heated discussion on Authoritarianism and Liberalism.

4.9.44 Travelled down to Prossen yesterday on the bar of the *Posten*'s bicycle and visited the three *Kommandos* and found them all in good order. Kron Prinz very happy in their new *lager*. New *Kommando* very well housed in the Prossen Gasthof. Lovely outlook on the banks of the Elbe. Long talk with Johnny, the Dutchman, and saw tail-end of an international concert. News comes in that big events are now going on in Belgium, and France is very nearly finished.

Today and yesterday, spiritually at a very low ebb. Realise my own utter futility and incompetence. Need of God in everything. Deepen faith, trust, dependence and committal. 'Restore unto me the joy of Thy salvation.'

5.9.44 Back in Hohnstein. Brussels fallen and today we hear that our troops have entered Holland. Go out for a spell to think. Get my head and mind clear again. Get right out of the 'trough'. Back to real efficiency and prayer. Our prayer life must be definite, purposeful and incisive; asking for definite things, definite needs to be met, defeats changed, real confession of detailed mistakes. Not so much of the hazy, casual approach. Definite claims, if we are to have definite answers. Prayer life is shadowed in the real life. Turn morbidity into activity.

6.9.44 Interesting talk yesterday with Polish chemist on the future of Europe. Polish point of view – so much still in the air. Russian system. Whoever wins the war, the Poles lose it. Drone of our planes now very high up. Yesterday advance in Holland, towards Rotterdam. Aix-la-Chapelle gone to Rhineland; bombardment has begun.

'With malice towards none; with charity for all; with firmness in the right, as God gives us to see the right, let us strive on to finish the work we are in; to bind up the nation's wounds; to care for him who shall have borne the battle and for the widow and his orphan, to do all which may achieve and cherish a just and lasting peace among ourselves and with all nations.'

Abraham Lincoln

7.9.44 These are startling days. Bulgaria now disposed of and the Allies have taken Rotterdam and Saarbrücken and are bashing the Siegfried line. Nervous tension. Planes over several times yesterday, though we are comparatively off the beaten track here, 40km southeast of Dresden.

Just received unexpected letters from home. Much news and much optimism, written from the security of White Park Bay. My old friend Fred Cromey has that restless feeling that I had in June 1940 and hopes to go further afield soon.

Today is simply idyllic. I'm sitting in the shade of an apple tree weighed down with fruit. Splendid sunshine and yet a cool, refreshing wind. Tremendous sense of peace here in Sächsische Schweiz. Distant hum of planes has become a background noise, just like the grasshoppers. The valley looks splendid today. One might almost be at home. News has reached a tremendous pitch now and once again we are in suspense. How long? Two weeks? Two months? Bing Crosby's 'I'll be home for Christmas' has come into its own. It certainly is some thought and I do wonder how I'll settle down and if, indeed, I'm meant to do so. I do feel greatly the sense of life as an adventure and in no way has this experience quenched that desire to get about. However, time will settle these things.

8.9.44 Prayers: Pray for those who have lost their husbands and fathers, who have received no news – in suspense and anxiety. All the women and children who have suffering in their homes. Smashed homes and lives.

Peace:
O Father who hast made us all members of the one great human family, cause this terrible strife to cease and when it comes to an end, may reason, foresight and justice prevail. Cleanse our hearts of

bitterness and hate. Help us to realise our common nature as Thy children. Give us the determination to live as individuals and as a nation that war may be outlawed from the world. Guide our lives more and more into the spirit of love and forgiveness. Amen.

POWs:
O God of our weary years, who hast been with us right through this experience – its hunger, thirst, depression, loneliness – be with us now in these days of suspense and waiting. As Thou hast been our Guide and Strength in the past, sustain us now. Give us the quiet mind of patience and confidence. May we remember that Thou hast said, 'Thou wilt keep him in perfect peace whose mind is stayed on Thee because he trusteth in Thee.' Amen.

12.9.44 Another short trip over. Trains very packed with weary, dispirited people. Stood all the way to Königswartha and most of it back again. *Sonderführer* Lammel is a psychological study in himself. Some of his lovely expressions: 'Do not walk so fast Mr Davey or we will transpire'; 'I will procure a chamber in the Gasthof'; 'I wish to organise some eggs.' After a considerable conversation with a German *fräulein* in the train, he says to me, 'That is the sort of girl I will like to marry, but she is already engaged. She looks so solid.' Then he leaves me in Dresden *Hauptbahnhof*, while he goes to 'advantage himself' in 'obtaining' soup from the Red Cross and gives me this note, just in case: '8.9.44 The British minister Raymond Davey finds himself on transport with me to Königswartha and waits on the 12.40 train.' He asked for return of the note later.

Looks as if Dresden is getting it now.

14.9.44 Big push on the Siegfried line has begun, so it looks as if things are coming to a head at last. Waiting for confirmation of my trip to Dresden Links. Now we hear three new Yank *Kommandos* are about to be opened. One raid yesterday. Wrote to Kathleen.

15.9.44 Yesterday saw another scrap with *Abwehr* [defence]. We tried to see the *Hauptmann* several times and finally succeeded after the fourth attempt. I had asked for eight days in Dresden Links. This was refused and I finally got two days. The *Hauptmann* had heard that the men in

Lobau Sugar Factory were somewhat restless after my last visit. He did not believe it, but he could not let me stay away for such a long time — these times in which we live — perhaps I could soon go out on my own. I protested against the idea that I caused unrest and said my job was directly the opposite and he could read what I had said, if he so wished. However, I accepted the two days, as I don't think this will go on so much longer and now our policy is to take what we get and be thankful.

18.9.44 These have been most strenuous and interesting days. Left Hohnstein on Saturday morning early. Travelled with Sgt. Smith (*Hauptvertrauensmann*, or Main Man of Confidence) and went straight to the new Yank *Kommando* in Dresden. Got an overwhelming reception there, as they'd seen no Englishmen and were in a pretty bad state. No parcels, no cigarettes, small rations, hard work, didn't understand Jerry *Posten* nor civilian gaffer. All of them were caught on the Cherbourg Peninsula. They reminded me of the French Foreign Legion — Chinese, Mexican, Spanish, German, Jewish; Levy, Alvarez, Brown, Burodini, etc.

20.9.44 Arrived back yesterday very early and spent the day in bed with a cold. Today I'm more or less mended. *Posten* who brought me to Bahnhof asked if I knew the Oxford *Bewegung* [Movement] and the YMCA. Did I what! He nearly kissed me when I told him I was a YMCA secretary.

News goes ever better. Complete Airborne Army landed in Holland and forces in the vicinity of Köln.

26.9.44 Really wonderful letter from Kathleen yesterday. It's grand to know that she got back to Ireland and had a holiday in old Donegal. It is just the right place after all the strain of Club work in Scotland. Date was 24 August, so the mail is beginning to flow again. The letter was a much-needed inspiration, as life is a bit ragged now, waiting in *stalag*. Just been reading over some of the notes of this time last year and it certainly was grim. So much to be thankful for now — conditions here, news, state of mind, providence of God in my stay in Germany. So many amazing experiences and new knowledge.

29.9.44 I'm in splendid form these days. The letters from Mother and

Kathleen have been a wonderful inspiration. It's amazing how they keep coming in. Grand to know Kathleen has been out to the Manse. It is all a remarkable climax and I believe it is the harbinger of the end. News is a bit slow now and Holland is seeing some heavy fighting, as is Germany. Some pessimism is beginning to spread around. Anyway, what does it matter? It certainly cannot last many months, and what's a few months! Though I do so wish it was over. In the hard times of life remember that God cares most of all for spiritual success, which is inward, and that He can help you to make even adversity contribute to character: 'To be faithless is to fail, whatever the apparent success of earth: to be faithful is to succeed, whatever the apparent failure of earth' (Maltsie Babcock). I think this sums up so much of what has been said by those who've had to speak to POWs.

I've tapped most nationalities on the theme of post-war reconstruction and about a federation. All are keen on it, but naturally not optimistic about its success. Russia remains the enigma. For myself, I believe Britain and the USA may form a federation of the English peoples; that will be the first step. Then many of the European powers may join. One possibility for preserving peace is that Britain and USA should remain very strong and more or less 'oversee' Europe, with a federation emerging in forty or fifty years' time, as the others tumble to the idea. There are many objections: violation of freedom, etc. But freedom is as yet an ideal and nations are like men, very selfish, and a certain amount of control is justified if it produces more freedom for more countries. Law is always necessary as a basis for freedom. Perhaps this is just a bit of British Phariseeism. But one year in Germany has made me 100 per cent more British, though we have a lot to put in order in our own house.

The Belgians say federation is impossible: in their country there are only two sorts of German – 'schlecht' and 'mehr schlecht' ['wicked' and 'more wicked']. The French agree with me that this attitude is senseless, and indeed a denial of democracy, which is based on the belief that all men are created equal. So much depends on England and America and how they will handle the situation after the armistice. You have only to talk with the POWs to realise how much this matters. We are apt to be so complacent and content in our mental as well as our geographical insularity.

2.10.44 Another letter from Kathleen, telling of her visit out home and meeting Mother. The two people who mean most to me in the world! What a dear she is and how I long for her now. I must be patient. Remember those who have been denied this experience, whose loved ones have not come home. What does a few months matter now? Her love is so sure. How wonderful life is, but I must not daydream. Put all the efforts into positive action here and now. Don't be selfish in my love. Kathleen writes so beautifully and naturally about the Manse and 'home'. I do think Mother and she have much in common and in a way are prototypes. I know Mother will love her so much. Now both families know, so the plot thickens. How amazing is God's love and providence! So often before I wondered about this business and stopped, attracted by people here and there, but always to move on again, as I knew somehow it was not here that I would find the one who was meant. And at last the way leads right home to Kathleen, the sweetest girl in the world!

3.10.44 Down from the heights – creative work. Surrender thoughts, restlessness, longing, suspense, waiting. Sincerity: *Matthew* 6:2–6. The secret of hypocrisy is the desire to appear well without paying the price that being right asks. Trying to cover the truth by the outward appearance. Surrender all future fears. Complete trust and adequacy will be given when the day comes. Beware of the way of ease and comfort. Easy position, job, etc. The ferment of my mind is tremendous. What are we to do in the future? That will have to be decided soon. There are several courses open, all of which basically amount to the same thing: church at home, mission field and China all the way; YMCA work in England or abroad (should I be accepted); or other possibilities may open out. Pray for God's guidance when the time comes. How wonderfully Kathleen is suited for all these things. She knows much more than I do on the social side.

6.10.44 Now in the Company in Dresden Rechts, waiting to go on to Gunther Werke. *Dolmetscher* Peter is an interesting chap. Member of the YMCA and also well read in theology. We had a long talk on Liberalism on the trip. *Kommando* in good form. Held a service, then a celebration of Communion. Feel strongly these days that I'm not using many of these opportunities to the full. Also my talks must be of a more direct and personal nature. Must keep the balance between liberal humanism and fundamental orthodoxy. Sense of the real function of the Church. In evangelism, calling men to the new life. Nothing must ever crush that out.

9.10.44 After my visit to the Company on the sixth, I went out to Gunther Werke with Peter and had a fine night with them. *Lager* in better order, boys all looking forward to the end. Interesting talk on the future. Held a service in the home and a Communion service. Then travelled across Dresden and out to Radeburg. Lovely run through the Weintraub hills, woodlands, lakes and Morizburg Schloss [castle]. Had the agreeable company of an *Oberfeldwebel*, who spoke some English and fell asleep on my shoulder. Arrived at Radeburg and an alarm went, and from the banks of the shelter I saw more planes *en masse* than I have ever seen before, silver specks in the sun, in batches of 10–15 over and over, fighters hovering round. Dresden AA. Bombs dropped; lots of silver paper dropped. This was the first raid on Dresden proper. Many think it was just the prelude, as it was very light, though a lot of *Ausländers* [foreigners] were killed. Boys provided me with a Red Cross armband, as we did not know how severe the raid had been. *Oberfeld* met me at station and we went into Postplatz, where there was evidence of bombing. Two streets were bashed up and controlled by police and Brown Shirts. Just like London in 1940; large crowds watched the work in progress from the end of the street. Ride to Pillnitz was deadly. Terrible crush, *Kinderwagens* [buggies], and I was glad to get out at Pillnitz.

Dr Whale's book *Facing Facts* has set my mind on real theological lines again, also the talk with Peter. Determination now to link up theology and life: to make the Gospel live, apply it to life.

13.10.44 Well, here I am in Erika. Yesterday I took the steamer down the Elbe. I think it will always be a lovely memory of my stay in Germany, sailing down through that wonderful scenery on a clear, sharp October morning. Lift into Dresden with French lorry, on their way to funeral of French POWs killed in the raid. Arrived here at 4.30pm. Special room outside the *lager* – in theory I'm not allowed into it without *Dolmetscher*. Boys in good form. Wally going great guns. Service on 'Dilemma of Today' and Communion. Now I'm in the delightful solitude of my room. Thoughts of Kathleen and a real sense of gratitude for her and her love.

15.10.44 Saturday was a busy day. Wally in for a yarn in the morning. He is likely to go in to the Methodist ministry and on his work he will be the real thing. Set off for Lohsa on the 1.30pm with bicycle, and cycled to Ostfeld through flat country as dreary as a wilderness. Good crowd, though somewhat weary after three years in the same *lager*. Parcels all being removed outside *lager*, which causes a lot of unrest among the boys. Service there and Sacrament, which they had not had for eighteen months. Gilbert, the 'Vicar', has done a fine job there. Violin helped the music and quite a good attendance. Spoke on 'Anxiety'.

Yesterday, off early by bicycle to Weidnitz, via Schwartz Kollm, and we lost the way and did about 20km before we finally got there. Very good spirit there, though, like Ostfeld, they have had a long stay. Service on 'Suspense'. Fine ride back. Really lovely mild days. Trees become more yellow and golden each day. Silver birches are lovely here. Crops are being brought in, fruit pulled and some ploughing going on. Then I passed through Lautawerk, which had been visited by the RAF about a fortnight ago and it certainly left its mark. Big damage on the main factory, small craters all over the place, houses smashed, windows gone and slates broken. One wooden billet was blown away.

17.10.44 What a day yesterday at Berghammer! My poor *Dolmetscher*, Herr Kaas! It was a chapter of accidents. Burst tyres, hair's breadth catching of trains, forestry, groans, *Gott verdammt!* Lost ways, rushed service and hectic ride back on the worst bicycle in the Reich. Flat tyre the whole way. Poor old Kaas was nearly finished on the way back, asking the way, pessimism, but in the end I did succeed in getting him to laugh when I said what I thought of the German roads and my bicycle.

19.10.44 Started off for Geisslitz yesterday. Really lovely run through the woods in a gloriously fresh autumn day. Firs, pines, rabbits, and the divine stillness of the forest. Little *Kommando* right in the middle of the forest. Fellows happy enough. Service and talk and back in the twilight. Kaas, nourished in body, was in good form on the run home.

New officer has instituted new '*ordnung*' in the camp: hands out of pockets, tunics. *Hauptmann* Ifford and Ginskye away to the Front.

21.10.44 News is very slow these days and many are beginning to think that it'll be a next-year finish now. Who cares anyway! It'll all come in good time. In the meantime: learn, live and serve. Captain Wykes got a large consignment of records yesterday, which he played over in the evening. Room upstairs is like a pub at night with its thick, hot, smoky atmosphere.

Psalm 139: The crowning Psalm of the Psalter for the loftiness of its thought and expression. God's infinite patrol pervades the whole of our existence. God knows absolutely everything about me, secrets and faults, all. He is around my life at every point in space and time. Heaven or hell, light or dark, in birth. All my body known to God. In sleep and waking.

'When I awake I am still with Thee
Search me, O God, and know my heart.
Try me, and know my thoughts
And see if there be any wicked way in me,
And lead me in the way everlasting.'

22.10.44 Sunday. 'He shall be like a tree planted.' Often we must fall back to that, to the roots of our lives: are they strong and steadfast? Will anything shake them? Enthusiasm, visions, dreams often break down; new ventures fail, hopes and plans cave in and we fall back on our reserve. Doubt, depression, sorrow, hardship, danger, insecurity.

Typical autumn day. We played a scramble of a football match, quite amusing, especially when Dodger, Best and I mixed in some rugger tackles. Serbs and Dutch played with us. It was splendid to feel the turf again and to speed along – my speed is not diminished altogether yet. Our guards here have been changed almost completely and there is certainly a definite stiffening in the air. Aix-la-Chapelle is now fallen, as is Belgrade, and Bologna is not far from the same state. Big argument on how we should treat the 'goons' after the war is over. I took my usual attitude, which was most unpopular. Various atrocity stories quoted – Crete – pre-war – Greece. I cannot but admit that these days are trying, all the expectations of a September or October finish were wrong and the winter slips on and we're still here, with the troops around Aachen and the border. But I'm still hopeful that it will finish this year.

27.10.44 Got off on Tuesday for the burial of Ronnie Wraight. Saw extensive damage done in Dresden air raid, especially around Wittingerstrasse. All glass in the roof shattered and many filled-in craters about. I sensed a stiffening in the attitude of the people. At Neustadt I saw a South African who was shot down eight days ago 3 miles from Russian Front. He believed that the war would be over in three months. Took his address in the hope of getting news of his safety back to Johannesburg. Funeral on Wednesday went off quite well, apart from the role of the Detaining Power. No volley allowed now; also, only one wreath. And the guard of honour they did send! Otherwise, all went off in a reverent and decent manner.

Letter from Protecting Power re. my status. Message from England: I'm a *bona fide* YMCA secretary, to be treated as an officer and rank as a captain! Many collapse and fall about! Have to stand much abuse in Hohnstein with salutes, etc.

29.10.44 Four British MOs and Swiss German Repatriation Board were here. Dr Ferguson was passed, so he'll soon be back to Erin and I'm giving him some addresses to look up. We feed in the Casino, where English and French officers muck in, and with the French cooking, the result is some very excellent food. Five Yanks arrived in yesterday, so there is now quite a colony here. We get up disgracefully late. Spiritually, I've been slacking and feel at a low ebb just now.

> *O God, help me in the strength of Thy Son to make this world in all its hardship, sorrow and tragedy my own. Teach me in these days to think deeper and straighter; to develop my philosophy and faith; to find my feet in life; to find the work I can do. Take away the old self of carelessness, slipshodness, laissez-faire, laziness. Give me real gladness in the bearing of the tasks and problems. I am so grateful for your providence in bringing me through all this experience. I pray that I may utilise it to the full when I go back. O give me then drive, energy, vision and faith to seize life by the throat, to use all that is in me, to surrender the various fears I have of myself and to do the work you want me to do. All this I pray may be possible, so I learn to serve and follow your Son. Amen.*

30.10.44 Today I arrived back from a tour of the two hospitals, Königswartha and Schmorkau. I find it hard to settle down after being so much on the move. The country seems to be pretty far through. People are very tired and browned off. Hungry, pinched faces, overcrowded trains, long hours. Dresden has suffered in the bombing, especially around Wittingerstrasse Bahnhof and the area towards Postplatz. It does seem to have changed the attitude of the people a little. Country is now being scraped and combed for manpower. *Volksturm* (16-60 years) has been formed and rigid economy imposed. No Firing Party now at the funerals of POWs. Only one wreath.

Life in our hospitals is a pleasant change from the *Kommandos*. One can wander round and talk to everyone. Königswartha is very pleasantly situated and was originally a home for the blind. All nationalities are treated. Most of the chaps are getting on well and their sole concern is of being sent out to work again. At present the British feed the Russians with Red Cross food, which is an absolute Godsend to them.

1.11.44 Read Government Social Security Scheme, which has been adopted. It is very close on the Beveridge Plan and differs only on a few details of money, etc.

9.11.44 Yesterday I went down to Hauptmann Zumpfe re. trip. Very nice, but nothing doing at present. These days are useful for the bit of reading I do, but they are thoroughly and completely selfish. There is still a very deep dissatisfaction in my heart, or perhaps it is more an urge to service and work. I realise that I must use these days for inward as well as mental growth. Sometimes in life one has to be content with limited circumstances and put them to the best use. I would rather bury myself in books than spend time with the boys in *stalag* at present.

13.11.44 Travelled to Dresden Links. My *Dolmetscher* was in USA for four years and in England and Australia, so is *ganz einverständlich* [quite understandable]. Showed me his shop in Dresden – *Lederwaren* [leather goods]. Visited the American *Kommando* and certainly it was a pretty raw effort. Bad conditions, roof sweats and large drops of water fall everywhere. Most of the men were unshaved and in a miserable state altogether. Took a note of service there, but the singing was like an aeroplane that wouldn't take off. It really was a most depressing place and I hope conditions will soon be improved.

14.11.44 Spent the night at Nicern, really lovely barrack, attached to the *Luftwaffe* school. Splendid food also, and the work is quite reasonable. Met many fellows from Lucca and Campo 70 – one who worked in the bakery in Fermo. Took service in corridor. Talk on 'Why does God allow war?' Worthwhile to give another talk on that.

17.11.44 Back in Hohnstein. I'm to go back to the old office with Captain Wykes and Sgt. Smith. Also, I'm now on roll call with the officers, which saves a lot of time and will open new doors in getting to know more of them. The last tour taught me much. I was fortunate in my guard, *Oberschutzer* Wilhelm Krumm, who had spent some nine years in English-speaking countries and was most helpful. It was a good tour, though pretty stiff going, and I was fairly dried out on Monday. Several points have been brought home to me. Need for much better preparation – vital in such services.

20.11.44 Much air activity yesterday – 150 planes flew over. Later came some German fighters. Weather is much cooler and today it is very windy. Armies in action along the whole Western Front and progress is being made.

23.11.44 Repatriation indefinitely postponed. Big push all along the line towards the Rhine. Heavy air raids. Horrible weather. No mail yet. Spiritual life is a bit scratchy just now.

24.11.44 Many searching questions pass through my mind these days. Ultimate questions about life; the fundamental issues of life. Time I had a coherent philosophy of life. Time all the strands began to fit into each other. Relationship of morality and psychology and religion. What is my *credo*? What do I wish to accomplish with my life? What is the *summum bonum*? Am I progressing, or merely marching time? Acknowledging and accepting what I have and what I am. Relate religion to my life and see how vital it really is. Religion and life to hang together as a great whole. Each one of us is a universe in himself.

27.11.44 Got four letters, as well as three the day before, so they come in gradually. Most grateful for the three snaps – lovely ones of Mother and Father and the dear old home. Talk on prayer: Is it any use? Why do we need to worship? God and war?

29.11.44 Another funeral in Dresden. Gunther Werke. Harvey Moore was shot while re-entering the *Kommando* with two others. They had been warned many times and this was the result. Tragic business. Had a really fine old *Posten*, Gefr. Karsh, who looked after me like a son. Owns an art shop in Dresden.

5.12.44 I write from Schlachthof. Spent yesterday at Dohna. I found it rather a drop after the other *Kommandos*. Men seemed unresponsive, though that may have been my fault, as I did find myself very tired, not so much with services as with endless talking. This has been an encouraging trip, though I realise my work has been but seed-scattering. Value of the life lived is what counts.

> 'Not merely in the words you say,
> Not only in the deeds confessed,
> But in the most unconscious way
> Is Christ expressed.
> For me 'twas not the truth you taught
> To you so clear, to me so dim,
> But when you came to me you brought
> A sense of Him.
> And from your eyes He beckons me
> And from your heart His love is shed
> Till I lose sight of you and see
> The Christ instead.'

6.12.44 Many thoughts arise in my mind now. How will I react after all this time away from home, this unsettled, irresponsible life? Four-and-a-quarter years away now. Who would have thought so? September 1940! But at present there is a deep sense of satisfaction, in that I did get out of the rut of orthodox clerical life and find an experience like this. I feel in many ways a rebel and hope for the courage to live out a true religion and faith. May reality, simplicity and service be ever my guiding stars.

This life is curious in its effects. I'm sometimes up and sometimes down, but I do realise what the antidote is. Must get my ideas, habits, beliefs, plans much more clear-cut. Life is still much of a drift to me. It is true that the spiritual world is very real to me and religion is certainly a power in my life – I've seen that through the experience of 1942, 1943, 1944. But I demand of myself a far deeper singleness of purpose: a more fundamental unity of my whole personality. I demand also the conquest of fear, which is largely of myself. I demand clarity in my beliefs: not a theological hotchpotch of different leaders of thought. Let my guiding star and criterion be experience both of myself and of other people. Gratitude to God for showing me so many remarkable and charming men of different nations.

13.12.44 Visited the two American *Kommandos* in the Richter School in Freital and to get there I passed through the bombed area. Found our Allies in fine fettle and had some good chats. Most friendly crowd and responsive, though time was short and I could not spend the night with them as I had hoped. All captured in France – Airborne – and tell of their ordeal in Paris when they were marched through the streets and were jeered at by the Vichy French. Many of these lads had been in Ireland – Armagh, Bangor, Portrush and Londonderry. One said, if you ever go to Portrush, 'Tell Mum I'm doin' swell. Gee, she and I got along swell.' Many anxious inquiries re. parcels, which run out everywhere just about Christmastime.

15.12.44 Most pleasant time in Cossebaude. A good lot of fellows! The records have been popular and I've acquired one of Vera Lynn's here. She is the Soldier's Sweetheart now in Blighty. Yesterday I shed, with regret, my *Dolmetscher Feldwebel* Hering, who is going to the *Strafofflag* of Colditz.

20.12.44 Life has certainly moved swiftly since I landed in Hontsch [an S.S. factory]. Had an enjoyable and, I believe, useful time there. Service and Communion both well attended. Dalton looked after me well and Connor and Curley were most amusing. On Saturday I had a good look round and saw the boys at work. Then in the afternoon I took my 'convoy' round to Sportsplatz – Dr Pfeifer and two of the boys with my records, gramophone and hymn books. Sportsplatz had a complete new staff since my last visit and only old Beakie, the guard, is left. Most of these boys were captured at Arnhem and some Canadians in Belgium. I felt almost fatherly, flaunting my two-and-a-half years (exact today, 20 Dec.) against their paltry two months. On to Goppeln and found them in great fettle preparing for Christmas – decorations and a band without any instruments. Returned to Hohnstein with a junior officer, leader of Hitler *Jugend*. When I got back, I found one letter from Kathleen and a photo taken in Donegal. It grows on me daily, so natural and unposed. She looks wind-burned and tanned, fresh, vital and radiant. These days I do realise what being in love is and I feel it is love all along the line – heart, mind, soul, strength. God's great gift to me and often I am lost in wonder and amazement. Why me? Why should I be the lucky one! I feel that this Christmas will be the happiest of all my life.

21.12.44 I've certainly learned a lot about Germany this year. Spoken with hundreds of soldiers of all types. Ration of two cigs a day hits them very hard. Now this area gets at least one *Fliege* alarm each day and often more. Different places in Saxony have received considerable attention and the latest news is that 140 of our boys got it in Brux Benzine Fabrik in Stalag IV C. We've heard many fierce bombardments and Dresden itself has had two minor visits. I've seen the RAF go over several times and it is a tremendous sight. They fill up the sky and come in in swarms. Sometimes far up in the stratosphere we see the Mosquitoes drawing vapour trails across the sky. The boys say, 'And those lads will be back in Blighty tonight.' And they like to say that our hosts cannot look above 1,000 feet. That is enemy territory.

Praise: Joy and zest of Christmas; thankfulness for sense of expectancy; health of body and pleasure of work; the inspiring hope of freedom. For the love and thoughts and backing of parents and family. For the surpassing joy and assurance of Kathleen and myself. For the stimulation and privilege of being allowed to work among 5,000 POWs. For the deepening knowledge and sense of the realness of the faith. For the loyalty of so many old friends and the making of so many new ones. For a surer touch in life, dealing with men and their problems. For all the mercies of the Red Cross – food, clothes; the YMCA, books, etc. For a deeper love of nature. Freedom from the old bonds.

Manhood's Greatest Task:

'To take up the purpose of God and work for it; work for it confidently and continuously as Christ worked for it: giving his whole life for it, even unto death. But today, who cares to this extent about the work of God? Or sees it as a glorious purpose, the only hope for mankind? Yet what is nationalism compared with God's will for the whole human family? What are political changes compared with the transformation of human nature and destiny? What is the value of a four-year plan compared with God's promise for today, tomorrow and forever? Yet to these man-made schemes men will give the strength and enthusiasm of their manhood.'

H.E. Fosdick

23.12.44 Well, yesterday turned out to be a real 'how do you do'. First, after several sessions, *Herr Major* Zumpfe decided that I could not travel to Königswartha and after lodging a protest, I had to accept his decision. However, *Arbeit* Einsetz was not informed of this and eventually I was allowed to travel. 16 degrees F below! I've never been so cold before. Good welcome here. Seen many of the Italian boys, severely wounded, one lad with both arms off and face very badly burned. Wonderful spirit. Restores one's belief in human nature. News seems to be that the Jerries are cut off in the big attack.

25.12.44 And so Christmas Day 1944 dawns and we are still POWs. But not too worried. I'm in Königswartha and in some ways there is a very unreal atmosphere around. I've put so much into these last few days that there's little time to think. Yesterday we had a memorial service in the Friedhof. Very cold, so I kept it short. Visited many wards. One hundred new cases from Italy; long yarn with officers. Then a carol service at night, very well attended by all nationalities. Today we've had a Christmas service, followed by Communion, and now preparation goes forward for the Christmas dinner. Sort of improvised concert all afternoon, tea at 4.30pm and then a four-and-a-half-hour show at night. A lot of organisation in it all. My thoughts go back and forward in time and space: Drogheda, 1939; Suez Canal, 1940; Tobruk, 1941; Italy, 1942; Mühlburg, 1943, Königswartha, 1944; ?? 1945 – 'Next year in Jerusalem'?

28.12.44 Still in Königswartha. News is up and down these days: attack and counter-attack near Saarbrücken and Alsace. Live here with Dr Devimeux of Paris, a very decent fellow. My return to Hohnstein has been arranged for tomorrow, so I must get all in order for that.

My Darling One,

I've just been reading through some of your letters I brought with me here to K. and indeed you seem very near to me. You've no idea how much thoughts of you help me these days. I believe I know some of your letters by heart … Temperature down to 17 degrees below. It has been an adventurous and interesting time, and enough to eat. One hundred new lads from my old home, some grievously wounded but with heroic spirits … Human nature is a remarkable thing. It is shame that we must wait still longer, darling, but though I do absolutely long for you, yet I have hardened myself for another six months. How are you? Did you have a decent holiday back home? … I do hope your mother and dad were well … I hope my letters are getting through again, though they don't say anything like what I really do feel, but I know you'll be able to read between the lines, and as you say, feelings are in expressions. Now I know that love must be mind, spirit and body – everything … I wonder were you out home again. It is wonderful that you and Mother get to know each other.

31.12.44 And so the end of 1944. What a year of hope, interest and experience. So much to be thankful for. Promise of the end soon. The New Year will bring me many changes. Prayer for adequacy and ability to face whatever comes, both of hardship and joy:

O God of every stage of life, I come to Thee now on the threshold of 1945. For all that 1944 has meant and done to me, I give Thee hearty thanks. And now as I look across into the future, untrodden and unknown, I realise how much I need Thee. It will bring me many opportunities of service. May I, in Thy power and spirit, seize them to the full. It will bring hardships. Give me Thy courage and patience and faith, not only to overcome them but to see that they

become stepping-stones to fuller service and deeper life. It will bring
new joys and happiness, may all such be in accord with Thy will and
service. I take this life, personality, with all its possibilities and
weakness, and through Thy power and in Thy companionship, I
would mould it to be an instrument fit for Thy greater service.
Amen.

2.1.45 Last night we had a mixed concert between the English and the
French. French put across their songs very well. Our lads, of course,
were complete amateurs, but the real difference was the matter of taste.
Our boys sing absolutely wooshy slush, while the French sing clear and
snappy stuff. Jumbo nearly brought the house down with his yodelling.
He is a good, honest Lancashire lad. It's a deep reflection on our social
system. Shows us up really badly.

7.1.45 The general knowledge bee went off quite well last night and
stirred up a lot of enthusiasm. Next we will have a lecture on 'Flower-
growing' and, later on, a debate. Service tonight into which I must put
all I've got. The positive outlook and action in any situation. I must
study what is the positive and creative thing to do. Seems that I only
begin to grasp the nature of my work now. Prayers, people, letters:

My Dear Mrs T.,

I've just received George's permission to write to you, so here
goes. First of all, very many thanks for all the good wishes you've
sent. I can assure you that they are all appreciated. You will want
to hear about George. Well, one thing about a letter is that one
can write just what one thinks without worrying about
embarrassment and I always try to give credit where and when it
is due. So I would like you to know that George has won for
himself a high place in the respect and affections of us all. I am
one of those odd POWs who believe that POWs' life, like any
other trying experience, can affect a man in two ways: either
bitter disillusion or the birth of a real, strong, vital personality.
Need I tell you how George has gone through his hardships?
Indeed, he is one of the few who helps me to believe in human
nature. I know that your part has been a hard one; we all realise

that those at home have the more difficult break, but I'm sure it will in the end work out for the greater good and this especially in the case of George and yourself. His pride and devotion to you and Ann is tremendous and, may I say, absolutely justified, judging by all accounts, second though they be. I send this off with great hopes that soon George will be with you and Ann.

With every best wish, I am yours most sincerely,

Ray Davey,
Padre

10.1.45 Today I'm thirty-years-old, though it is really difficult to realise so.

11.1.45 Yesterday I left Hohnstein with *Ober Gft* Mie as my *Dolmetscher* and walked to Porschdorf and took train for Neukirch Kofferfabrik. Here I had a really good night with the boys. Mr Mie is a tragic figure, lost his only son in Russia in September 1943 and has not got over the loss yet. Extremely nice man. Nineteen boys on light work in the Fabrik and in good heart. Very cold and snowy. Today I go on to Kirschau, where several difficult cases await me. Prayer: adequacy for all situations; grateful for service last night, which seemed to get home. Consider Mr Mie and the tragedy of life for many people now.

16.1.45 Yesterday, the long-expected happened at last. Dresden was very heavily bombed, at midday and at night. The night raid was very heavy and lasted a considerable time. The noise shook the Burg here and flak guns [anti-aircraft fire] were clearly audible and flashes were visible across the sky. In the midday raid one plane came down near Siebnitz and the crew of seven baled out around this area, causing great excitement. Later they were rounded up, parachutes and all, and were brought in here. They were kept specially guarded and shipped off in the early hours. All passes are now forbidden. We await news from Dresden, where some 3,000 of our boys are held.

15.2.45 Events move fast now to a crescendo. Dresden was very heavily bombed four times in two days. First two raids, 1,600 and 800 bombers. They shook this place in every sense as they passed over. The Russians are now around Gorlitz and moving towards Dresden each day. The roads are filled with evacuees and *flüchlinge* [refugees]. Yesterday the sky was dark with smoke and dust, though we are approximately 40km from Dresden. Considerable excitement and speculation now. 'Will they attempt to evacuate us?' 'How long will these people fight on?' Many French *Bombe beschädigt* arrived today, about 100. Stories of Dresden damage terrific. All told, we've had eight heavy raids in three days. These seemed to start just after the Three Power Yalta Conference. These are times which remind one of Italy in September 1943. Once again, we must keep cool and ready for any emergency.

19.2.45 These are nervy days and we live from hour to hour wondering what is about to happen. The Russians seem to be east of Dresden and we hope that any time they'll make another big and fast push and our day will have dawned. But that is almost too good even to hope for. All sorts of rumours filter in of evacuation – 'heard' artillery fire, etc. But externally life goes on here quite as usual. Frequent air raids in this area, though we don't hear so many rumbles.

My heart is very sick for the American boys in the *lager* at Lilienstein. Two of them have already died and the others are in a very bad way indeed. Their conditions and work put slave labour in the shade and the weather once again has become bitterly cold. Most of these boys were captured on 19 December and they have not yet become accustomed to POW life. At times one does feel very bitter against the enemy and nothing inspires it more than to see the shape of these boys. It becomes just a picture of desolation and misery. But I daily pin my hopes on a quick end to all this suffering.

Last night I had a service for the boys on 'In quietness and confidence', and it seemed to be the right idea for these days of waiting. The boys are beginning to speculate on what will happen and news is at a premium. At least I feel that something decisive is about to happen and that another decade of *Gefangenschaft* is certainly coming to a close.

12.3.45 Events have moved on in the West and the Russians have advanced on the North but left our sector (Breslau), more or less around Gorlitz. We have established a bridgehead over the Rhine and have cleared the West Bank.

Today I visited Dresden again and saw the ruins of that city in daylight in contrast to the ninth when I saw them in the cover of evening. I walked for about an hour and a half from Plauenstrasse to the *Hauptbahnhof* and saw what modern bombing does. It looked as if some supernatural giant had taken up the town and shaken it and then set it on fire. I walked for a very long time without seeing a house fit for habitation. I've never seen such absolute devastation on such a wide scale. Nothing but the casing of the houses remains, charred walls, even the trees are battered; here and there, the wreckage of a tram, which had been caught on its way during the raid. Not many people around and those who were about were either the police or civilians looking over the remains of their homes. On each wall names were chalked up and addresses: the idea seemed to be to let others know where the surviving residents had gone. Casualty figures now range from 80,000 to 300,000, and I don't think we will ever know correctly.

We finally arrived at the station and found that only the shell remained; the inside of the building had totally collapsed and only a few of the outside platforms were usable. The synchronised clocks bore mute witness to the fact that the destruction had descended at 3 minutes to 11 o'clock. It is reckoned that 16,000 perished in the station alone. There was a ghostly quiet about this usually so busy centre and the whole Main Halle was boarded off. Lines of burnt-out trains were visible at the other end of the platforms. All around lay the wreckage of burnt-out fire wagons and cars. It was a terrible fact to realise that many thousands of bodies were still entombed under the debris. I did realise then what total war means.

No one bothered with me at all. I felt that somehow the people didn't have any more emotions left. They simply wait, fatalistically, for the end of it all. I left Dresden with no regrets. It was good to see complete houses again where the families lived on just as usual. One amazing feature from our point of view is that we have only lost three men in all the raids. The French, I believe, lost five, and the Dutch, fourteen.

The devastated city of Dresden after the intensive Allied bombings of February 1945

Chapter Nine

LIBERATION AND HOME

15.3.45 New book for a new start. Get down to living boldly and courageously. So much to face up to and sort out. The herald who is not sure of his message.

19.3.45 Away from Hohnstein since Friday. Left on the 4.20pm with my *Begleiter* [companion] Johny Schartz and went to Reich Dresden and eventually got connection across to Radeburg Ost and arrived in *Kommando* about 11 o'clock. Funeral of Ken Funnell next day at Standort Friedhof. Back to *lager*, where we had two long *Fliege* alarms and at last we had the German skilly at 2 o'clock. Later I travelled through ruined Dresden to Schlachthof and now I'm at Omsewitz, where another death has occurred. On Sunday visited Wölfnitz and saw all the wounded, and went up to Reichbahn on the way back. Frank Philip in their *lager* was killed. A 1,000-pounder landed about 60 yards from the *lager* and knocked it out of shape. The atmosphere in Dresden brings one back to the reality and grimness of war, which one does not realise in Hohnstein. In Schlachthof, one sees where it has received seventeen direct hits and tremendous damage done everywhere. All the men jump into action as soon as the alarm goes and beat it with kit already packed for the shelter. We were down one-and-three-quarter hours just now and the atmosphere was very warm and stuffy. Most interesting talking to the boys and finding their reactions to the raids, which would shake a lot of people at home and outside of Dresden. Many of the people they knew and worked with have been killed and practically everybody has lost everything they possessed. I wonder about it all. Each of our four casualties now was the result of carelessness and refusal to go down into a shelter during the raids. A very big price to pay!

Meantime, the news is the big relief from all this and soon all the West Rhine will be free. At present Patton is carving up the Saar with his columns, the bridgehead at Remagen is being steadily extended and each day brings us more and greater hopes of better days in the very near future. Another problem now is food, which is very short in the *Kommandos*. Hohnstein has lived better, with the remnant of parcels, and many of the *Kommandos* are fortunate in their 'rackets'. But we all hope and pray that the Red Cross will deliver the goods once again.

20.3.45 Today I went down into Dresden again. All the buildings I had come to know so well – the Zwinger, Hochkirche, Frauenkirche, Rathaus, Oper, Schloss, etc., are now at best shells and mostly rubble. Postplatz is unrecognisable, the Zwinger is burnt out and looks like an ancient monument just unearthed. In the streets there is an unusual silence, few people about; scattered groups of British or Russian POWs leisurely working on the ruins. Practically no traffic and here and there the shell of a burnt-out tram. All the tram wires are gone and it will be a long time before trams pass to and from Postplatz again. I felt strangely uncomfortable walking around the sorrows of this once-beautiful city. In some of the streets it was like climbing on the Giant's Causeway. Places that had been the hub of human activity and action are now still and few people pass by. I don't think one could find a habitable building in some 10 square miles in the central area. I 'climbed' round to the remains of the Domkirche a month ago, probably the most beautiful church in the city. Now it is but a mass of ugly masonry, with the statue of Martin Luther, legless, lying face down in the street, blown 10–15 yards from its pedestal. In the square in front of the Dom a group of demolition workers camp out in a tent.

22.3.45 Yesterday was a day of alarms and travelling. Bit of an argument with *Posten*, who wished to spend another night out. Two hours in Prossen. Back to Hohnstein at night and got letters from John and Jim Barker, both in splendid form. Now today comes the wonderful news that Red Cross parcels have arrived in Prossen. I cannot describe what this means for morale, health and human life itself.

23.3.45 News is verging on the sensational. I do find it terribly hard to settle down just now, so many things are in the air and life seems rapidly coming to a climax. Perhaps it is the atmosphere, news, activity of *stalag* life. Little or no peace by day now. The room is a sort of Reception, Mess and committee centre. Also news from home: Emily's marriage, John on the way home, and the prospect of my own return very soon now, and of course the natural high vitality of spring in one's blood. These beautiful days show Hohnstein at its best, and apart from a nippy freshness in the air, it might be June. Today, as ever, there was much air activity, several alarms and American planes overhead in formation after formation. The new sport on Hohnstein is 'Pamphlet Hunting'.

Easter comes again. Surely the loveliest festival of the year: everything renews its youth and the world is young again. The pure joy of life fills my veins and I almost feel it wrong to be glad at such a time, in such a place. So many thousands die each day and the ashes of Dresden lie 20 miles away. Many of our boys have passed on since the year began. I would almost be inclined to leave it as the ancient festival of spring, but somehow I can't. Amid all the joy of spring and its special promise for a prisoner this year, there is an emptiness if one stops at mere *joie de vivre*; one knows that soon the weather will change and Easter's freshness will pass. For me, it means that I want God and when I interpret Easter in terms of God, then I get peace: somehow it fits into the realness of things – its tragedy, despair, death, sorrow, all re-echo the feelings of so many millions today in our world of destruction, hate and greed. Somehow here we see into the very nature of things; our faith is grounded in life, blood, sweat and tears. It's not an escape from the mystery of evil and pain: it's God's answer to it. It's not an attempt to take us from the grimness of our twentieth-century world but a call to face it and see through it and see God. Like our world, the drama moves down into the valley of death and destruction, but it climbs up the other side into life and victory over death. Here God sets His stamp on the real inward qualities of life's character of love, joy and courage, and shows us that these are the final things of life.

25.3.45 Palm Sunday. Lovely weather. News of five bridgeheads now across the Rhine.

Easter 1945
It's Eastertime in Hohnstein;
The spring is here to stay.

The siren calls o'er prison walls,
The RAF is on its way.

It's Eastertime along the Rhine
Where eager youths do die.
Mid shot and shell our modern hell,
Victims of a shameless lie.

It's Eastertime in Lilienstein
And prisoners cry for bread.
Doing heavy work they dare not shirk
Already eight lie dead.

It's Eastertime in Palestine,
The lilies bloom again.
And Christ is there, His Cross to bear
And shed His tears of pain.

27.3.45 John 13: 1–17: Jesus washes the disciples' feet. Great sacramental act. It reveals His spirit of humility and His desire to serve the disciples. Revolutionary idea of leadership. Such an incident shows more clearly than much talk the Spirit of Christ and what it means for us. How far we have got away from that. We fight for our rights and squabble over precedent and rank. We are hurt when people do not acknowledge us properly. Often we look on such work as menial and despise it. Surely this is the great sacrament of social workers, but it is very important to grasp the proper motive that inspires such an action, otherwise our work becomes condescension. 'Look at who I am and yet what I do.' But the Master's life was so complete, so consistent and sincere, so much one with His mission that His action was one of the master touches of His life. It was the sort of thing one would expect to come from such a life because he had real inward humility.

We go on to ask then, what is humility? Consider its opposite – pride, self-sufficiency. The point about the proud man is that he cannot see the world apart from himself, he gets in his own light. He's got himself all out of proportion, like a badly taken photograph. Everything is completely self-related. This naturally results in distorted values, all his interests are rationalised. He cannot be objective, he cannot lose himself in something really big and great.

Consider Christ, on the other hand. How He lived an extended life, in the problems, hardships, joys and pleasures of those around Him. How He could see the world apart from Himself and yet realise the part He had to play in it. How His life was 'lost' in the great cause of the Kingdom of God. So He was able to see all life in proportion and when He saw that, He knew how unimportant mere prestige, dignity and office are, in comparison to the big things of the Kingdom.

28.3.45 News is striking a very high pitch now and we are beginning to expect things any day. In the meantime, I must try and collect myself and do the little that has to be done. Letters to relations, finish sermon, letters home, prayers for peace, talks to boys, future. Splendid letter from K. God bless and keep her.

Jesus' new commandment of love. This was to be the hallmark of the Christian. 'By this shall all men know that ye are my disciples, if ye have love one to another.' This is the distinguishing characteristic of those who seek to follow Him. Often we are known for other qualities – morality, conscientiousness, loyalty, sincerity, honesty, etc., but the touchstone of all is love. If it is not there, all the others go sour. A moral life without the warmth of love is precarious and does little to attract men and so often repulses and repels.

30.3.45 Good Friday brings a typical example of German administration. All teed up to go to Lilienstein for a service, but I'm told now I can't go. Looks also as if all the other arrangements go by the board. News continues epic.

Amid all the distractions and realities of this present time, I lift my heart back to the Central Theme – the Cross and all it means – and I pray that in some way its message may meet my life, mind, will and feeling. Great belief that Christ is the Victor; challenge to make the Cross our own. So today I bring myself back to consider my relationship with God and ask His forgiveness:

> *Selfishness in so many ways,*
> *Cowardice in avoiding so many vital issues,*
> *Allowing feeling of hate to arise,*
> *Negation of love by tattle, laziness,*

> *Indiscipline in thought and life,*
> *So many opportunities missed of service,*
> *Work carelessly done.*

1.4.45 Gratitude to God for the great message of Easter Day. Had a service and spoke on hope – 'Wherefore turn ye to the stronghold ye prisoner of hope' – and I felt that God did speak through my feebleness.

A note from Harold Barker yesterday mentions that Mr Christiansen has asked him and, he believes, me to stay on in Germany after the end of the war, but I shall have to do a spot of thinking about that before I make any decision. Five years is a long time to be away and I have to remember the home folk.

3.4.45 Ephesians 2:8: 'For by grace are ye saved through faith; and that not of yourselves: it is the gift of God.' How often do we need to remember this? We are apt to take so much on our own shoulders: to worry and to fret. But here we see it is something given, a message of God's grace: nothing we can do can win it. So I would open up my life to that grace. I would give up all my fears to God: all my intellectual worries and doubts; all my emotional life with its uncertainty and lack of balance; my bad habits, laziness and indiscipline, capitulation to my environment; lack of real interest in men; undue sensitiveness, lack of reality. Idea of Grace: Are the best things in life not really undeserved, unwon, unbought – beauty, love, etc?

4.4.45 On the road once more. This time to the Column at Bautzen and Hoyerswerda. Need to get back to the real life that one sees here in these *Kommandos*, which are indeed 'living' under pressure.

9.4.45 The days pass and I'm back at Erika. On Saturday visited Lohsa and Ostfeld. Both places were in top spirits, and at Ostfeld we could hear the guns on the Eastern Front. Shared a bicycle with my *Begleiter*, much to the amusement of the boys.

10.4.45 Good trip and visit to Weidnitz yesterday. Boys in good spirits now. News is splendid and boys look for the big day soon. Some have been down with swelling due to malnutrition, but are OK again. Parcels have been a merciful providence.

14.4.45 The boys are nearly here. Leipzig has fallen and the troops are on their way to Dresden, and the people here are in a terrible flap about things. They have been told that on no account are they to become POWs of the Russians and just now comes the unofficial news that the Germans have packed in to us. It surely will dawn any moment now and how we all look for it. It seems more than likely that we have to move across the Elbe. In the meantime, however, excitement mounts up. Need to keep steady and cool now. Keep busy and occupied. Deep regret at the death of President Roosevelt. We can ill afford the loss of such international figures at this critical stage.

Later. The hour of the end seems near. We're told that our forces are 15km from Dresden and moving on. I feel as yet strangely unmoved. Hohnstein is lovely in the freshness of spring and the people, though obviously under strain, carry on as usual. I do admire their spirit and feel for them now, though surely it is for their best also. Where will it all lead and what sort of a climax awaits us?

16.4.45 O tempora, O mores! The battle of nerves is at its height. The end seems very near and all sorts of news is coming through. Allies very near Berlin. We are more or less on the *qui vive* for a move across the Elbe on very short notice, as it seems likely that the Allies will come up to the West Bank and the Russians to the East. Père Huby, French Man of Confidence, has been told that we will be escorted to Anglo-American troops by 'friendly' *Postens*, who will have orders not to shoot when they see the Allied forces. Wise men, too! The boys find it impossible to settle and are very much on edge.

17.4.45 All to be made ready for the possibility of a quick move. Held a memorial service last night for President Roosevelt and had a good attendance.

18.4.45 Yesterday depressed the boys a bit, as they heard our forces had been pushed back. But I think this has been without foundation. Bring forces of the Spirit into play now as one waits. Two prayers:

> *Father, these are tremendous and yet difficult days. The spirit of hope is in the air, but it is mingled with suspense, anxiety and strain. We know not what each new morning will bring forth. Rumours and*

alarms excite us by day and disturb us at night, but we would turn in confidence to Thee. Through all the vicissitudes of army and wartime life Thou has been ever our Guardian and Guide. Thine unseen presence has garrisoned our spirits with courage and when the lights were low and hope burnt weak in faith and trust, Thou didst ever walk before us. And now we make the old surrender of ourselves, our fears, our doubts and all the difficult problems we face in the innermost part of our lives. Lead us on now and bring us in Thine own good time, from the darkness of this long captivity to the light of home and freedom, where we shall worship Thee with a more understanding love. Amen.

O God, in these last days as we see the fate of a great nation, keep our hearts and spirits set on the highest truths. May we ever be magnanimous in victory and give all the praise and glory to Thy glorious name. In the hour of victory we would remember all who have suffered in this terrible war. In this country we remember all the real patriots who love their country with a sincere love and who suffered in imprisonment and exile. We think of all the simple, decent folk who have been deceived by propaganda. At this time give us a fundamental sense of humility in our gratitude. Inspire in our hearts the burning desire to put our own house in order, to fight for a more righteous social order, to seek for a real understanding among the nations, and in all things to realise that the only final remaking of men and changing of human nature is in the forgiveness and grace of God. Amen.

19.4.45 Yesterday brought us a two-and-a-half-hour air raid in the afternoon. Bill Shack and I saw it in the open, as we had gone for a walk. First of all, the smoke flares were dropped and then squadron after squadron came in and the noise of bombs and flak mingled in a great rumbling. Once again it was on Dresden and seems to be a preparation for the occupation of that city – so we hope! Then one of the four-engined bombers flew on its own out over us and it seemed to be moving very slowly. Then out of the blue came a fighter, the new jet-propelled type, I believe, and there was a flash beside the bomber and the fighter veered off like a shooting star. The bomber limped round for a few seconds, then began to lose height and went into a spin, and three small spots suddenly appeared, only three. The plane finally hurtled in a nose-dive to its doom. It was queer to hear the sounds follow at such an interval after the incidents. In the background the raid on Dresden went on and dirtied the clearness of the sky with smoke and dust. Then six fighters began to play over Bad Schandau behind us and did some absolutely vertical dives, coming up again like a child on a swing just when we thought they had had it. We could hear that shuttle-like noise that told us they were strafing the roads. Later, the doctor, who'd been down, told us that they'd machine-gunned the roads and got every vehicle around. It looks as if once again we are near the Front.

21.4.45 These have been hectic days. Russians are on the move, as also the Allied forces in the West. So we had all the rush of packing and deciding what to take and what not. Yesterday I got a stomach upset and stayed in bed the whole day without food. Now I feel much better and hope to be fit for the march, if it should come today. The road is completely packed with transport, helter-skelter, everywhere. Mostly horse transport, mixed up with civilians getting along as they can. Surely we are nearly through now.

22.4.45 Weather has gone bad. Still we stay here. News is that Allies and Russians are on the point of meeting around Dresden and Berlin. Our roads are simply stifled with traffic. Mostly cavalry, and motorised troops look much the worse for wear. Telephone communications are *kaput*, so we don't get air alarms and on the whole this is to the good. I have disposed of most of my stuff now, given most away, left a few books with the dentist and stored others in the Magazine in a suitcase with my name on the lid, but I reckon I'll not see either again. These are difficult days of suspense, but I believe it is in our interests to stay here as long as possible. Indeed to me it is equal whether we are retaken by the Red Army or the Americans, except that the latter would probably get us home more quickly. Everybody's nerves are taut and much is made of the most childish arguments and people get annoyed at very little, but of course 3–5 years of this life begins to tell its tale. Now I am two years and ten months 'in the bag' [captured]. This is what we've longed for, for so many months and years. It is terrifying to see a country fall, but somehow it underlines the moral laws of the universe.

Eternal God, be with us now in these breathtaking days, when so much is happening, when old things are passing away, old frontiers, old customs, old ideas, when Europe is solvent and, for us, the clouds are lifting and the path towards home seems to open up to us at last. Give us the consciousness of Thine abiding presence in the ups and downs of this waiting: may we in joy come to Thee in thanksgiving and in hardship come to Thee in dependence. Keep us from all smallness, pettiness and selfishness: may the flame of comradeship and brotherhood burn at its brightest now. Save us from petty irritations, quickness to take offence and dangerous credulity. Inspire us with a deep faith in Thyself, in Thy purpose of love for us in Thy protecting care and guiding providence. Amen.

23.4.45 Late in the day I saw with my own eyes (the only way to be sure now) the puffs of smoke rise over the valley towards Stolpen and this smoke originates from Russian shells. So they must be very near us indeed. Yesterday the whole east of the *stalag* area caved in – Hoyerswerda, Kamanz, Bautzen, Schmorkau and Königsbruck, all gone – and forces expected to meet at Dresden. Russians 5km from the centre of Berlin. Terrific amount of troops have passed through, but now it seems to have slackened off. Boys are naturally very strung up and it looks as if we'll stay here and be retaken by the Russians. Perhaps that is better than wandering round on the west of the Elbe with a large area in the south, into Sudetenland, still unoccupied. It seems really to be near the end now.

25.4.45 Yesterday afternoon I visited Frau Weisheit and had a most unforgettable time, though it brings home the drama and sadness of the situation. A real example of living and cold-blooded heroism: son missing in East since June, husband on Eastern Front, daily expectation of the Russians, and yet she is as charming and composed a hostess as I've ever met. Listened to her daughter, who is church organist, play some of Bach's 'Chorales'. Took coffee with the family and heard the tragedy of the Ukrainian girl who lived with her family in Dresden for four-and-a-half years. Lost her father and sister in the raid and has not seen her mother since and believes she is also dead. Was wounded in the raid herself and now wishes she was on the other side of the Elbe, which will be occupied by the Allied forces, we believe. I did feel like Job's comforter, as I speculated on what the Red Army will do when they arrive. Somehow that overshadowed everything that was said.

For our boys, things get worse. Freital *Kommando* is a few kilometres beyond the Elbe, practically starving. Peter Phillips has put down a ground sign, 'POW Camp', and now says he will add 'S.O.S. FOOD', though he will wait 'until the first death' before he does this. The boys are sleeping in barns and only receive bread and that not regularly. Dr Wykes was in and his crowd got out of Berghammer *Kommando* just in time, as the Russians flattened the *lager* and village with low strafing, many of the villagers being killed. They are about 500 on the march and are badly treated. All this underlines just how lucky we are to be allowed to stay here.

News is slow. Russians have one-third of Berlin and also 'hit the Elbe at Mühlburg'. Resistance now has become very feeble around here. Also, the Germans have said that all POWs will remain in their camps and not be moved, so it looks as if we'll not move, after all our preparation. Yesterday a crowd of most dishevelled Polish POWs arrived in, part of the army fighting with the Russians. They are in a mess, rags, unshaven and thin. Some were supposed to be taken only a few kilometres away.

26.4.45 My mental state these days is a mixture of many, many emotions. Sgt. Smith saw *Oberst* Kratz, who was most reasonable and will certainly do his best for us. Now we hear that the Allies and Russians have met at Riesa Torgau. Two-thirds of encircled Berlin is taken, so the Big Day moves nearer.

28.4.45 Yesterday I tried to get out but without success, so I must settle down to *stalag* life and wait patiently for the end. News – Stettin and Bremen taken, Berlin far through and Yanks meet Russians on Elbe at Torgau, north of Dresden. So events should shape themselves now.

1.5.45 After the refusal, the authorities relented and asked where I wished to go. The result was a small but worthwhile *Dienstreise* [official travel], on foot to Prossen, Königstein, Lilienstein. Went with *Sunderführer* Herschell and we got on well this time and kept completely clear of politics. All sorts of news around and it looks as if the end may come literally any hour. This was a good trip and the visits were well appreciated in all the camps and I believe did some little good.

I spoke on 'Waiting', *Isaiah* 40, and it seemed to be the right line and certainly all listened. Must pursue the prophets and get to know their message more and more. Met several fellows in Königstein who'd been in Lucca. Yesterday they shot a German soldier here in Hohnstein and displayed him on a kitchen table at the crossroads: 'He who runs away from death will meet a death of shame.' Grim days now.

Today is May Day. All the world is in suspense and the air is tense with expectation. Will it be capitulation or not – to all three powers? I hear of Mussolini's bloody end and wonder if his better half still lives here in the Kleine Reich.

Feel now that I need some touchstone to bind all my life into one again; some flame to ignite the whole fire of my life. I think it will take a big job to do this. Much I would like to say if I could only articulate it and put it into an ordered whole, a philosophy of life, a *credo*.

4.5.45 Events for us have developed at last. Yesterday we were told to '*fertig machen*' [make ready] and once again, half-incredulous of anything happening, we made ready. However, things moved with a more businesslike swing and we saw that we were really for it this time. One of the lads, a Kiwi, was grievously ill with complications from tonsillitis and Dr Clay had to stay behind to look after him. We set off in column about 5pm, after the inevitable army 'messing around' – and preceded by the Russians – we left the Burg, with a considerable gathering of the villagers to see us on our way. Several Nazi flags were displayed at half-mast. Heath Robinson would have had nothing on some of the conveyances used, all home-made, groaning under monstrous loads. We were in high spirits, for we felt that at last we were on the way home and all sorts of rumours float round about our eventual disposition. Some even hope we'll be sent to our own lines! Anyway, real optimism is in the air now.

The lovely countryside of the Sächsische Schweiz looked at its best, the apple blossom was bursting out and the fresh green of spring was everywhere. The air was sweet with blossom scent and new-mown grass. So we left Hohnstein, my home for sixteen months. We toiled down and up the Sepentine Road and then on, via Waltersdorf, to Königstein, to the ferry, where we had an interesting talk with some SS blokes, but they all suffer from fixed ideas and propaganda. Poles, Dutch and the German *Postens* all found the pace too heavy and I saw one 'Froggy' arrive with his wagon in his arms. At last we arrived at a *Papierfabrick* [paper factory] near Königstein, where we were greeted by bright lights and our *stalag* officers. It was like a homecoming and it was notable just how friendly the Detaining Power is now. We were agreeably surprised by the accommodation – we slept in a storing shed and made up very excellent beds from stacks of fine white rag. Events move quickly in the outside world. Italy is finished and part of Austria. Hamburg is an open town and Prague is a hospital town.

5.5.45 We find ourselves still in the *Papierfabrik*, under the shadow of the once-mighty fortress of Königstein. Many SS troops in this area, now practically the last to hold out in the whole Reich. I believe we are in a small pocket, an oasis in the desert. It looks as if we'll trek along the Erzgebirge and one day walk into our own lines. Meanwhile, our time here is not unpleasant, but I long for the end and to step into another atmosphere. I do hope the folk at home are not unduly worried these days. Let's hope the BBC is not putting over too much horror stuff.

6.5.45 Still domiciled in the *Papierfabrik*, but with considerable changes. Early this morning all the Confidence men and some hangers-on were ordered off to Schneeburg and so Sgt. Smith and the others of the combine left. So I am alone now with the boys and somehow it has been a bit of a release. Smith is not the easiest man to live with as intimately as POW life demands. Later, all sorts of speculation goes round and the camp here is now in the hands of a *Feldwebel* and things are very loosely organised. *Oberst* appeared today and assured us that all his desire was to get us to the Americans. Then he ordered all doctors and ministers to go on to Schneeburg, but I'll certainly not go if I can possibly help it. We hope to take off on our own, seventeen English and Americans, and get through to the lines with a German *Posten*. It now seems that our area is practically the last to hold out. Trust Saxony. Even now we hear the Russian guns near Dresden. Also we hear that Patton's Army is cracking on Czechoslovakia. We got bread for two days and believe it to be the last, but the boys keep in good spirits and I am sure that 'we ain't got long to stay here'. All the German guards are at sixes and sevens and are very glad to take off with us. May it be soon now!

8.5.45 Victory in Europe day. Up at 6 o'clock, coffee, kit, roads, refugees, lovely weather down into this plain. Teplitz Schönau Stalag IV C. Walked through the town. Bombs and strafing, artillery, battle: our quarry, city falls, the capture, our surrender and handover, flag, Russian troops, the road and what a road. The night by the roadside. The women in great fear.

9.5.45 On the road to Komatov, where the Yanks are, Czechs, and welcome, towns, flags, Russians. Our transport, Froggies, *cherchez les Américains!*

10.5.45 Lovely weather. Off for Karlsbad in tiptop form. We meet the Yanks and what a thrill! Our entry to Karlsbad, we meet the Yank Colonel. Trip out to meet doctor, good quarters and sleep.

11.5.45 Food, Yank breakfast. Off to Allied Waiting Camp. Meet some of the boys. Swim. Lovely sleep on stretcher.

12.5.45 Vehicles and vehicles, announcement, stand by, on the way to Nürnberg. What a trip.

13.5.45 Nürnberg. Lovely sight on the 'drome. Douglas Dakota. Flight to Brussels 9.45–11.00. Brussels reception. YMCA. Accommodation, money, people, good sleep.

14.5.45 Two-and-a-half hours over the Channel. Oakley, fine reception. Off to Camp 95, soon clear, London, Mr Scott and Betty. Hotel guests.

15.5.45 Much to get clear today. Clothes: suit, shirts, underwear, socks, shoes. Arrangements for travel home. Haircut and toilet articles, presents, cash, new digs.

Real sense of gratitude to God for all.

16.5.45 Clothes coupons, passport photos, battle jacket pressed and badges sewn on, trousers altered, shirts and pyjamas, beret, hair oil, shoes. Ring K. Now at last I relax and wait for the 10.40am train to Gloucester to see Will for the night. This will be the first of the reunions. How tremendous it has been to hear all on the phone – Mother, Father, Beth, John and Kathleen, and today Will. His call so strange and yet thrilling, it has happened so swiftly. But it is tremendous and I'm grateful to God for so much. Must get back to normal spiritual life. Today I had to go through a lot, saw a pressman, liaison for the YMCA. I do wonder what he'll write! If it helps the Y, it is all to the good. No news of Barker yet. How wonderful it is to be back to it all: to talk to non-POWs; to hear the news; to see happy faces; to eat white bread; to wear new clothes; to bathe often; no more guards; decent bed; solitude.

17.5.45 War in Europe is finished, all the horrors. Next step is reconstruction and planning, so that people will be able to live happier lives, free from want, fear, hate, suffering, destruction. Government plans, social security, housing, education. Will all this be enough? What is the answer? Change people's hearts. Things that make wars and unhappiness are not just Hitlers and Mussolinis, but are things in our own lives – greed, pride, dishonesty, lack of consideration. If we are to overcome these things, we must become different ourselves.

18.5.45 Beth and Kathleen. What a day!

29.5.45 Lovely Dunmurry Sunday. Lisburn Road buzzes with traffic and the old crows cackle, but all around there is that sense of peace and home. I suppose it's just as well I can feel this all too intensely, but my heart is filled with a profound sense of gratitude. I don't think there's much more I could ask for, except perhaps the knowledge that Barker is home.

1.6.45 Release, homecoming, family, Kathleen. Old things have passed away; new confidence, courage and hope. I feel one of the high-watermarks of happiness. I realise it is one of life's happy times, one of the sunny patches, and I praise God for it.

EPILOGUE

On returning home in 1945, I became Presbyterian Chaplain at Queen's University in Belfast. My experience of ecumenical community in Tobruk and the devastation of Dresden had made an indelible mark on me, and seemed particularly relevant to the situation at home in Northern Ireland. In the 1950s and '60s I returned to Europe several times with groups of students, visiting the Agape, Taize and Iona communities, amongst others. For almost two years from autumn 1963, a group met regularly to discuss how we could apply these experiences closer to home.

On 30 October 1965, the Corrymeela Centre was opened on the site of an old holiday fellowship centre, near Ballycastle on the north coast of Ireland. Tullio Vinay, founder of the Agape community in Italy, presided over the opening ceremony. My hope back then was that Corrymeela might come to be known as 'the Open Village':

> 'open to all people of good will who are willing to meet each other, to learn from each other and to work together for the good of all; open to all sorts of new ventures and experiments in fellowship, study and worship; open to all sorts of people ... This is part of our vision. We know that we are only at the beginning and there is so much to be done.'

Today Corrymeela continues to thrive as 'a community of people of all ages and Christian traditions who, individually and together, are committed to the healing of social, religious and political divisions that exist in Northern Ireland and throughout the world.' It has bases in Belfast and Reading in England, and a greatly expanded centre in Ballycastle. The dispersed community has 165 members alongside many Associate Members and Friends of Corrymeela worldwide.

In Ballycastle the centre is run largely by a community of volunteers from Ireland and overseas, working alongside permanent staff. Its activities have ranged from providing cross-community residential projects for families and young people, conferences for the discussion of social, political and religious issues, a refuge for victims of the 'troubles', and a forum for speakers from as far afield as Mother Teresa of Calcutta.

Sometimes my mind goes back to my lowest moment of the war, after the fall of Tobruk. I was cooped up in the midst of a sandstorm, in the searing heat of the desert, with Italian and German forces flying overhead. I had to decide whether I should use my predicament as an excuse to go under and put in my time as a prisoner-of-war; or to see the situation as a challenge and make something positive of it. I opted for the latter.

Ray and Kathleen on their wedding day